Crisis and Breakdown of Non-Democratic Regimes

Crisis and Breakdown of Non-Democratic Regimes:
Lessons from the Third Wave

Editors
Pietro Grilli di Cortona
Barbara Pisciotta
Eric R. Terzuolo

NEW ACADEMIA
PUBLISHING

Washington DC

Library of Congress Control Number: 2016938346
ISBN 978-0-9966484-9-3 paperback (alk. paper)

NEW ACADEMIA
PUBLISHING

4401-A Connecticut Ave., NW #236 - Washington DC 20008
info@newacademia.com - www.newacademia.com

To Pietro Grilli di Cortona
Esteemed colleague, teacher, and friend

Contents

Acknowledgments

This book was made possible by a 2011 grant from the Ministry for Education, Universities, and Research of the Italian government, as part of its program to support "research projects in the national interest."

The co-editors and authors also would like to thank the Department of Political Sciences at the University of Rome 3 for its kind support, in particular following the untimely death in summer 2015 of the senior co-editor, Prof. Pietro Grilli di Cortona, a long-time member of the faculty.

Many colleagues, too numerous to cite individually, have provided moral and substantive support to this project, but Prof. Giampiero Cama of the University of Genoa made a particularly important contribution with his ideas and observations.

Deborah Perrie Park, who translated several of the chapters, devoted great care to rendering the original Italian into English that respects both the voice of the authors and the style that English-language readers expect. With her broad experience in the foreign affairs field, plus in-depth knowledge of Europe, Latin America and the Caribbean, and the Middle East, she also provided valuable substantive insights.

Finally, gratitude goes to our publisher, Anna Lawton of New Academia, who has been unfailingly supportive and responsive, and very sensitive to the impact of Prof. Grilli's death on those of us left to continue the project.

Introduction

Barbara Pisciotta and Eric R. Terzuolo

"Discarding Democracy: Return to the Iron Fist" was the discouraging subtitle of Freedom House's 2015 *Freedom in the World* report.[1] The document went on to underline that, for nine years in a row, freedom in the world had declined, with the Middle East and North Africa, followed by Eurasia, as the worst-performing regions, and five out of ten "Worst of the Worst" countries in Africa. The "international backlash against liberal democracy has grown and gathered momentum," according to Cooley (2015, 49), with authoritarians finding ways to "erode the norms that inform and underlie the liberal international political order." A dire picture indeed, and one the 2016 Freedom House reporting would largely echo.

Students of democratization (generally also sympathizers) who lived through all or part of what Samuel Huntington so memorably named "The Third Wave" perhaps became a bit spoiled along the way. The democratization processes that touched over 80 countries, beginning in 1974 and ending in the late 1990s or early 2000s, even though not uniformly "successful," certainly raised expectations. And by extension the perceptions of democratic backsliding so commonly expressed over the last decade were probably inevitable.

This is not to question the value of reflecting on the continued utility of the "transition paradigm," which Carothers already called into question in 2002, stressing the importance of a case-by-case approach, given "the importance of starting conditions and the fact that not all countries have equal chances to make democracy work" (Diamond, Fukuyama, Horowitz, and Plattner 2014, 91). Perhaps, as Donald Horowitz suggests, the transition paradigm was really more a "set of ideas about how democracy might happen" and those in the field "should avoid *a priori* standard formulas" (Diamond et al. 2014, 89, 100).

Another metaphor that perhaps has become too reified is that of the "wave." A quick Google search will identify considerable discussion of exactly what wave of democratization we are in, assuming we are indeed experiencing such a wave. By the 2010s we reportedly had moved from Huntington's three waves to five, with a fourth wave having followed an authoritarian counter-wave in the mid- to late 1990s[2] and designation of a fifth wave necessitated by the difficulty of fitting events in the Arab countries since 2010 into any preceding wave of democratization (Szmolka 2013). But we should avoid giving too much substance to the term "wave," and fretting excessively over how to define and delimit whatever number of democratization waves we personally are convinced have washed over the international community. In the following essays, "Third Wave" appears with some regularity, but largely as a convenient way of referring to the remarkably large number of attempts at democratic regime change over roughly forty years following Portugal's 1974 Carnation Revolution.

What seems unavoidable, however, is the question of whether, leaving aside the matter of paradigms and catchy metaphors, the "transitions era" is simply at an end (Plattner 2014). It is hard to argue that the broad democratizing trend that started in 1974 has not lost momentum. But media analyses of the Arab Spring and its aftermath, or of the Russia/Ukraine crisis, tend toward the breathless and over-simplified. Passing judgment on the end of the transitions era requires more in-depth and multi-faceted analysis.

A good illustration of the complexity of that challenge came in the 25th anniversary issue of the *Journal of Democracy*,[3] in which a number of leading experts addressed the question: Is democracy in decline? The variety of answers to the question was striking. Levitsky and Way wrote about "The Myth of Democratic Recession," arguing that "even the Freedom House data show only a very slight decline in levels of freedom since 2000" (Plattner 2015, 6), while Diamond in "Facing Up to the Democratic Recession" found an incipient decline in democracy over the preceding decade. Other contributors focused instead on the threats to democracy from weak stateness and poor governance or accentuated the recent successes of authoritarian regimes.

Even the undeniably "sad outcome of many of the recent Arab revolts" (Plattner 2014, 15) does not close the book on democratization, but rather merits careful and nuanced analysis, aimed at drawing useful analytical and practical lessons. An October 2015 collection of articles in the *Journal of Democracy*, for example, challenges aspects of the emerging common wisdom regarding the outcome of the Arab Spring. Marc Lynch, for example, points to a "trashing of the transitions" in the media (cited in Dunne 2015, 77), while Michael Robbins, director of the Arab Barometer polling organization, points to continuing robust Arab public support for democracy. Other essays provide complex and nuanced perspectives on Islamist parties, the actual degree of their electoral success, and their relations with other political forces (Dunne 2015).

Ahmed and Capoccia (2014, 30), in a separate analysis, underline the complexity of events in Egypt since the 2011 uprising, focusing on the role of enduring structural conditions and the uneven and asynchronous changes in different institutional sectors. Their approach is rooted in the "historical turn" in democratization studies, based on "re-examining the dynamics of democratic development among early democratizers."

Said historical turn further emphasizes the continuing importance of understanding the "Third Wave," defined here as including cases from 1974 into the early 2000s, over 80 in total. This is a uniquely large and variegated body of data against which to test and further refine our intellectual tools for analyzing current and future democratization attempts (which undeniably will come) and projecting their outcomes.

Munck (2007, 45) distinguishes three "agendas" in democracy studies, focused on "democratic transition, democratic stability, and democratic quality." The essays in this collection all fit firmly into the first of those agendas, inspired by belief that "the continued significance of democratic transitions...should not be underestimated" (Munck 2007, 47). The essays originate in a comprehensive set of brief, but systematically structured, analyses of all the aforementioned national cases (see footnote 8), with careful attention to the process and specificities of democratization in each case. Each essay treats specific factors thought to condition democratization process, factors both external and internal to the countries in question. The objective in each essay is to use the body of case studies to assess and refine generalizations about a given factor, such as the role of the international system, internal political dynamics in a given country, or the influence of geography. The study of democratic transitions certainly does grapple with an "unwieldy proliferation of explanatory factors" (Munck 2007, 67), including structural, institutional, and human agency factors, and proposing an integrated and parsimonious theory of democratic transitions, assuming such a thing is even feasible, is beyond the scope of this work. There is still enough work to be done in analyzing and assessing the explanatory factors that are currently on the table.

Hale (2013, 333) points to "regime change cascade" as a "nascent notion" that scholars, the media, and the public are adopting when discussing events such as the Arab Spring, taking also the 1848 revolutions in Europe, the fall of Communism, and the "color revolutions" as key, related reference points. Though regime change cascade is a narrower concept than "wave," further analysis of the body of post-1974 democratization efforts seems an appropriate way to address many of the key questions Hale raises regarding the cascades. What, for example, is the role of demonstration effects? What is the role of human or institutional agency in promoting them? What are the relative roles of internal and external causes? Hale also underlines that regime change cascades do not necessarily result in democratization. In fact, looking at a large number of national cases, as we do in the following essays, can offer insights into why discontent and protest can have dramatically different political outcomes in different settings.

This work is explicitly *not* intended as a critique of democracy as it currently exists. In a review of studies on democratization in Latin America, for example, Anderson (2005, 399) underlined examples of *ideological* critiques of existing democracy by Latin American scholars, based on idealism that omitted "a sense of real-world process whereby we can understand the conditions that facilitate or hinder...democracy." She stressed instead "the value of broad, cross-regional and historical reach, and intellectual command of detail" (392) and it is our hope that the following essays to a reasonable degree reflect all those qualities. But, while it is certainly important to consider what indicators of democratization to employ in research (Munck 2007), it is not our intention to offer here any abstract formulae about what democracy *should* be.

One important objective of this collection is to make available to a broader audience the analyses and reflections of scholars from non-Anglophone Europe. The scholarly literature on democracy and democratization is very heavily the product of scholars in English-speaking countries, or of countries in Northern Europe where English is widely spoken and functions as a lingua franca in many scholarly and technical fields. But elsewhere in Continental Europe as well, democratization can attract significant attention and generate provocative analyses.

An interesting example came with the 2012 publication of Sophie Baby's *Le mythe de la transition pacifique: violence et politique en Espagne (1975-1982)* (The myth of peaceful transition: violence and politics in Spain, 1975-1982).[4] Baby forcefully challenged the accepted view of Spain's transition as a highly successful and consensual process, engineered via elite negotiations that avoided violence. She documented, for example, over 3000 acts of violence, involving a wide range of public and official actors, with an estimated 700 deaths.

In academic political science, broadly speaking, there may be two relevant geographical dividing lines. While still a postdoctoral fellow at Harvard and UC Berkeley in 1960-61, the distinguished Dutch scholar Hans Daalder (later the first head of political and social sciences at the European University Institute in Florence) took a stab at explaining the difference between European and American political scientists. In the US, he noted the "seduction of science," the "gigantic" scale of the political science profession, the "itch of interdisciplinarity," the "magic of methodology," and an adoption of complex words from expatriate German social scientists, all increasingly making political science writing "unintelligible except to the initiated" (Daalder 2014, 98-101). More than 50 years later, Daalder described his paper as explicitly "satirical" (97) though it seems fair to suggest there still may be something to his analysis. And yet, alongside some questions about the institutional culture of political science in the US, one also finds visible admiration for the scholarly productivity of US political scientists, sometimes depicted as a standard their European counterparts should seek to emulate (Schneider 2007). Gleditsch (2007), for example, noted the low incentive for Norwegian political scientists, as compared to their American counterparts, to publish in high-quality channels as their careers advanced.

Perhaps the most sustained and clear-eyed analysis of the state of the political science discipline in Europe can be found in *European Political Science*, the journal of the European Consortium for Political Research, an association founded in 1970, currently with 300 institutional members. Its purpose is to "promote the development of political science in Europe, in particular by fostering collaboration between universities and other European institutions active in political research."[5] Indeed, one could characterize its primary objective as the creation of a "specifically *European* political science," that is "more than just a collection of disparate national political science disciplines" (Bull 2007, 427).

It would seem, however, that in political science, as in many other sectors, efforts to build a common, integrated European approach have encountered a stubborn attachment to national specificity.[6] A survey of political science faculty in the US, Continental Europe, the UK, Canada, Australasia, Asia, and the Middle East indicated great divergence of views on the meaning of political science, its future direction, and the defining works in the field, along with only "only limited insistence upon the quest for overarching unity" within the field (King and Marian 2008). In the more strictly European context, a comparison of "European" political science journals with the *Revue Française de Science Politique* between 1973 and 2002 pointed out "how much the [European Consortium for Political Research] political science differs from national political science traditions" (Boncourt 2008, 366). A separate comparison of the French journal with its closest British counterpart, *Political Studies*, the main journal of the Political Studies Association, underlined how political science in France and the UK emerged from different disciplines: "law, sociology, and geography in France; history and philosophy in Britain [which] led to the building of two different national communities" (Boncourt 2007, 292). The internationalization of the political science profession had produced some signs of opening between two political science communities that had been "largely unaware of each other," but it was far from clear that "antagonisms between national traditions" would soften.

The Italian situation as well includes notable specificities, which have hindered the rise of the empirical study of politics. Among conditioning factors one could cite the prevalence of a juridical approach to the study of politics, the stultifying impact of Fascism, and cultural dominance in the postwar period of

> Marxism and of the neo-idealistic Hegelianism of Benedetto Croce. Both these approaches made it impossible to pursue the independent study of politics: political phenomena were continually perceived as either the product of structural economic factors, or as a kind of contingent interruption to the ongoing pursuit of the unity of spirit (Capano and Verzichelli 2010, 103).

Within the faculties of political *sciences* at Italian universities, now replaced by a department-based structure in a recent university reform, political scientists broadly speaking have occupied modest roles, with legal scholars, political historians, economists, and sociologists much more prevalent. A 2010 state of the field assessment noted continuing challenges on a number of fronts: resources; the visibility of political science practitioners, both domestically and internationally; the ability to attract students; perceptions of the field's utility (Capano and Verzichelli 2010).

A more recent analysis, however, finds greater internationalization of Italian political science research, including an increase since 2006 in the number of articles in international publications by Italian political scientists, including those holding tenure. Although an asymmetry persists between universities in Northern/Central Italy and in Southern Italy, attention to internationalization of political science is increasingly widespread. Younger scholars in particular are becoming more ambitious with respect to international publishing visibility, and are increasingly attuned to the spread of English as the lingua franca in political science. Other positive factors for Italian political science, even in the face of financial constraints stemming from the international economic crisis, have included the establishment and consolidation of some PhD programs and "the prestige of many Italian scholars involved in the international disciplinary organizations" (Verzichelli 2014, 27).

For part of this both challenging and promising period, leadership of the Italian political science profession rested with Pietro Grilli di Cortona, professor of political science at the University of Rome 3, who also served as president of the *Società Italiana di Scienza Politica* (Italian Political Science Association) from 2013 until shortly before his untimely death on July 16, 2015. In their published message of condolence, his colleagues in the university's Department of Political Sciences pointed out how he had faced his final illness "with exceptional lucidity and laudable dignity" and that he still had "many plans after having been a protagonist and a pillar of [their] academic community for almost twenty years."[7]

This volume is a concrete demonstration, we hope, of precisely the qualities Prof. Grilli di Cortona's colleagues highlighted. He devised the concept and structure of this collection with the goal of bringing wider attention to the key conclusions of a major, internationally comprehensive analysis of democratic regime change carried out primarily by his team at the University of Rome 3, which had received Italian government funding as a project of vital national interest. The first volume, including the country-by-country analyses, appeared in Italy in 2014.[8]

This volume in fact includes a chapter by Prof. Grilli di Cortona on domestic political determinants of democratization. Despite being already gravely ill, he completed a draft in mid-May 2015, with the intention of making further edits directly to the English translation. Unfortunately, by the time the translation was ready, his health had deteriorated to the point where he was not able to work any more. We present here Prof. Grilli di Cortona's final scholarly work, reflecting years of sustained reflection on democratization processes, in translation but with only minimal edits. (Note also his contribution to the chapter on stateness challenges and change in non-democratic regimes.)

After studying at the distinguished political science institute at the University of Florence, where he wrote his thesis on political power in the Soviet Union, Prof. Grilli di Cortona took his first academic posting in 1983 at the historic University of Rome "La Sapienza." After three years at the University of Trieste (1993-6), he moved to the new University of Rome 3, becoming full professor in 2000.

His first book, published in 1989, carried the prescient title *Le crisi politiche nei regimi comunisti* (Political crises in Communist regimes). In 1997 he also published *Da uno a molti: Democratizzazione e rinascita dei partiti in Europa orientale* (From the one to the many: democratization and rebirth of parties in Eastern Europe). In fact, democratization and political transitions would remain a principal focus for the rest of his career, as exemplified also by *Come gli Stati diventano democratici* (How states become democratic) of 2009. Closely related was his interest in political party and electoral systems, reflected for example in the co-authored *Evaluation and Optimization of Electoral Systems* (Philadelphia: SIAM, 1999). His 2007 book on political change in Italy, *Il cambiamento politico in Italia: Dalla Prima alla Seconda Repubblica* (Political change in Italy: from the First to the Second Republic), went through several printings.[9]

A tribute to Prof. Grilli di Cortona, published in leading Italian daily *Corriere della Sera*, had a very telling title, best translated as "Grilli di Cortona, freedom without utopias."[10] In fact, he succumbed to neither the Marxist nor the Hegelian-idealist utopias that long prevailed in the study of politics in Italy. He prized individual liberty above all, and regarded that as the ultimate and crucial measure of democracy. In the Hobbesian world of Italian university politics, he was known for challenging prevailing trends that he believed risked devaluing educational institutions, and as an advocate of the free and mutually respectful exchange of ideas on the challenges facing Rome 3 and the university system as a whole.

His students recall him as an exemplary teacher: always correct in his dealings with them, always available and ready to provide valuable suggestions and to stimulate their interest in research. He was also an irreplaceable friend, ready with a joke to make difficult situations seem less dramatic. His academic and life lessons left an indelible mark on his students and on his colleagues, who remember him with great affection. In recognition of his many contributions, the Department of Political Sciences, with the support of the

University of Rome 3, renamed its library of political studies in his honor, especially appropriate since he had served as chair of the library's scientific board until his death.

Prof. Grilli di Cortona's chapter here focuses on the three main internal determinants of democratization: legacies of the past; civil society and anti-regime mobilization; elite internal dynamics and succession crises. By no means does he discount the role of external factors in democratization, or of the interaction between internal and external factors. But he rejects the possibility of constructing a general theory that explains all regime transformations, underlining instead the importance of understanding specific national paths. Why, for example, did certain autocracies survive the Third Wave of democratization largely intact, despite broad trends favoring democratization? Internal factors intertwine with international factors, in his view, to promote diverse and distinct outcomes.

Reviewing a large number of national cases, Grilli di Cortona points out how autocratic regimes can filter and interpret legacies of the past, i.e. experiences, values, traditions, practices, and historical memory, in different ways. Such legacies can condition and limit the paths toward political change, but their impact is not always unidirectional or simple to discern. Even having a democratic experience prior to the installation of autocracy, though it generally has some positive implications, does not play out in the same way from one country to the next. And a history of colonialism can either promote or, perhaps more frequently, hinder the building of democracy. In other words, the impact of historical legacies is specific from one national case to another.

Though sometimes decisive, civil society and anti-regime mobilization are not always key elements in the crisis/collapse of autocratic regimes. The reasons for mobilization are very diverse, including, for example, disappointed economic expectations and ethnic, religious, or other cultural factors. The nature and quality of leadership also can determine the effectiveness of mobilization. While examples of significant civil society mobilization seemingly can be found in all world regions, Prof. Grilli di Cortona estimates that they affected only about half of the countries involved in the Third Wave, and were not highly significant, for example, in the important democratizations of Spain and Greece in the 1970s.

Elite internal dynamics also can pose varying challenges to the stability and continuity of authoritarian regimes. Palace conspiracies and other intra-elite battles, generally characterized by conflict between hard-liners and soft-liners, are one possibility. Individual leaders may launch a more or less sincere and extensive democratic transition. Or change may be a consequence of a leader's death and a resulting succession crisis. All such dynamics can influence ways of dealing with international factors, e.g. a loss of outside support or a wave of change that seems irresistible. In sum, Prof. Grilli di Cortona provides a strong demonstration of how internal factors contribute to specific, national democratization outcomes, even when states face a largely shared international context.

Luca Germano also devotes attention to the role of civil society in regime change during the Third Wave, along with the role of economic conditions in promoting change, and in conditioning the potential role of civil society. Broadly speaking, his analysis suggests that a country's relative level of economic *development* is a less reliable indicator of prospects for democratic regime change than the literature would seem to suggest. A state of economic *crisis* seems like a more reliable precursor of regime change. A country's level and type of economic development does influence the nature of pre-transition civil society, and hence the role civil society can play in a transition. Still, civil society can have an important role in *both* developed and developing countries.

Germano uses three pairs of democratic regime changes to highlight how the roles of economics and civil society, and the interactions between these factors, can differ: Portugal and Spain; the Philippines and South Korea; Ghana and South Africa. In both Portugal and Spain, for example, the economic and social crisis stemming from the 1973-74 oil shock contributed to destabilizing the authoritarian regimes. But Spain's higher level of economic development had facilitated the growth of a large middle class and of civil society organizations, unlike in Portugal. And the role of civil society in the democratic transitions consequently was different.

Though the Philippines and South Korea also differed markedly in pre-transition economic development, both encountered economic difficulties in the early 1980s. Despite its low level of development, however, the Philippines had a very lively civil society, thanks to a long democratic experience before the installation of authoritarianism. South Korea as well had preserved a well-networked civil society culture. Civil society played a major role in both countries' democratic transitions in the second half of the 1980s, illustrating that the role of civil society in democratic regime change is not necessarily determined by a country's economic development level.

In both Ghana and South Africa as well, civil society was quite vigorous. Economic crisis played a major in creating conditions for ending the apartheid regime in South Africa. But the authoritarian Rawlings regime in Ghana did not face significant economic problems, and was able to coopt many potential opposition groups, at least through the 1980s. Civil society later was able to organize and play a significant role in promoting democratization, with Rawlings himself ultimately investing in a democratic project. The Ghana/South Africa pair highlights, among other things, how, even within the same world region, economic trends can play out quite differently in promoting democratic regime change.

The chapter by Pietro Grilli di Cortona and Nicoletta Di Sotto focuses on how the weakness or fragility of states can condition prospects for the crisis and collapse of non-democratic regimes and for successful transitions to democracy. Among multiple potential sources of state fragility, they focus in particular on the presence of ethnic groups on the territory of a state with which they do not in fact identify, and on threats to territorial integrity. During the Third Wave of democratization, this factor was extremely important in Eastern Europe, which saw the collapse of three multi-ethnic states, most importantly the USSR and Yugoslavia (as well as the Czech and Slovak Federal Republic). In many of the successor states, inter-ethnic differences continued for some time to pose challenges to full democratic transition, and in countries like Ukraine they remain today a source of stress on the political system and of challenges to the territorial integrity of the state.

The importance of the stateness variable, however, varies between and within world regions, making generalization difficult. Asia includes a number of countries in which interethnic differences have posed challenges to both non-democratic and successor democratizing regimes, plus Taiwan and South Korea, which continue to face very significant external challenges to their territorial integrity, but have managed highly successful democratic transitions. In Africa, the remarkable ethnic diversity of populations is an important contributor to endemic weak stateness, though many other factors also have a role in hindering change in non-democratic regimes or completion of democratic transitions. In Latin America and the Caribbean, challenges to stateness have been relatively modest, and economic and social class differences have tended to be more important drivers of democratic change. Among the countries touched by the Arab Spring, only ethnically homogeneous Tunisia, which also has no external challenges to its territorial integrity, can be considered a democratization success (so far).

Turning to international sources of regime change, Barbara Pisciotta develops an analytical framework that starts with a distinction between structural (or long-term) and conjunctural (or short-term) factors. The former include the configuration of the international system, international economic trends, geopolitical position, and regional integration processes. The latter include military outcomes, the momentary diplomatic context, and what can be termed *Zeitgeist*, the spirit of a given historical moment.

It is important to distinguish as well between the spontaneous spread of democracy due to international conditions, e.g. via "contagion," and voluntary international interventions to promote or protect democracy. Spontaneous international factors are more difficult to study than voluntary ones, but it is clear that democratic contagion during the Third Wave benefited from new and improved means of communication. The so-called "color revolutions" of the post-Cold War era, and the rapid if problematic expansion of the Arab Spring, had a precursor in the much earlier spread, for example, of democratic regime change from Portugal to Spain and on to Latin America.

Voluntary interventions, on the other hand, come in three distinct types: military intervention, conditionality, and democracy assistance. The first two are coercive, albeit one entails use of force, while the latter involves a bargain: "credit in exchange for democratization." Democracy assistance, on the other hand, is a consensual intervention. The distinction between consensual and coercive interventions is a key element of Pisciotta's analytical framework.

This attention to international factors is not to deny the role of internal factors, which in Pisciotta's view "filter" the impact of international factors and account for differences in the democratization process from one region to another and between countries in a given region. At the same time, the international system can either limit the range of options for national leaderships, or sometimes provide unique opportunities, as with the collapse of the Soviet Union and its sphere of control. Like Grilli di Cortona, in his chapter on internal factors, Pisciotta underlines the complex, *multicausal* nature of democratic regime change, and urges caution regarding the feasibility of a general theory of democratization.

Antonino Castaldo focuses specifically on international interventions, introducing the concept of the Proactive International Dimension (PID), broadly defined as including the international actors and their actions that, intentionally or not, cause or contribute to the crisis, breakdown, and transformation of non-democratic regimes. It excludes, in other words, the spread of democracy via spontaneous processes, e.g. contagion or emulation. The Proactive International Dimension can include both state and non-state actors, with objectives including the spread of democracy, preservation of their own security, or preserving the stability of the international system. Some PID actions can threaten the formal sovereignty of the target countries. Overt resort to military force, however, may or may not include regime change among its objectives. International actions that do not formally undermine the sovereignty of the target country can include covert operations, sanctions, positive conditionality, diplomatic pressure, and democracy assistance.

In a detailed review of around 30 cases of Third Wave regime change, Castaldo illustrates how the Proactive International Dimension can play either principal, concurrent, or marginal roles, and how its influence has differed from one world region to another. He finds a very limited role for the PID in Asia (except for Afghanistan), with a greater role in regime change for international factors *not* linked to explicit actions by an international player, along with internal factors. In East Central Europe and the Balkans, the PID played on the whole a concurrent role, as it did in Southern Europe. The situation was more complex in Latin America and the Caribbean and in Africa, where, from one country or sub-region to another, the PID played all three possible roles.

The PID role was especially strong in: small countries with weak economies, dependent on international assistance, with traditions of outside interference; situations of heightened geostrategic significance, especially where so-called "black knights" were not active in bolstering authoritarian regimes; where an external hegemonic power withdrew its support for authoritarian regimes, as the Soviet Union did in East Central Europe at the end of the Cold War; cases of weak stateness and civil conflict. The presence or absence in a given region of a hegemonic international actor, able and willing to act, is another important consideration. The US, for example, was more able to exercise influence in Central America and the Caribbean than in South America. In turn, absent international actions that overtly undermine its sovereignty, a target state regime is more likely to resist the PID effectively if it benefits from: strong coercive ability; a very weak internal opposition; the support of black knights; geostrategic importance; valuable natural resources. The concept of the PID seems highly relevant to analyzing the results of more recent attempts at regime change in regions such as North Africa and the Middle East.

The democratization literature, when it does make reference to "geopolitics," usually uses the term as a synonym for "great power politics." Eric Terzuolo proposes an alternative geopolitical approach to democratization, drawing on the work of Yves Lacoste, the innovative and controversial French geographer. Lacoste's version of geopolitics is genuinely political *and* geographical, focusing on how geographical factors, including cultural and economic ones, shape rivalries for power on given territories, helping define competing interests and creating or constraining political options. Terzuolo proposes a geopolitical "approach" to democratization (not a "theory") that entails considering three main types of geographical factors: 1) location, viewed on a series of different geographical scales; 2) identity, size, and territorial distribution of populations; 3) resources and how they are distributed. This is not an argument for geographical determinism, but simply for viewing such geographical factors as crucial parts of the context in which human and organizational agency plays out in democratization.

Lacoste's core idea of "geographical reasoning" stresses the need to examine situations on multiple geographical scales, which can bring to light different intersections between competing groups. What looks simple on a large-scale map may prove a great deal more complicated as one moves to smaller scales. The largest scale appropriate for geopolitical analysis of democratization is probably the continental/world region scale, which can bring to light significant differences. But other scales, including sub-regions, regional organization membership, individual countries, and "dyads" of closely related countries, all can highlight important specificities and outliers. Distribution of democracy at the sub-national level also merits attention, as can differential distribution of economic and natural resources.

The nation state has been the primary container of democracy, as it actually has existed. But one should not overlook the specific ethnic identities of component population groups, whether located entirely *within* or ranging *across* national borders. That said, interpretations of the impact of ethnolinguistic fractionalization on regime change and transitions to democracy diverge significantly, as do assessments of religion's impact.

Lipset's analysis of the connection between prosperity and democracy remains a major influence in the democratization literature, but one should be wary of economic determinism (of which Lipset himself in fact was not guilty). Poor countries sometimes have taken democratic paths, while internal differences in wealth distribution have fueled political turmoil and secessionism in some relatively prosperous states. There is a case to be made that natural resource wealth, notably oil and gas, is negatively associated with democracy. That said, the effect is not uniform, and Ross, whose widely referenced article from 2001—"Does Oil Hinder Democracy?"[11]—remains a major point of reference, in fact gave a less emphatically positive answer to that question a few years later.[12] Water is another scarce and inequitably distributed resource that is a potential object of intrastate and inter-state conflict. Not surprisingly, there is a positive association between good availability of fresh water and democracy.

A final note. While Prof. Grilli di Cortona conceived this project, designed the structure of the volume, identified the authors, provided initial rounds of guidance, and contributed one chapter and part of another, his death prevented him from participating in the final editing of the volume and preparation for its publication. The remaining co-editors sorely missed the benefits of his sage advice and deep knowledge of democratic regime change. Without a doubt, the final product would have been much stronger had Prof. Grilli di Cortona been able to participate further in its preparation. Responsibility for any shortcomings rests solely with the remaining co-editors.

Endnotes

[1] Retrieved from https://freedomhouse.org/report/freedom-world/freedom-world-2015#.ViZikrSdLvk.

[2] Daniel W. Drezner, "The Fourth Wave of Democratization?" *Daniel W. Drezner* (blog), March 24, 2005, http://www.danieldrezner.com/archives/001960.html.

[3] Also the basis for Larry Diamond and Marc F. Plattner (eds.), *Democracy in Decline?* (Baltimore: Johns Hopkins University Press, 2015).

[4] Published in Madrid by Casa De Velazquez.

[5] See http://ecpr.eu/Filestore/Files/ECPR/ECPR_Constitution.pdf.

[6] At the risk of sounding a Eurosceptic note, it is worth considering that distinctive national traditions in scholarly fields may not be entirely a bad thing, and that resistance to the homogenizing aspects of European integration may have some legitimacy.

[7] See http://necrologi.corriere.it/defunti/pietro-grilli-di-cortona-00001.

[8] Luca Germano, Pietro Grilli di Cortona, and Orazio Lanza, eds. *Come cadono i regimi non democratici: Primi passi verso la democrazia nei paesi della "terza ondata."* Naples: Editoriale Scientifica, 2014.

[9] For a more exhaustive listing of his many publications, see http://scienzepolitiche.uniroma3.it/pgrilli/.

[10] Federigo Argentieri, "Grilli di Cortona, libertà senza utopie," *Corriere della Sera*, August 14, 2015, http://archiviostorico.corriere.it/2015/agosto/14/Grilli_Cortona_liberta_senza_utopie_co_0_20150814_cb6ca66a-4247-11e5-b9b6-28ac3b03d756.shtml .

[11] *World Politics* 53: 325-61.

[12] Retrieved from http://www.sscnet.ucla.edu/polisci/faculty/ross/Oil%20and%20Democracy%20Revisited.pdf.

Reference List

Ahmed, Amel, and Giovanni Capoccia. 2014. "The Study of Democratization and the Arab Spring." *Middle East Law and Governance* 6: 1-31.

Anderson, Leslie E. 2005. "Idealism, Impatience, and Pessimism: Recent Studies of Democratization in Latin America." *Latin American Research Review* 40 (3): 390-402.

Boncourt, Thibaud. 2007. "The Evolution of Political Science in France and Britain: A Comparative Study of Two Political Science Journals." *European Political Science* 6: 276-94.

_____. 2008. "Is European Political Science Different from European Political Sciences? A Comparative Study of the *European Journal of Political Research, Political Studies* and the *Revue Française de Science Politique* 1973-2002." *European Political Science* 7: 366-81.

Bull, Martin J. 2007. "Is there a *European* Political Science and, if so, what are the Challenges Facing It?" *European Political Science* 6: 427-38.

Capano, Giliberto, and Luca Verzichelli. 2010. "Good But Not Good Enough: Recent Developments of Political Science in Italy." *European Political Science* 9: 102-17.

Cooley, Alexander. 2015. "Countering Democratic Norms." *Journal of Democracy* 26 (3): 49-63.

Daalder, Hans. 2014. "The Plethora of Polysyllables: A Behavioural Approach to the Frequent Use of Jargon in American Political Science." *European Political Science* 13 (1): 97-102.

Diamond, Larry, Francis Fukuyama, Donald L. Horowitz, and Marc F. Plattner. 2014. "Reconsidering the Transition Paradigm." *Journal of Democracy* 25 (1): 86-100.

Dunne. Michele. 2015. "Caught in History's Crosswinds." *Journal of Democracy* 26 (4): 75-79.

Gleditsch, Nils Petter. 2007. "Incentives to Publish." *European Political Science* 6: 185-91.

Hale, Henry E. 2013. "Regime Change Cascades: What We Have Learned from the 1848 Revolutions to the 2011 Arab Uprisings." *Annual Review of Political Science* 16: 331-53.

King, Ronald, F., and Cosmin Gabriel Marian. 2008. "Defining Political Science: A Cross-National Survey." *European Political Science* 7: 207-19.

Munck, Gerardo L. 2007. "Democracy Studies: Agendas, Findings, and Challenges." In *Democratization: The State of the Art*, 2nd rev. and updated ed., edited by Michael Stein and John Trent, 45-68. Opladen, Federal Republic of Germany: Barbara Budrich Publishers.

Plattner, Marc F. 2014. "The End of the Transitions Era?" *Journal of Democracy* 25 (3): 6-16.

_____. 2015. "Is Democracy in Decline?" *Journal of Democracy* 26 (1): 5-10.

Schneider, Gerald. 2007. "Why is European Political Science So Unproductive and What Should Be Done About It?" *European Political Science* 6: 156-9.

Szmolka, Immaculada. "¿La quinta ola de democratización? Cambio político sin cambio de régimen en los países árabes." *Politica y Sociedad* 50 (3): 893-935.

Verzichelli, Luca. 2014. "Signs of Competitiveness? The Presence of Italian Research in International Political Science Journals." *Italian Political Science* 9 (2): 27-43.

Why Do Autocracies Fall?
Internal Political Factors

Pietro Grilli di Cortona

The goal of this chapter is to explore the internal political dynamics that led to the fall of autocratic regimes during the Third Wave of democratization. I will not deal with economic causes (see the chapter by Luca Germano) or those concerning stateness, (see my chapter with Nicoletta Di Sotto). Instead, I will discuss internal political factors, though not "structural" factors such as levels of development, class structure and income inequality (Mainwaring and Pérez-Liñan 2013, 5). Although important in any study, these factors tend to be overrated, especially with respect to Latin America and Africa, and we will see that they are not of primary importance in regime transformation.

Although recognizing how difficult it is to draw a clear line between internal and international factors, in other chapters Barbara Pisciotta, Antonino Castaldo, and Eric Terzuolo deal with the international dimension. All issues concerning stateness straddle that line. Even when you speak of the spread of a regime from one country to another, it is often difficult to distinguish between cross-national transmission of values and institutional models and the introduction of a concomitant concentration of emerging factors in a region (Brinks and Coppedge 2006, 465). In addition, the precise intersection of internal and international dimensions is often very difficult to pinpoint, since causal effects can go in both directions. The "Carnation Revolution" in Portugal (1974) was an internal event caused by armed forces exhausted by colonial wars (external factor), while Greece's military adventure in Cyprus (1974) and Argentina's in the Falkland Islands (1982) were international events determined by internal causes (essentially, the two military regimes' loss of prestige and consensus).

Despite these various causal combinations, the division between internal and international factors, and the attribution to one or the other of a major explanatory role, has solid roots in the international literature that has evolved over time. The 1986 work edited by O'Donnell, Schmitter, and Whitehead seemed to emphasize internal aspects, while Whitehead's 1996 work emphasized the importance of the international variable that clearly emerged in the regime transitions of the 1990s. From the 1990s on, the international variable, and its entwinement with internal factors, has received a great deal of attention (see the bibliographies of the chapters in this book that deal with this issue). The works by Magen and Morlino (2008) and Levitsky and Way (2005; 2010) are particularly interesting, and the "international-domestic nexus" is central to the analyses in Stoner and McFaul (2013).

The wave of transformations that occurred beginning in the first half of the 1970s overturned 83 regimes, producing significant change, but not always in a democratic direction. In reality, the various democratic results (consolidated democracies, relatively stable or intermittent) amounted to only 43 out of the 83 countries involved. The remaining 37 were mostly hybrid regimes and some were regressions toward new authoritarian forms (Grilli di Cortona 2014). If we add to these cases the so-called Arab Spring of 2011-2013, only Tunisia seems to have taken a credible democratic path. In the other cases the results, at least to date, seem to be civil war and the partial or total collapse of the state (Syria, Libya, Yemen) or the transition to new authoritarian forms (Egypt).

The End of Old Regimes

At the theoretical level, it is evident that there are three crucial aspects in the study of the crisis and fall of political regimes. The first is to identify indicators or signals that the old regime is about to end. When can you effectively say that it has entered its final crisis? How do you recognize it? Secondly, one must identify the principal motivation for change, with the understanding that the end of a regime can never be attributed to a single cause. (Scholarly explanations are never monocausal.) The reasons are almost always in reality a concatenation of causes. It is evident, though, that in each case there are causes that are more important and significant, and that sometimes these can become truly decisive. The third crucial aspect is the outcome of the regime's transformation, or rather the end point, which offers us the opportunity to understand, for example, whether it is a democratization or not.

I will make only a few observations on points 1 and 3, and concentrate on point 2. Concerning point 1, you can say that a regime falls and ceases to exist in the presence of two possible groups of circumstances. First and foremost, when it is overthrown by illegal and violent means, for example, a coup d'état, revolution, civil war, or foreign invasion. The most traumatic event indicating the end of a regime can be the ouster of the dictator with whom the regime is identified. A study of cases between 1946 and 2004 (Escribà-Folch 2013) found that, in regime change, 47% of dictators were imprisoned, killed, or sent into exile.[1] In all cases in which the transition is discontinuous and traumatic, it is very easy to identify when the regime collapses and the new political order begins. Changes in the elites, the rules, and institutions go at the same speed. Although the modalities differed greatly, the end of the Caetano regime in Portugal in 1974-1975, of the Somoza regime in Nicaragua in 1979, and of the Communist regime in Czechoslovakia in 1989 all belong to this typology. In totally different conditions and with different results, the end of the old regimes decreed by the Arab Spring in 2011 and 2012 occurred in the same manner. The traumatic nature and rupture with the past marking a political change are especially evident when accompanied by a change in the form of the state, as occurred in all the former Soviet republics (Way 2005).

A second type of change is instead more subtle, with all or some of the old regime's elite managing the change. In this case, transformation is less traumatic and more continuous (Morlino 2003; Grilli di Cortona 2009). There are no drastic ruptures. Rather than being replaced or abolished, norms and institutions are integrated, bent, and adapted to the new situation. Most administrative and even some political personnel remain in play, albeit with the collaboration of parts of the political opposition. In Spain and Hungary, for example, it was the old elites that launched the change, attempting to combine real and important transformation with some continuity. In fact, this type of transition should not be underestimated. The change is real, it is just more difficult to pinpoint the moment when the autocratic regime ends. At a certain point, however, the transition is complete. In the case of democratization, this is demonstrated by competitive elections, the restoration of civil rights and political freedom, and the reform or creation of democratic institutions. In the case of other types of transitions (for example, towards new types of authoritarianism or hybrid regimes) it is demonstrated by the formation of new pacts, changes in the composition of the elites (even if sometimes the personnel do not change), and often even a change in "political formula," i.e. the regime's political culture and ideological configuration. The transitions in the 1990s of certain post-Soviet republics and African regimes come to mind (Carbone 2005; Grilli di Cortona 2014). Other factors, including the context in which the change takes place, require consideration. Authoritarian leadership can consist of a single or hegemonic party, the armed forces, a royal family and its entourage, a group that identifies with a leader's personal power, or a combination of these actors. The transition from one actor to another indicates a significant change, but sometimes even the perpetuation of a dominant actor can entail a considerable shift, if accompanied by changes in other dimensions. A royal family can support the transformation from a despotic monarchical regime to a constitutional monarchy, as in Nepal in 1990, or a military leader may alternate with another from the same inner circle (same national, religious or ethnic group), changing the person but not necessarily the regime.

As for the transformation's results, we already have seen how, despite the sweeping movement of nations towards democracy during the Third Wave of democratization, not all countries became democratic. To be systematic, the results can be categorized thus: regime survival, perhaps under a partially renewed leadership; democratization, to a variable extent; replacement of the old autocratic regime with a new one (Geddes, Wright, and Frantz 2012).

Internal pressure for change can originate from three different and distinct groups of sources, often capable of interacting, nurturing each other, and melding: the legacy of the past; civil society and an organized opposition; elite internal dynamics. Each of these sources of change develops thanks to a situation favorable to the weakening of the regime. During the Third Wave, among the factors included in such a favorable context, we must consider the international ones discussed in other chapters of this book, as well as the failure of the legitimizing role of the great ideologies of the 20th century (Fascism, Communism, Corporatism, etc.) on which many of the world's authoritarian regimes long rested, having been presented as alternative models to fragile Western democracies. After World War II, when some of the old ideologies collapsed or lost momentum, democracy was again proposed as a successful model, and many surviving authoritarian political regimes justified themselves as transitional regimes, their existence aimed at restoring social peace, the pursuit of economic development, combating corruption, etc. (O'Donnell and Schmitter 1986, 15).

The role of ideologies at the global level is also a subject of interest for Linz and Stepan (1996, 74ff.), who assert that the difference between the 1920s and the 1970s consists in the fact that, in the 1920s, the *Zeitgeist* (spirit of the times) saw competition among at least five ideological models: the Soviet Union's Communism, Italy's Fascism, Catholic integralism (i.e. belief in an integral unity of faith with political thought), a conservatism that still considered authoritarian and pre-democratic constitutional monarchies as valid models (for example, Imperial Germany), and finally democracy, which began to establish itself in a dozen or so countries that had no previous democratic traditions. In these conditions, the authoritarian models still seemed to be successful and enjoyed the support of significant parts of the population and, in some cases (especially Communism and Fascism), exercised a certain attraction outside of the countries where they were established. Undemocratic ideas circulated with success, and not just in Europe. In Latin America they supported institutional experiences such as Vargas's *l'Estado Novo* in Brazil, beginning in the 1930s, or Peronism in Argentina after the Second World War. Indeed, despite the collapse of Fascism at the end of the war, authoritarian institutional models survived up to the 1960s, making the prospects for the spread of democracy rather remote (Maier 1994; Bell and Staeheli 2001).

Beginning in the 1970s the situation was very different. As we have seen, authoritarian ideologies lost all prestige and were discredited even among the middle classes that often had promoted them. After Vatican II (1961-1963) the Catholic Church increasingly developed positions in harmony with democratic concepts (Huntington 1991; Linz and Stepan 1996). With a lag of more than 20 years, Communist ideology as well suffered a drastic reappraisal and weakening in regimes that based their legitimacy on it. Marxism-Leninism had already lost its vigor by the 1970s and for younger generations had no appeal whatsoever. The Communist model appears to have missed most of the objectives that had promoted its expansion and rise to power in many countries, ending up by legitimizing repressive regimes dominated by tiresome rituals that publics considered increasingly anachronistic. Some attempts at innovation and reform were successful, such as the New Economic Mechanism in Hungary, which introduced typical free market criteria to the management of factories (Hankiss 1990). Others were destined to fail, at least in the short term, such as the economic reforms in Czechoslovakia that culminated in the tragic end of the Prague Spring in 1968, and the birth in August 1980 of the free labor union in Poland, then outlawed in December 1981. After these events, a crisis in Communist regimes was fairly predictable, only a matter of time (Grilli di Cortona 1989).

For its part, compared to the 1920s and 30s, the democratic model strengthened and became attractive pretty much everywhere in the world. All regimes sought, not always successfully and often rather hypocritically, to don democratic clothing. One reason the Colonels' regime in Greece had difficulty in solidifying and establishing itself at the end of the 1960s was the greater prestige of the democratic model at the international level, a model that was distinctly on the defensive in the 1920s and 30s when the authoritarian regimes of the Iberian peninsula were developing (Diamandourous 1986, 145). We can say the same about the Chilean junta and Pinochet's attempts at institutionalization beginning at the end of the 1970s. As in the 1990s, it was evident that the "spirit of the times" was clearly in favor of democracy. Authoritarian and totalitarian forms were generally viewed negatively. One cannot overlook this change in ideological and cultural orientation when studying the crisis of autocracies from the 1970s on.

Coming to the sources of change, except for the legacies of the past, the other factors are all connected to the role of political actors (leaders, elites, political parties, unions, associations, groups, the military, organized movements) capable of controlling political resources and exercising influence on the direction and extent of political change. Along with international influences, whether political actors take moderate or radical positions, or prefer democratic or authoritarian institutional models, has great importance in explaining political change, its success or failure and its outcomes. Legacies play a conditioning role, with the past offering a variety of models on which to draw: the presence of institutions that are part of the country's historical tradition; a political experience to look to as a model to revive or as a negative model to avoid; the legacies of a previous colonial occupation; historic memory. Specific situations influence the degree of popular mobilization, and organized oppositions, legal or semi-legal, assume particular importance when the old regime appears weak and incapable of controlling the development of civil society, with alternative organizations taking form, e.g. political parties, unions, movements, and pressure groups (sometimes even within the establishment).

Finally, the internal dynamics of the old regime's elite (of whatever variety) hark back to many factors, from the nature and solidity of the pacts and alliances on which the coalition in power stands, to problems of succession (a real thorn in the side of many authoritarian regimes), and to the birth of out and out conflicts within the elite that can weaken or send it into crisis. For example, it is well known that military regimes have a shorter duration than single-party regimes (Nordlinger 1977; Geddes 1999; Hadenius and Teorell 2007; Kailitz 2013) and that democratization is the most likely outcome once the stimuli that originally induced the armed forces to seize power have been exhausted (Geddes, Wright, and Frantz 2012). The following section addresses in more detail the three main sources of internal pressure for change: legacies; civil society and anti-regime mobilization; internal dynamics of elites.

The Role of Legacy

The legacy of the past is that patrimony of experiences, values, traditions, practices, and historical memory that is transmitted to old and new political actors, restricting their choices and behavior, and that ends up conditioning the character, path, and results of political change (Grilli di Cortona and Lanza, 2011; Lanza 2012). Each change is also the product of so-called *confining conditions* (Kirchheimer 1965), namely that combination of influences, conditioning, and limitations that must be overcome or adapted to, but that in any case determines successive choices and decisions. The reference here is specifically to the legacies of experiences that preceded the autocratic regime and that obviously contribute to its weakening and delegitimization. Some of the conditions that favor regime change are inherited from the past: influences of the colonial experience or the role of certain cultural and religious factors (for example, ethnic composition and attending hostility between different linguistic, national and tribal groups, discussed in my chapter with Nicoletta Di Sotto). The endurance and cohesion of the state and its structures, the organization of civil society with its greater or lesser potential for mobilization, also are factors that can explain the differences between countries in the push for change and its efficacy. These are variables that can positively unite with an innovative process and bring the authoritarian experience to an end, sometimes with an opening towards more democratic institutions.

The weight and power of legacy depend on how the different legacies are filtered and reinterpreted by autocratic regimes: the longer such regimes last, and the more they display internal innovative and transformational characteristics, perhaps fed by strong ideological motivations and the ability to mobilize, the more the legacies of the past are conditioned and funneled in specific directions. In the USSR, Portugal, Spain, and the countries of Eastern Europe, non-democratic regimes had more than 40 years to mold new generations, impose behaviors and values, and consolidate institutions. The Communist regimes added heavy-handed internal transformations (of civil society, the economic system, cultural aspects) dictated by the revolutionary force of Marxism-Leninism. In Greece, on the other hand, the limited duration of the authoritarian phase (seven years) and the general ideological inconsistency of the Colonels' regime did not permit the military to influence either society or the state deeply. Brief duration of the non-democratic phase can facilitate the rapid reconstitution of political parties and institutions, with the eventuality that individual political representatives can even reclaim their roles in the political arena (Grilli di Cortona 2011).

The legacy of a colonial past comes in various forms, and often with contradictory influences. This can be read as a variable straddling internal and external factors. The crucial question is the following: Can a colonial past constitute a legacy that is a negative factor in terms of the stability and duration of an autocratic experience? On this point, according to Diamond (1988, 6-10) and referring to Africa, we can make the following observations. First of all, even when a colonizing country has comparatively liberal institutions, in the colonized country political participation can be attained only after many years, is limited to a small elite, and certainly is not for the majority of the population. Secondly, the colonizing country always introduces a model of political relations that is based on violence, in the form of repression and coercion, rather than on dialog and negotiation. This has a direct influence on how the new indigenous political class exercises power when the colony becomes independent. In essence, a colonial past establishes power management practices that are coherent and compatible with an authoritarian order. Thirdly, the colonial experience is not only authoritarian, but fundamentally statist. Control is imposed on commerce, agriculture, and the exploitation of raw materials. Various types of monopolies are imposed on most of the internal sources of income. Finally, the participation of locals in the higher levels of public administration is generally discouraged and seen with diffidence, with the result that, once independence is obtained, most of these countries are unprepared to create and manage the mechanisms of government. This also explains the fragility of public institutions, an effect of choices made during the colonial era which remain a negative legacy, responsible for difficulties in the *state building* set in motion with independence.

Despite these negative legacies, especially advantageous for the preservation of an authoritarian order, the colonial experience also can contribute to limiting the authoritarian characteristics in a newly independent state, and sometimes even weaken them. This can occur when certain institutions are created, even at an embryonic level. The transfer of power in British colonies was accomplished via constitutional mechanisms and logic. In the French colonies, Africans with high levels of education were allowed to enter the French National Assembly. The pattern in Portuguese colonies was different: their democratization was more the product of emulating what was occurring in Lisbon in the 1970s than of the presence of prior institutions and practices. Diamond (1988, 9-10) calls attention to the nature and manner of the decolonization process. Where independence came without extensive mobilization of the masses and, especially, without an armed struggle for national liberation, the new state was born without a potential source of anti-democratic pressure. A comparison between Algeria and Senegal illustrates this point well. While in Algeria there was a long and bloody anti-colonial revolution that led to the formation of an authoritarian regime, largely dominated by the military heirs of the National Liberation Front, in Senegal the absence of a war of liberation, significant mass mobilization, and sanctioning of violence as a method of political expression allowed for the development of a more democratic style and behavior in the new political elite, facilitating the abandonment of authoritarian characteristics initially present in the newly independent state.

In many African countries, the duration and the characteristics of colonial control not only shaped the structuring of the political system and public administration, but also the culture of each individual country, and thus had important repercussions for the configuration of the political institutions that were formed after independence. Sometimes it is the colonial power that directly or indirectly creates conditions favorable for democratization. The choices and political evolution of the colonizing or occupying country can have an important explanatory role. The United Kingdom was influential in Botswana's political development, beginning contact in 1959 with the internal elites to draft a constitution that gave birth to an independent nation with democratic institutions. It was also the United Kingdom that left a partially trained and autonomous administrative class in Ghana and elsewhere in West Africa that helped in the development of democratic institutions. In Namibia, South Africa's own internal evolution was notably influential. It explains why South Africa was not able to delay granting independence and beginning a political transition. Portugal's transition was strictly tied to colonial issues. The "Carnation Revolution" originated largely in the armed forces' unwillingness to continue colonial wars where there was absolutely no prospect of victory. As mentioned earlier, political change in Lisbon was concurrent with the beginning of the dismantlement of Portugal's colonial empire, and in turn represented an important opportunity for various countries. Leaders in what became independent Cape Verde, Guinea-Bissau, São Tomé and Príncipe, Mozambique, and East Timor took advantage of the changes occurring in Lisbon to initiate their own internal changes. Thanks to French influence, the establishment of democratic practices in Senegal dates back far to the past, when the French granted participation in municipal governments and even the election of a representative to the parliament in Paris.

Previous democratic experiences also can have a role in weakening a non-democratic regime (Grilli di Cortona and Lanza 2011; Lanza 2012). As Huntington (1991) pointed out, past existence of a more or less embryonic democracy, pluralism, and market economy makes an authoritarian regime's stability less probable and fosters conditions more favorable to its obsolescence and collapse. A certain number of states that saw regime change during the Third Wave had some democratic history (Grassi 2008). This group included Spain, Portugal, Greece, South Korea, Turkey, Czechoslovakia, Poland, the Baltic countries, East Germany, Hungary, Argentina, Brazil, Chile, Ecuador, Peru and Uruguay. These countries were able to rely on a patrimony of past experiences that potentially could weaken non-democratic regimes. These included institutions and institutional models, clandestine leaders or exiles ready to step in and provide an alternative to the authoritarian political class, and political party or union organizations, whether clandestine or abroad, ready to revive at any time and contribute to organizing protests and to the rebirth of the opposition, historic memory, and political learning. In the transition to mass democracy, even countries where there was a "racial oligarchy" made use of strong democratic institutions originally reserved for the white minority.

Some countries admittedly had only fragile and brief prior democratic experiences, the only trace of which remained the historic memory of the errors committed, explaining the weakness, ephemeral nature, and fall of the democratic experience.[2] These are past experiences that members of the opposition harken back to as points of reference and institutional models (political learning). For example, the rather ephemeral democratic experiences of the Baltic countries in the 1920s provided an incentive to return to being independent democratic states, as well as institutional and constitutional models for the new democratic phase. It is no coincidence that Estonia and Latvia relied on reinstatement of their 1920s constitutions. This is what Huntington (1991, 42) describes as the *second try pattern*, which can explain the success of certain democratizations as a result of learning from past errors.

On the other hand, in certain circumstances legacies carry more weight, such as when democratic structures and institutions are not completely eliminated, and perhaps continue to operate under the radar, even with a certain amount of tolerance (perhaps intermittent) on the part of the regime. According to O'Donnell and Schmitter (1986, 19-21), political parties, social movements, interest groups, autonomous agencies, forms of local government, and other institutions that are able to survive, even in a clandestine form, contribute to eroding an autocratic regime, and in certain cases can demonstrate an extraordinary capacity to reemerge. In Brazil, the generals who took over in 1964 ruled largely by distorting the basic institutions of political democracy, rather than by dismantling them (O'Donnell and Schmitter 1986, 22). Officially, political parties were illegal, but their reemergence was tolerated. Parliament had no real power, but continued to carry out certain functions and, over time, recovered a certain amount of authority. This made the transition from authoritarianism to a democratic regime easier and less traumatic. In Greece, the authoritarian experience under the Colonels was very brief (1967-74) which in part facilitated the return to power of the same political actors, and even of the same pre-1967 political alignments. The democratic legacy experienced in different forms in Hungary, Czechoslovakia, and Poland between the two world wars clearly reemerged at times under the Communist regimes formed after World War II. During the Hungarian uprising in 1956, many Hungarian political parties from the 1930s and 40s reappeared. During the Prague Spring in 1968, the strong influence of the traditions of political pluralism and market economics found in the territories that became part of the Czechoslovak Republic in 1918 were evident, in addition to the legacies of the interwar period. The whole story of *Solidarnošč* in Poland (1980-

81) had solid roots in the tradition of the "White" and "Red" union movements of the 1930s (Grilli di Cortona 1989).

Civil Society and Anti-Regime Mobilization

The resurrection of civil society and mass mobilization can seriously undermine a regime and create significant cracks within the elite. Like rifts within elites, civil society and anti-regime mobilization are only one link (even if in some cases decisive) in the chain of events that leads to a regime crisis. Reasons of an economic nature, others tied to ethnic, religious, and linguistic identity, and various kinds of political issues also can promote mobilization.

Economic development has always contributed to the growth of the middle class and to forging civil society. If development fails and the economic crisis is so grave that it affects the citizens' quality of life, the latter will mobilize via civil society organizations (unions, political parties, movements, groups) and challenge the regime. This sequence (first development, which creates rising expectations, then crisis and the fall of all socio-economic indicators) is relatively frequent, and often a contributing factor in the end of authoritarian regimes.

Ethnic, religious, and cultural causes also can have strong potential for mobilization (Way 2005, 238). If opposition leaders can appeal to sentiments of identity, mass mobilization against the regime becomes more probable. In some Communist regimes, the effectiveness of the opposition's actions depended greatly on its ability to make itself the standard bearer of the struggle for national liberation. In these cases, the emotional tension reaches its peak and the response of the masses is ready, as in the case of the huge demonstrations in the Baltic countries in 1989-90. The importance of the nationalist and patriotic call fades or assumes problematic connotations when two nationalist poles face off, as in Moldova, Ukraine, and Georgia, where the pro-Russian and pro-Western poles were at odds. The first to mobilize are usually artists, intellectuals, students, human rights movements, unions, and political parties, with demands for civil rights, freedom of the press, the right to strike, free elections, etc.

Popular mobilization is often driven and fueled by a leader able to catalyze, unify and guide the opposition. Mobilization can come in various forms, depending on whether or not it is violent, its duration and repetitiveness, if it involves labor organizations (therefore, with strikes in various sectors), how large and extensive it is, and how much support it attracts from internal and international organizations. Violent mobilization can alienate sectors of the population that fear a breakdown in public order and security, and can provoke the opposite of the intended effect, a strengthening of the authoritarian regime. On the other hand, a large, peaceful, widespread, and continuous mobilization creates conditions favorable to a crisis in the authoritarian regime (Schock 2005; Bermeo 2003), unifying the opposition and institutionalizing an eventual emerging leadership. If the regime's reaction is violent, mobilization can expand further and create conditions for opening negotiations in which a third party (a religious organization, foreign country, nongovernmental organization, etc.) can acquire a mediating role. Negotiations de facto legitimize the opposition (as occurred in Poland in 1980) making it costly and difficult to turn back.

In half of the countries involved in Third Wave, transformations featured grassroots mobilizations, which were to varying degrees peaceful, effective, and connected with sectors of the elite trying to control the change. In Spain and Greece these phenomena did not occur to any great extent (except for the Greek student demonstration in fall 1973), while in Portugal mobilization was in large part generated and encouraged by revolutionary members of the military, with the goal of creating for external consumption the image of a popular revolution. In Argentina, something of a mass uprising occurred when, after the defeat in the Falklands War, a process of change was clearly beginning. Limiting ourselves to a few examples, important mobilizations were seen also in Peru, the Philippines, Nepal, South Africa, Czechoslovakia, and Chile at the end of the 1980s.

The economic crisis in Peru in the 1970s was decisive for the development of an increasingly active popular movement. General Velasco Alvarado's removal in 1975 created high expectations in the population, spreading the feeling that they were entering a new era. There was new unrest among political parties, movements, and unions, with increasing protests and demonstrations. These did not cease even with repression by the regime. (Velasco Alvarado had been replaced by General Morales Bermúdez, who announced the beginning of a "second phase" of the Peruvian revolution). Civil society initiatives, publications, and protests continued to proliferate, culminating with the 1977 strike to which all opposition political forces adhered. It was a resounding success (Cotler 1986). The government's attempts to open to the business class and to political parties traditionally sidelined by the regime, such as the center-left *Alianza Popular Revolucionaria Americana* (APRA) and *Acción Popular* (AP) not only did not obtain the desired results, but de facto helped unite the opposition in a loud demand for the return of democracy. Even the *Partido Popular Cristiano* (PPC), an expression of the right-wing middle class, joined in this demand. There is no doubt that the series of civil society mobilizations induced the government to seek an agreement with the two major political parties (APRA and PPC), consisting of a promise to transfer power to civilians after the election of a constituent assembly.

In the Philippines, the Marcos regime ended because of its inability to contain and repress the Communist guerillas and to handle the economic crisis. The first problem began at the end of the 1960s, with the birth of the New People's Army, the armed wing of the Communist Party of the Philippines, an increasing worry for the United States. In fact, guerrillas were present in most provinces, controlled about 20% of the country's villages, and were responsible for innumerable acts of violence, especially in Mindanao province (Jackson 1988). The economic crisis began to make itself felt in the second half of the 1970s, especially hitting the incomes of the lower classes. It became increasingly dangerous for the regime's stability when, between 1983 and 1986, it began to hit the upper middle and business classes, which until then had supported Marcos. The 1983 assassination of Benigno Aquino, exponent of a growing democratic opposition, contributed to the regime's increasing unpopularity, and its loss of support from the United States and the Catholic Church. Hundreds of thousands of people mobilized for celebrations and funerals. In the fall of 1983, weekly anti-Marcos demonstrations began to give the first push to the regime. By the fall of 1985, the regime's legitimacy had been eroded by the popular protests, leading to the decision to call a new presidential election in 1986. Marcos's fraudulent electoral victory did nothing but exasperate the opposition and, following the elections, Corazon Aquino, widow of the politician assassinated in 1983, announced a campaign of non-violent civil disobedience. Attempted military coups, the continuing demonstrations, the strong support of the Catholic Church for the opposition, and the end of US support finally convinced Marcos to leave.

After the democratic interlude of the 1950s and the installation of an authoritarian monarchy in 1960, opposition mobilization in Nepal intensified in the 1980s, when the Congress Party, the major clandestine organization, allied itself with some Communist groups. The most important demonstrations began in February 1990: a peaceful demonstration of over ten thousand people in Kathmandu, and a general strike that the regime violently suppressed. The demonstrations did not end even when, in April, the king tried to pacify the masses with various promises of reform. A new constitution in 1991 that limited royal powers and provided for free elections seemed to be the turning point for the regime. (The monarchy persisted, however, until declaration of a democratic republic in 2008.)

Fueled by the economic crisis of the 1970s and 80s and the collapse of legitimacy of internal power, other forms of prolonged mass mobilization were seen in Latin America (for example, Argentina, Bolivia, Chile, Mexico, Nicaragua, Paraguay, Peru, and Uruguay) and in East Central Europe (especially Poland, Czechoslovakia, East Germany, Romania, and the Baltic countries). Among the Communist regimes, the most interesting case was that of Czechoslovakia, where the old elite, led by Gustáv Husák, seemed totally impervious to calls for moderation coming from Moscow and Mikhail Gorbachëv. The revival of civil society and the population's mobilization around two leaders, Havel and Dubček, had a particularly dynamic role in the fall of the regime. Active clandestine political groups were already a reality at the end of 1988. In mid-1989 there were 27 independent political groups and movements and more than 40 *samizdat* periodicals (Grilli di Cortona 1997, 24). Public demonstrations became the only real method of applying pressure for change, and in the second half of 1989 there were three demonstrations in Prague (August 21, October 28 and December 10) in which thousands participated. The inability of the elites to respond by beginning negotiations with democratic reformers provoked the collapse of the old regime, with Husák's resignation in December 1989, and produced a higher level of participation in the process of change than in countries like Hungary and Poland, where reforms launched by the respective Communist leaderships had allowed them to control the transition's initial phases.

Chile's case is very unusual and its inclusion in cases of civil society mobilization is debatable. In reality, this mobilization was initiated by the authoritarian regime itself, when, in 1980, in an effort to strengthen, re-legitimate, and re-institutionalize the regime, General Pinochet decided to launch a constitutional reform and submit it to a referendum (something similar was also happening in Uruguay), feeling certain of the population's approval. Unlike in the rest of Latin America, where even rightwing movements were aligned against the military (for example, in Uruguay), in Chile the traditional Right and the business world still supported the military (Linz and Stepan 1996, 206). The 1988 referendum was to decide if the person unanimously chosen by the military junta (Pinochet) would govern as an "elected president" for 8 years. This constituted both a way of measuring the level of support for Pinochet and an opportunity to reorganize the opposition. The dictator obtained a modest success (44% of the vote), but not the absolute majority desired. This represented the beginning of the regime's transformation.

Not even Africa was completely immune to pressure from below. The case of South Africa was important, with growing mass mobilization (in addition to other factors, starting with the sanctions and the country's international isolation because of its internal apartheid policies) being decisive in persuading part of the White elite to begin negotiations with the Black opposition. The 1980s were particularly important for popular mobilization against the regime, although such mobilization was already visible in the 1970s. Besides the African National Congress (1912), other organizations were born, including the United Democratic Front (1983) and the Congress of South African Trade Unions (1985). 1985-86 and 1989 saw various waves of demonstrations, during which protest spread rapidly and mobilization involved ever more sectors of society, until de Klerk announced the release of Nelson Mandela, the start of negotiations, and the dismantlement of apartheid.

Sub-Saharan Africa has one of the weakest traditions of civil society among world regions (Leon 2010). One notes limited mobilizations in Benin, the Comoros Islands, Lesotho, Mali, Malawi, Niger, Tanzania, Togo, and Zambia. The principle protagonists were tribal or ethnic groups, social groups, political parties, unions, churches, and religious groups. Sometimes these mobilizations occurred with the support of parts of the power elites that (via national conferences or referenda) were trying to promote reconstruction of the state, for example in Benin, Malawi, Mali, Niger, Togo, and Zambia at the beginning of the 1990s. As highlighted by Huntington (1991), churches and religious groups were much more active in mass mobilization of civil society during the Third Wave than in previous democratization waves. In particular, alongside other Christian churches, in the 1970s the Catholic Church assumed an increasingly critical position towards authoritarian regimes and played an important role in Poland, Central America, Chile, Brazil, the Philippines, South Korea, East Timor and some African states. In many cases, representatives of local churches took direct initiatives to weaken the existing regimes by convening national conferences (Benin), mediating between the government and opposition (Nicaragua, Poland, Zambia), or applying direct pressure with speeches, pastoral letters and sermons (the Philippines, South Africa). Obviously, internal religious structure is not always decisive. As stated in Joseph (1991) and Carbone (2005, 173) concerning African countries, there also were many cases of failed or interrupted political change (for example, Angola and Burundi) despite strong Catholic majorities.

Elite Internal Dynamics and Crises of Succession

In general, the leadership's internal dynamics are one of the decisive factors in political change. The nature and traits of elites can be very diverse, as are the pacts and coalitions that form the basis of non-democratic regimes. A regime crisis often derives from internal changes in the elite and alliances, which in turn are often the product of economic problems and international crises. These dynamics can take three different forms. First, most challenges to the stability of non-democratic regimes come from palace conspiracies and battles within the elite (Frantz and Ezrow 2011). They almost always take the form of a split between hard-liners, who seek to perpetuate the old regime at any cost, and soft-liners (O'Donnell and Schmitter 1986, 15-17) who are prepared to concede some change to respond to the demands of the masses and opposition, but remain firm in their desire to safeguard the regime. Second, for various reasons, individual leaders sometimes decide to initiate change, for example, by launching a more or less wide-reaching democratic transition, which is more or less sincere and genuine. Finally, the decline or even the fall of a regime can be caused by the death of the leader and the resulting succession crisis.

The formation of rifts within the elite is rather common in military regimes, whose origins are often linked with short-term factors and not with long-term ideological projects. In military regimes, the elite is often composed predominantly of members of the armed forces, plus civilian consultants, technocrats, bureaucrats, and representatives of the business and financial world under military influence. In addition, an ideological justification for military regimes is generally nonexistent, replaced by values such as national interest and unity, order, security, fighting corruption, efficiency, and patriotism (Linz and Stepan 1996). Sometimes legitimizing ideological forms are adopted that are clearly specious in nature. The case of Jerry Rawlings is typical. The young Ghanaian officer established a military regime, initially populist and socialist in tone, but then converted to free market policies once he realized that the international order made it worth his while. The objectives of military regimes are often specific, limited in time, and generally have to do with safeguarding the state's integrity from internal threats (guerrillas, rebellions, social disorder, secessions, incompetent politicians, corruption, and illegality) that often come in conjunction with situations of economic crisis, or to defend the military's own corporate interests or those of some particular social group (financial, industrial or agricultural elites). Mostly found in Latin America and Africa, military regimes also have surfaced in Asia (Bangladesh, South Korea, Thailand) as well as in Europe (Greece, Turkey). In Chile under Pinochet and Uganda under Amin, the military regimes became personalistic. In such cases, the military tends to lose power to a leader who establishes himself as the *dominus*, even if always with the armed forces' critical support.

As highlighted by many authors (Huntington 1991; Linz and Stepan 1996), a peculiarity of praetorian regimes derives from the relative ease with which military regimes can abandon political power and return to the barracks. Nordlinger (1977) observed the tendency of military regimes to last for less time than other kinds of regimes. Authors like Geddes (1999), Hadenius and Teorell (2007), and Kailitz (2013) agreed in finding that military regimes do not last as long as single-party regimes. It is worthwhile to note that officers consider themselves servants of the state, with enduring interests, a permanent role, and high social standing. An evaluation of the costs versus the advantages of remaining in power is often present, and, in any case, given the military's privileged position because of their monopoly on force, a return to power is always possible if any threats should arise to their institutional autonomy. At the same time, one should remember that armed forces are often internally divided, and that these divisions are accentuated in moments of crisis and difficulty, due to policies the armed forces themselves set in motion.

Bolivia's bumpy and irregular journey toward a more democratic order is a crystal clear demonstration of how political change is in many cases determined by the internal dynamics of the elite. Despite factionalism within the armed forces, divided along ideological, generational, and hierarchical lines (Gamarra 1989), the Bolivian military regime lasted for nearly 20 years, until 1982. This long period was characterized by a series of coups and counter-coups, in which 10 military governments of various political orientations, and two weak civilian governments, alternated power. Inside the Bolivian military elite, alliances had to be renegotiated constantly, and the armed forces remained permeable to outside influence, especially from civil sectors, and completely unpredictable in their dealings with other organized groups in society (Whitehead 1986, 54). The Bolivian transition to democracy was therefore tortured and tortuous and finally ended with the military regime's collapse (O'Donnell 1986; Mayorga 2005). The transition began in 1978, but only in 1982 could we speak of actual regime change towards a fragile democracy.

In Brazil, economic crisis accelerated the erosion of the social base supporting the regime (businessmen and the middle classes), altering relations within the elite. The recipe imposed by the International Monetary Fund to deal with the crisis called for cuts in public spending, and consequently in subsidies to private businesses. That alienated the regime's entrepreneurial base, which had provided very extensive, if passive support. Hit hard by the crisis, the middle classes that had been the backbone of the regime during its expansionary phase (1968-1974) were transformed from active supporters to passive dissidents (Martins 1986, 91). In addition, the crisis intensified the rift between hard-liners and soft-liners in the military. Even if the hard-liners threatened another coup d'état to halt the ongoing change, the situation remained within the limits of relative calm, also thanks to a dialog between moderate opposition party leaders and the armed forces. In that sense, Tancredo Neves played a key role when, to obtain the backing of moderate military officers, he promised, in case of an electoral victory, not to support the formation of a constituent assembly independent of the Congress, and accepted the military's demand not to cancel any military decrees (law on national security, anti-strike legislation, press censorship laws, and limitations on Congress) before the promulgation of the new constitution (Fleischer 1998). Intra-elite agreements and alliances were therefore central in the Brazilian transition process (O'Donnell 1986, 12).

In Uruguay, by the time the military took power, the glue that held the military together already had disintegrated. As Linz and Stepan (1996, 153) underline, the guerillas already had been defeated when the military took power in 1973, and by 1980 were no longer a significant presence in the country. In addition, all of the upper classes were convinced that a political opening would contribute to economic recovery, much more than the perpetuation in power of a military class devoid of an economic strategy. Constitutional reform began in 1977, and the subsequent plebiscite of 1980, won by the democratic opposition, further convinced part of the military of the necessity of transferring power to civilians. This deepened the divide between the "military as government," looking for any solution that would guarantee their power, and the "military as an institution," desirous to open contacts with the opposition to organize a gradual transfer of power that would guarantee the institutional integrity of the armed forces. In Argentina as well, quarrels within the armed forces had an important role, generating internal instability that between 1976 and 1983 saw numerous turnovers at the top of the armed forces (Videla, Viola, Galtieri, and Bignone) culminating in the failed attempt to recover the Falklands and the subsequent collapse of the regime. In Ecuador, the lack of internal cohesion in the armed forces was evident as early as the 1963 coup that put an end to a fragile and unstable democratic phase. New prospects for democratization opened when agreement within the armed forces definitively fell apart. The triumvirate composed of the heads of the three services installed with the January 1976 coup declared its intention to return power to a civilian government.

In the first half of the 1970s in Peru, the high cost of investment, the hike in prices of petroleum and imported technical goods, plus the collapse in the price of exported raw materials, led to a serious trade deficit, financed by enormous foreign bank loans taken out by the military. The explosion of the foreign debt began to undermine the faint prosperity that previous reforms by the military junta had made possible, exacerbating the discontent of both the middle and lower classes, and laying the basis for democratic transition. The economic crisis of the 1970s ended with a worsening contrast within the armed forces, between the radical faction, led by General Velasco Alvarado, and the more moderate faction that favored reforms to encourage both internal and international private investment. Velasco was deposed in 1975, and followed by General Francisco Morales Bermúdez who announced the beginning of a "second phase" of the Peruvian revolution. In any case, military power seemed destined to end, and did end in 1979-80 (Cotler 1986, 156).

In Greece, internal divisions were rooted in the clash between monarchists and republicans within the armed forces, accentuated by the crown's rather tardy opposition to the 1967 coup d'état. In part, this division was at the root both of the failed attempt to form a proper governing coalition and the inability of the Colonels' regime to institutionalize itself despite two new constitutions (1968 and 1973) and a controversial referendum that abolished the monarchy, also in 1973. The student demonstrations in November of the same year represented yet another challenge to the regime, and led to a coup by hard-liners and the ouster of Papadopoulos by General Dimitrios Ioannidis, after a stand off between different components of the armed forces. This was a prelude to the military adventure in Cyprus that ushered in the end of the military regime.

In Lesotho, internal frictions in the military elite led to the April 1991 coup that was the final push toward a transition. When an elite's homogeneity ends, it is usually due to negative economic events, failure of an "internal enemy" strategy, the effects of international isolation, or erosion of the regime's bases of social support.

In Sub-Saharan Africa, as of 1999, 23 military leaders had been in power for more than 10 years, and 9 for more than 20 (Carbone 2005, 77). It is easy to understand how regime changes have occurred during the tenures of some of those leaders. In Togo, for example, during Colonel Étienne Gnassingbé Eyadéma's long rule, the regime experienced military and civilian phases, attempted coups, popular revolts and faint democratic openings. As repeatedly stated by Bratton and van de Walle (1997) and Carbone (2005), in Africa the military is central to democratic transition. When they oppose it (Nigeria 1993) it fails. When they are in favor, the transition is launched and has a greater chance for success (Ghana and, once again, Nigeria after 1998).

An interesting question is what induces certain authoritarian leaders to change direction and strive to reform the regime. Despite widespread high levels of unscrupulousness and opportunism, of the "things must change, in order to stay the same" variety, the most common motivations are loss of international support or an attempt to ride the wave of a change that appears to be inevitable, while also looking after their own interests and guaranteeing their personal security and that of their entourage. From this viewpoint, we can ascertain that sometimes it is the new generation of authoritarian leaders that brings about this turn in policy, and other times it is the product of conversions or political recycling fueled more by opportunism than by a sincere desire for reform. Mikhail Gorbachëv's decision to reform the Soviet system in the second half of the 1980s was surely the underlying cause of the landslide that rolled over the European Communist world. He did not foresee that this decision would further weaken the Communist empire's last frail pillars. Even with a long preliminary period of weak attempts at dialog during the 1980s, in 1990 Frederik Willem de Klerk had the courage to begin negotiations with Nelson Mandela and the African National Congress and decreed the end of apartheid, extending rights to the entire non-White population. Although they were prominent representatives respectively of the Soviet leadership and of the White elite in power in South Africa, Gorbachëv and de Klerk belonged to a new generation of leaders that not been governing long and had what it took to launch a reform. This is not always the case. In Burkino Faso, Blaise Campaoré's conversion from military dictator to elected president was astonishing and not very believable. Similar observations can be made for Jerry Rawlings in Ghana, Hastings Banda in Malawi, and for the still unclear democratic transformation/conversion of the Communists in Romania.

Most especially in personal dictatorships, the death of the leader and a succession crisis can represent opportunities for change. Precisely because of this, many autocracies (even very different from one another) have revived (or a least attempted to revive) old hereditary traditions, to guarantee a dynastic succession for a son or at least a trusted member of the dominant clan (Brownlee 2007). There are many examples of this: Nicaragua (1956), Dominican Republic (1960), Haiti (1971), Taiwan (1975), North Korea (1994 and again in 2011-12), Syria (2000), Azerbaijan (2003), Singapore (2004), Togo (2005) (Brownlee 2007, 601). In many other countries the desire to ensure a dynastic succession was equally evident, e.g. for Ceauşescu in Romania and Qaddafi in Libya. The fact remains that the death of a leader always represents a critical moment for the regime. Despite differences in conditions and timing, the deaths of Antonio de Oliveira Salazar in Portugal (1968), Chiang Kai-shek in Taiwan (1975), Francisco Franco in Spain (1975), Jomo Kenyatta in Kenya (1978), Sani Abacha in Nigeria (1998) and Franjo Tuđman in Croatia (1999) accelerated or caused the end of their respective regimes.

The death of a leader becomes a source of change for at least two reasons. The first is that, in any case, it is a change that produces realignments, shifts in alliances, and fear among individuals, structures, groups, bureaucrats, and institutions of losing privileges and income from positions obtained under the previous leadership. Then there is dissatisfaction on the part of those who feel underappreciated by the new leadership. All this can induce the new leader to look for different alliances (perhaps with civil society or opposition groups). The second reason is that, once a new leader is designated, they rarely maintain total continuity with their predecessor. The temptation to somehow differentiate oneself can be very strong, and the designated successor can decide to pursue new policies and radically innovate, as happened in Spain with Juan Carlos, or perhaps less dramatically with Caetano at Salazar's death. Even though the change was barely perceptible and the discontinuities of little importance, even in this second case the prospects for change could make headway within civil society and elite milieus, and prepare the ground for further transformation.

Personal dictatorships have difficulty in envisaging institutionalized procedures for succession. Succession usually comes in one of three ways: 1) the old leader's nomination of a successor while still alive; 2) following a natural course via the predictable accession to power of the leader's deputy or an old collaborator; 3) a power struggle among various personalities, all of whom try to come out on top. Spain and Taiwan provide examples of the first option. The reasoning was different, but the results were similar. Francisco Franco already had designated Prince Juan Carlos de Borbón in the 1960s, but the project of restoring the monarchy at the end of the Franco era dated from many years earlier. Two days after Franco's death on November 22, 1975, Juan Carlos was crowned king of Spain. Despite the fact that this was an agreed and non-traumatic transition, intended to ensure continuity, this new political path's break with the past was evident from the outset. To name only a few of the key changes that confirmed the end of Francoist Spain and the breakthrough of democracy: the Cortes's approval of the *Ley para la Reforma Política* in November 1976; the first post-Franco democratic elections in June 1977, establishing a parliament that de facto became a constituent assembly; and the king's firm stand against the attempted coup in 1981.

In Taiwan, Chiang Ching-kuo succeeded his father Chiang Kai-shek, who died in 1975. He had already held high government positions and had emerged as the designated heir. In this case as well, we are dealing with a transition guided by reformist sectors of the old leadership that, within a few years, produced clear breaks from the authoritarian regime of Chiang Kai-shek and the Kuomintang. The 1987 repeal of martial law, in effect since 1949, was among the most incisive actions. The death of Chiang Ching-kuo in 1988 did not lead to any regression towards authoritarianism, and political change set down roots.

In Kenya, we saw the second mode of succession, the rise to power of an old collaborator of the deceased charismatic leader. Under personalistic and charismatic leadership, Jomo Kenyatta ruled uncontested from independence in 1963 until August 1978. He governed via a single party, the Kenyan African National Union (KANU) and the predominance of the Kikuyu ethnic group. After Kenyatta's death, power passed to Vice President Daniel arap Moi in October 1978. He distinguished himself from his predecessor via a series of policies, redistributing benefits to the Kalenjin, his own ethnic group, and starting a slow transition, marked by frequent interruptions, violence and regressions, that never accomplished a complete democratization of the country. In Serbia and Croatia, the beginning of democratization was closely linked to the departure of charismatic leaders who seemed to be the main obstacles to political change. While in Serbia Milošević was removed by defeat in the October 2000 elections, in Croatia change followed Tuđman's death. Guided principally by the authoritarian elite, the transition phase was short-lived. It concentrated predominantly on electoral reform, given that the principal democratic institutions already had existed, at least formally, in Tuđman's time. The transition concluded with the first free elections, won by the political parties that had opposed Tuđman.

The third mode, a power struggle after the leader's death, is the most common in Communist regimes. Even if out of context for the Third Wave of democratizations, a classic model is that of the USSR after 1953. With Stalin dead, the proclamation of a collective leadership in reality was camouflage for a power struggle that, in the end, was won by Khrushchev.

Conclusions

Even though the number of countries involved in the Third Wave was undoubtedly high (83), the question at the center of comparative studies is always the same: why have certain autocratic regimes remained stable and have, without any particular damage, survived the innovative push of the Third Wave, while others have collapsed? An important point concerning the countries of the Third Wave is that all kinds of regimes were involved in transformations of the political order. From the quantitative point of view, plebiscitary single-party regimes (40) and military/civilian-military regimes (25) outnumbered the others. To these were added more or less competitive single-party systems, personal tyrannies with sultanistic characteristics, colonial regimes, traditional monarchies, racial oligarchies, and theocracies. Certainly there exist long-term factors, universally valid, that explain the greater or lesser longevity and stability of regimes, as well as incidental causes that help us understand discrepancies and the specificities of individual paths. This question often reoccurs in the literature (for example, recently, Gerschewski 2013). Other authors have asked themselves the same question about democracies (Przeworski et al. 1996). Let's begin with the first part of the question: How do we explain the persistent stability of so many autocracies?

According to Gerschewski (2013), from a solely internal perspective, the pillars of autocratic regimes are legitimization, cooptation, and repression. As we have seen in the preceding pages, in reality the Third Wave needs clear and better developed explanations, such as international causes (both political and economic) and internal factors that intertwine and blend, generating those different and distinct causal concatenations to which we have referred. We once again confirm that it is impossible to construct a general theory, valid *urbi et orbi* for all regime transformations. Exactly like those for the *decline and fall*, the reasons for the *persistence* of regimes vary notably, according to different spatial and temporal logics. The Third Wave is characterized by the end of the Communist regimes, but few take note (among these Saxonberg 2013) of how Communist regimes that are very important on the international chessboard have managed to survive, e.g. in China, North Korea,

Cuba, and Vietnam.[3] It is unthinkable to get away with saying that only European Communist regimes fell, but not those outside of Europe, given the fate of Communist regimes in Cambodia, Ethiopia, Grenada, Mongolia, and Nicaragua (Saxonberg 2013).

There is no lack of attempts to explain these differences in persistence/decline. Brown (2009) cites the capacity of some Communist regimes to transform the old ideology and resurrect nationalism, an explanation that does little, however, to explain the results of the Croatian, Serbian, and Romanian transitions. Levitsky and Way's theory (2005; Way and Levitsky 2007) is certainly more developed and convincing. Using the concepts of *Western leverage* and *linkage to the West*, it re-proposes international factors. The first concept describes the degree of each country's penetrability and vulnerability to outside pressure, determined by the subject country's economic and military size and strength, the nature of the West's strategic and economic interests, and the presence or absence of possible alternative pressures. Great powers like Russia and China, and regions like the Middle East, where there is an extensive network of competing international interests, are in the end less pervious to Western pressure for democratization. The concept of *linkage to the West* refers to the strength and depth of a country's ties to the United States, European Union, and other Western-led multilateral institutions. These ties have five dimensions (Levitsky and Way 2005, 22): economic (credit, investment, assistance); geopolitical, such as agreements and alliances with Western organizations and states; social (tourism, immigration, Western education and training of internal elites); communication (Internet, Western media penetration); transnational civil society (religious organizations, NGOs, political party organizations, etc.). The stronger and more rooted the ties, the higher the "costs of authoritarianism," making Western denunciations and condemnations more likely and effective, and increasing the likelihood of protest and dissent within the country involved. This type of theory helps us not only understand the varying results of change (the post-Soviet Asian republics vs. the Baltics, but also Ukraine, torn apart by the pull of the West in its western half and the lure of Russia to the east) but can also explain the persistence of autocratic regimes where Western leverage and linkage to the West are practically nonexistent or of low intensity: China, North Korea, Cuba, and Vietnam.

If among the Communist systems we find only a few cases where political regimes resisted the shocks of the Third Wave, countries whose economies are dominated by energy resources are generally much more impervious to change. This kind of economic arrangement almost always ensures a regime's long life and stability. For example, in the case of the "traditional regimes" of the Gulf, petroleum enables elites supported by familial or tribal networks to use "modern" political structures, like public institutions, to reinforce their power without having to change their social contract with the governed. Enormous oil wealth facilitates state centralization and the expansion of the state's role in society. It requires the leadership to spend heavily, maintaining vast client networks to prevent the formation of independent groups in society, thereby inhibiting the growth of opposition movements and dissent. At the same time they must use that mechanism to co-opt social groups that might sooner or later organize an opposition and challenge the regime (Ross 2001). Oil wealth needs a strong authoritarian state, which in turn needs oil. One of the first analyses of the regime born of the 1979 Iranian revolution (Skocpol 1982) revealed how much of the new Islamic Republic's oil income was diverted to bolster the armed forces and internal security.

Are the factors that lead to democratization the same that cause the crisis of the old regimes? Not always. Military elites, for example, might be a factor in the crisis and transition of an autocratic regime, but not necessarily a factor in the consolidation of democracy (Linz and Stepan 1996, 66ff.). Mass mobilizations weaken and destabilize the old regime, and represent an ever more frequent crisis factor, but, if extremist or radical passions triumph over moderation, not only does the road towards democracy become more difficult, but there is a risk of all change stalling. The same is true for economic crises and other causal factors. It is clear that an autocratic regime entering into crisis is a necessary but insufficient step for the realization of a democratization process.

What we aimed to document in this chapter was that, referring to the various processes involved in political change, some prevalent cases can be identified that represent real internal pressures for change. As seen in Table 1, destabilizing legacies from the past, mobilization of the masses and of civil society, and elite internal dynamics and succession crises constitute the principal internal sources of change, and combine with other factors analyzed in this volume: external pressure and obligations, state-building process-es, or at least the reconstruction of state organizations.

It is evident how the development of mass politics during the 20th century explains the growth and frequency of mass mobili-zations and the active role of civil society, in contrast to the tran-sitions of the Second Wave (Huntington 1991; Stoner, Diamond, Girod, and McFaul 2013, 15). Irrespective of the end results, about half of the states involved in the transformations of the Third Wave saw the development of protest from below. This was a geographi-cally widespread phenomenon, occurring almost everywhere, even in Africa. Equally strong was the role of the old elites. In a series of countries (Spain, Brazil, Ecuador, Mexico, Uruguay, Mongolia, Russia, Slovenia, Hungary, Benin, Burkina Faso) the old elites took the initiative for change. In others, the conversion to change was the product of pressure from below or outside, but in the end the elite went along with the regime's transformation, perhaps *obtorto collo*. This proves the importance of pacts, crucial for understand-ing the transitions in Southern Europe, Latin America, East Central Europe (the "round tables"), South Africa, and other African cases.

Endnotes

[1] The fate of dictators depends on both the outgoing regime, since military leaders have a greater probability of being arrested than heads of single-party regimes, and the incoming regime. In democratizations, for exam-ple, exemplary punishment of dictators is less likely (Escribà-Folch 2013).
[2] Here we mean mistakes by democratic political forces as well as the dem-ocratic regime's institutional structure that contributed to the crisis and fall of democracy. See Linz (1978).
[3] Lambie (1999) provides an unusual, and rather debatable, explanation of the Cuban case.

Table 1. Internal Causes of Regime Crisis in States Involved in the Third Wave

	AFRICA	LATIN AMERICA AND CARIBBEAN	ASIA	EASTERN/CENTRAL EUROPE	SOUTHERN EUROPE
Importance of legacy	Botswana, Ghana, Senegal	Argentina, Brazil, Chile, Ecuador, Peru, Uruguay	South Korea, Turkey	Czechoslovakia, DDR, Estonia, Hungary, Latvia, Lithuania, Poland, Slovenia	Greece, Spain, Portugal
Role of elites or individual leaders more or less favorable to change	Burkina Faso, Ghana, Kenya, Lesotho, Malawi, Niger, São Tomé and Principe, South Africa, Tanzania, Togo, Uganda		Indonesia, Mongolia, Taiwan, Thailand, Western Samoa	Bulgaria, Hungary, Montenegro, Romania, Russia, Serbia	Spain
Succession crises with conflicts and divisions within the civilian and military elites	Kenya, Lesotho, Malawi	Argentina, Bolivia, Brazil, Ecuador, Peru, Uruguay	Taiwan	Croatia, Serbia	Portugal, Spain
Mobilization of civil society and demands from below	Benin, Comoros Islands, Lesotho, Malawi, Niger, South Africa, Tanzania, Togo, Zambia	Argentina, Bolivia, Chile, Ecuador, Haiti, Mexico, Nicaragua, Paraguay, Peru, Suriname, Uruguay	East Timor, Indonesia, Mongolia, Philippines, South Korea, Thailand	Croatia, Czech Republic, DDR, Estonia, Georgia, Kosovo, Latvia, Lithuania, Macedonia, Moldova, Poland, Serbia, Slovakia, Ukraine	Greece, Portugal

Reference List

Bell, James E., and Lynn A. Staeheli. 2001. "Discourses of Diffusion and Democratization." *Political Geography* 20: 175-95.

Bermeo, Nancy. 2003. *Ordinary People in Extraordinary Times: The Citizenry and the Breakdown of Democracy*. Princeton, NJ: Princeton University Press.

Bratton, Michael, and Nicolas van de Walle. 1997. *Democratic Experiments in Africa*. Cambridge: Cambridge University Press.

Brinks, Daniel, and Michael Coppedge. 2006. "Diffusion is not Illusion. Neighbor Emulation in the Third Wave of Democracy." *Comparative Political Studies* 39 (4): 463-89.

Brown, Archie. 2009. *The Rise and Fall of Communism*. London: Bodley Head.

Brownlee, Jason. 2007. "Hereditary Succession in Modern Autocracies." *World Politics* 59 (July): 595-628.

Carbone, Giovanni. 2005. *L'Africa: Gli stati, la politica, i conflitti*. Bologna: Il Mulino.

Cheibub, Jose, Jennifer Gandhi, and James Vreeland. 2010. "Democracy and Dictatorship Revisited." *Public Choice* 143: 67–101.

Cotler, Julio. 1986. "Military Intervention and 'Transfer of Power to Civilians' in Peru." In *Transitions from Authoritarian Rule: Latin America*, edited by G. O'Donnell, P. C. Schmitter, and L. Whitehead, 148-72. Baltimore: Johns Hopkins University Press.

Diamandouros, P. Nikiforos. 1986. "Regime Change and the Prospects for Democracy in Greece: 1974-1983." In *Transitions from Authoritarian Rule: Southern Europe*, edited by G. O'Donnell, P. C. Schmitter, and L. Whitehead, 138-64. Baltimore: Johns Hopkins University Press.

Diamond, Larry. 1988. "Introduction: Roots of Failure, Seeds of Hope." In *Democracy in Developing Countries: Africa*, edited by L. Diamond, J. J. Linz and S. M. Lipset, 1-32. Boulder, CO: Lynne Rienner Publishers.

Escribà-Folch, Abel. 2013. "Accountable for What? Regime Types, Performance, and the Fate of Outgoing Dictators, 1946–2004." *Democratization* 20 (1): 160-85.

Fleischer, David V. 1998. "Government and Politics." In *Brazil: A Country Study*, edited by R. Hudson, 253-332. Washington, DC: Federal Research Division, Library of Congress.

Frantz, Erica, and Natasha M. Ezrow. 2011. *The Politics of Dictatorship: Institutions and Outcomes in Authoritarian Regimes*. Boulder, CO: Lynne Rienner.

Gamarra, Eduardo A. 1989. "Government and Politics." In *Bolivia: A Country Study*, 3rd ed., edited by R. A. Hudson and D. M. Hanratty, 149-218. Washington, DC: Federal Research Division, Library of Congress.

Geddes, Barbara. 1999. "What Do We Know About Democratization After Twenty Years?" *Annual Review of Political Science* 2 (June): 115-44.

Geddes, Barbara, Joseph Wright, and Erica Frantz. 2012. "New Data on Autocratic Regimes." Unpublished manuscript. http://dictators. la.psu.edu/pdf/pp9.pdf.

Gerschewski, Johannes. 2013. "The Three Pillars of Stability: Legitimation, Repression, and Cooptation in Autocratic Regimes." *Democratization* 20 (1): 13-38.

Grassi, Davide. 2008. *Le nuove democrazie: I processi di democratizzazione dopo la caduta del Muro di Berlino*. Bologna: Il Mulino.

Grilli di Cortona, Pietro. 1989. *Le crisi politiche nei regimi comunisti: Ungheria, Cecoslovacchia e Polonia da Stalin agli anni '80*. Milan: Franco Angeli.

———. 1997. *Da uno a molti: Democratizzazione e rinascita dei partiti in Europa orientale*. Bologna: Il Mulino.

———. 2009. *Come gli Stati diventano democratici*. Rome: Laterza.

———. 2011. "Il passato che non passa: il ruolo delle eredità nelle democratizzazioni." In *Tra vecchio e nuovo regime: Il peso del passato nella costruzione della democrazia*, edited by P. Grilli di Cortona and O. Lanza, 11-39. Bologna: Il Mulino.

———. 2014. "Crisi e crollo dei regimi non democratici. Condizioni e tendenze nella terza ondata." In *Come cadono i regimi non democratici: Primi passi verso la democrazia nei Paesi della "terza ondata,"* edited by L. Germano, P. Grilli di Cortona, and O. Lanza, 2-36. Naples: Editoriale Scientifica.

Grilli di Cortona, Pietro, and Orazio Lanza, eds. 2011. *Tra vecchio e nuovo regime. Il peso del passato nella costruzione della democrazia*. Bologna: Il Mulino.

Hadenius, Axel, and Jan Teorell. 2006. *Authoritarian Regimes: Stability, Change, and Pathways to Democracy, 1972–2003*. Kellogg Institute Working Paper No. 331. Notre Dame, IN: University of Notre Dame.

Hankiss. Elemer. 1990. *East European Alternatives*. Oxford: Clarendon Press.

Huntington, Samuel P. 1991. *The Third Wave: Democratization in the Late Twentieth Century*. Norman, OK: University of Oklahoma Press.

Iqbal, Zaryab and Harvey Starr. 2008. "Bad Neighbors: Failed States and Their Consequences." *Conflict Management and Peace Science* 25 (4): 315-31.

Jackson, Karl D. 1988. "The Philippines: The Search for a Suitable Democratic Solution, 1946-1986." In *Democracy in Developing Countries: Asia*, edited by L. Diamond, J. J. Linz and S. M. Lipset, 231-65. Boulder, CO: Lynne Rienner.

Joseph, Richard. 1991. "Africa: The Rebirth of Political Freedom." *Journal of Democracy* 2 (4): 11-24.

Kailitz, Steffen. 2013. "Classifying Political Regimes Revisited: Legitimation and Durability." *Democratization* 20 (1): 39-60.

Kirchheimer, Otto. 1965. "Confining Conditions and Revolutionary Breakthroughs." *American Political Science Review* 59 (4): 964-74.

Lambie, George. 1999. "Reinforcing Participatory Democracy in Cuba: An Alternative Development Strategy?" *Democratization* 6 (3): 30-61.

Lanza, Orazio. 2012. *Eredità del passato e democrazia: La Spagna e il Portogallo.* Soveria Mannelli, Italy: Rubbettino.

Leon, Tony. 2010. *The State of Liberal Democracy in Africa: Resurgence or Retreat?* Washington, DC: The Cato Institute, Center for Global Liberty and Prosperity.

Levitsky, Steven, and Lucan A. Way. 2005. "International Linkage and Democratization." *Journal of Democracy* 16 (3): 20-34.

_____. 2010. *Competitive Authoritarianism: Hybrid Regimes After the Cold War.* Cambridge: Cambridge University Press.

Linz, Juan. 1978. *The Breakdown of Democratic Regimes: Crisis, Breakdown, and Reequilibration.* Baltimore: Johns Hopkins University Press.

Linz, Juan, and Alfred Stepan. 1996. *Problems of Democratic Transition and Consolidation: Southern Europe, South America, and Post-Communist Europe.* Baltimore: Johns Hopkins University Press.

Magen, Amichai, and Leonardo Morlino, eds. 2008. *Anchoring Democracy: External Influence on Domestic Rule of Law Development.* London: Routledge.

Maier, Charles S. 1994. "Democracy and Its Discontents." *Foreign Affairs* 73: 48-64.

Mainwaring, Scott, and Pérez-Liñan, Anibal. 2013. *Democracies and Dictatorships in Latin America: Emergence, Survival, and Fall.* New York: Cambridge University Press.

Martins, Luciano. 1986. "The 'Liberalization' of Authoritarian Rule in Brasil." In *Transitions from Authoritarian Rule: Latin America*, edited by G. O'Donnell, P. C. Schmitter, and L. Whitehead, 72-94. Baltimore: Johns Hopkins University Press.

Mayorga, René Antonio. 2005. "Bolivian Democracy at the Crossroads." In *The Third Wave of Democratization in Latin America: Advances and Setbacks*, edited by F. Hagopian and S. Mainwaring, 149-77. New York: Cambridge University Press.

Morlino, Leonardo. 2003. *Democrazie e democratizzazioni.* Bologna: Il Mulino

Nordlinger. Eric A. 1977. *Soldiers in Politics: Military Coups and Governments.* Englewood Cliffs, NJ: Prentice-Hall.

O'Donnell, Guillermo. 1986. "Introduction to Latin American Cases." In *Transitions from Authoritarian Rule: Latin America*, edited by G.

O'Donnell, P. C. Schmitter, and L. Whitehead, 3-18. Baltimore: Johns Hopkins University Press.

O'Donnell, Guillermo, and Philippe C. Schmitter. 1986. *Transitions from Authoritarian Rule: Tentative Conclusions about Uncertain Democracies.* Baltimore: Johns Hopkins University Press.

Przeworski, Adam, Michael E. Alvarez, José Antonio Cheibub, and Fernando Limongi. 1996. "What Makes Democracy Endure?" *Journal of Democracy* 7 (1): 39-55.

Ross, Michael L. 2001. "Does Oil Hinder Democracy?" *World Politics* 53 (April): 325-61.

Saxonberg, Steven. 2013. *Transitions and Non-Transitions from Communism: Regime Survival in China, Cuba, North Korea, and Vietnam.* Cambridge: Cambridge University Press.

Schock, Kurt. 2005. *Unarmed Insurrections.* Minneapolis: University of Minnesota Press.

Skocpol, Theda. 1982. "Lo stato 'rentier' e l'Islam sciita nella rivoluzione iraniana." *Rassegna italiana di sociologia* 23: 177-200

Stoner, Kathryn, Larry Diamond, Desha Girod, and Michael McFaul. 2013. "Transitional Successes and Failures: The International-Domestic Nexus." In *Transitions to Democracy: A Comparative Perspective*, edited by Kathryn Stoner and Michael McFaul, 3-24. Baltimore: Johns Hopkins University Press.

Stoner, Kathryn, and Michael McFaul, eds. 2013. *Transitions to Democracy: A Comparative Perspective.* Baltimore: Johns Hopkins University Press.

Way, Lucan A. 2005. "Authoritarian State Building and the Sources of Regime Competitiveness in the Fourth Wave: The Cases of Belarus, Moldova, Russia, and Ukraine." *World Politics* 57 (2): 231-61.

Way, Lucan A., and Steven Levitsky. 2007. "Linkage, Leverage, and the Post-Communist Divide." *East European Politics and Society* 21 (1): 48-66.

Whitehead, Lawrence. 1986. "Bolivia's Failed Democratization." In *Transitions from Authoritarian Rule: Latin America*, edited by G. O'Donnell, P. C. Schmitter, and L. Whitehead, 40-71. Baltimore: Johns Hopkins University Press.

Whitehead, Lawrence, ed. 1996. *The International Dimensions of Democratization: Europe and the Americas.* Oxford: Oxford University Press.

Social and Economic Factors in Regime Change during the Third Wave of Democratization

Luca Germano

Although the precipitating event of the Arab Spring was the self-immolation of a young Tunisian man frustrated in his efforts to earn a decent living, economic drivers for regime change in the Arab world, and the economic consequences of such change, have received only modest academic and journalistic attention (Winckler 2013). And one can argue that, when commentators have mentioned economic factors, they have focused excessively on unemployment, when inflation actually may have had the greater impact (Byun and Hollander 2015). The following analysis of key national cases in the Third Wave of democratization suggests that economic crisis is a more significant determinant of democratization than is a country's relative level of economic development. Level and type of economic development, however, can influence the shape of civil society before a country's transition to democracy actually begins, with important consequences for the transition process. That said, civil society can exercise a crucial role in transitions in both developed and less-developed countries.

Theoretical Considerations

To explain the underlying conditions for change (crisis-collapse/transformation) in non-democratic regimes, several levels of analysis are necessary. If international factors are a fundamental point of departure, it is still essential to identify their interaction with internal factors. External developments often trigger crises, but variations in the speed, pace, and the relative ease with which the regime changes can be ascribed to internal factors. In the so-called

Third Wave of democratization, the relative importance of external and internal factors varied notably from one geopolitical area to another, based especially on when the wave struck. This chapter focuses on the role of two important interconnected internal factors in producing conditions favorable to the crisis-transformation/collapse or to the eventual survival of a non-democratic regime: socio-economic conditions (development/crisis) and civil society. First of all we must define the concepts of socio-economic development, crisis, and civil society. Then we will turn to analyzing the weight of these variables in six specific cases, and then draw some conclusions.

Socio-Economic Development and Crisis

When we speak of socio-economic development in relation to democratization processes, we must necessarily refer to the theory of socio-economic modernization originally formulated by Lipset (1959, 1960), then further expanded by Russett (1965), Dahl (1971), Cutright (1963), Londregan and Poole (1990, 1996), Diamond (1992), Przeworski and Limongi (1997), and Przeworski, Alvarez, Cheibub, and Limongi (2000). The theory identifies a positive correlation between the level of socio-economic development and democracy, beginning with the historic observation that most wealthy countries are democratic. According to Lipset, a country that has high levels of per capita wealth, industrialization, urbanization, and education has a high probability of being democratic, because socio-economic progress leads to diversification of interests and to the diffusion of power in ways resistant to state monopolization. The basic idea is that development leads to a modification in the social structure, thanks to the action of correlated factors. By promoting wellbeing and a rise in the level of education, development contributes to changing citizens' values, making them more inclined toward tolerance, moderation, and respect for the opposition. Higher income levels and economic security extended to a large part of the population reduce the intensity and effects of class struggle, allowing citizens to develop more gradualist political views over the long term, and change the outlook of the upper social classes, encouraging them to see lower social classes as non-threatening and worthy of political rights and the possibility of sharing power. More generally, the spreading of wealth brings a reduction in objective levels of inequality and, consequently, a diminution in class differences, increasing the size of the middle class. The middle class tendency to contain conflict rewards moderate and democratic parties, resisting the call of anti-democratic and radical parties and ideas.

Economic development and the spread of education also promote the birth of autonomous and voluntary social organizations that can act as a control on government actions, increase political participation, improve political skills, and create and disseminate new opinions. Economic development therefore contributes to the emergence of civil society (Lipset 1959, 1960; Diamond 1992).

The theory of modernization does not explicitly deny that democracy can develop in poor countries, but considers it an arduous endeavor, holding that transitions to democracy are easier in countries that have at least a medium level of economic development. Various authors have supported and further developed this hypothesis. Dahl (1971) maintains that countries that exceed a threshold of per capita GDP between 700 and 800 US dollars (in 1957 dollars) have an elevated probability of becoming polyarchies, while countries with thresholds below 200 US dollars do not have much of a chance. Despite this, aware of the multiple exceptional cases,[1] he is very cautious about identifying a direct causal nexus between development and democracy. Relying on Dahl, Diamond (1992) maintains that there is an upper limit beyond which the probability of a democratic regime is so high that an increase in wealth has no effect, while Przeworski and Limongi (1997) maintain that, above that threshold, all kinds of regimes are able to stabilize, and hence authoritarian regimes that have survived to the medium income threshold have good prospects for lasting. In any case, everyone seems to be in agreement that, below said threshold, increases in wealth increase the probability of a democratic regime. However, as observed by various authors (Dahl 1971; Diamond 1992; Huntington 1991; Seligson 1997; Vanhanen 1997; Landman 1999; Smith 2005) correlation is not automatically causation, because one also finds the reverse situation: some countries, even in the absence of economic development, can democratize, and economic development can be a consequence of democratization rather than its cause.

In other words, though economic development can be a necessary condition for democratization, it is not a sufficient condition. We can deduce that a democracy can arise at any level of economic development and it is not necessarily the product of modernization (Diamond 1992), because it can develop, even with more difficulty, in countries in which the indicators of social development (as well as per capita wealth) utilized by Lipset (industrialization, urbanization, education) are not on the high end of the scale. That means that a combination of other factors could explain the change (Grilli di Cortona 2014).

As Huntington (1991) authoritatively observed, the economic dimension is not important only when the indicators are positive, but also when they decline after crises and resulting recessions. In other words, in addition to the effect of economic development on the erosion of non-democratic regimes, it is essential to look also at the effect of economic decline, or, eventually, at the combined effect of both. The development-recession-economic crisis sequence often constitutes the mix that destabilizes non-democratic regimes (Grilli di Cortona 2014). More specifically, economic difficulty and a non-democratic regime's inability to confront it call into question the regime's competence in the economic sphere and, consequently, its right to govern. This aspect can have limited importance if the regime has total control over society. But, if not, the government can find itself facing protests and uprisings by the sectors most damaged by the economic problems. In this instance, the onset of economic crises brings with it the need to adjust public policy, which can undermine the interests of groups—often in the commercial and entrepreneurial sectors—that usually are part of the regime's social support base. These groups, deprived of the material resources usually assigned to them, can rethink their support, seeking new political pacts (Haggard and Kaufmann 1995). They often form organizations to put pressure on the government for political change, to improve the environment for advancing their own interests.[2] In addition, disagreements and battles for supremacy over policy decisions can produce divisions and fractures within the authoritarian regime,[3] introducing fragmentation within the governing elite and further diminishing the coherence of the regime's actions. Also, since many non-democratic regimes base their legitimacy on *performance*, a substantial dip in services because of economic crisis can generate questions concerning the regime's adequacy and its remaining in power, especially when the crisis shows the inefficacy of the economic model the regime promoted[4] (Gill 2000). All these factors do indeed create interaction between economic and political crisis (Gonzalez 2008).

On the other hand, along with authoritarian regimes that destabilize following economic crises, others are able to survive, thanks to a strong state or the presence of a cohesive hegemonic party that put the rulers in a position to prevent defections within the elite, discourage protests, or win or fix elections despite citizens' obvious discontent (Pepinsky 2009, 271; Levitsky and Way 2010, 77). Still, waves of economic crises often have been important turning points, contributing to the liberalization or collapse of various autocracies: Latin American and Africa in the early 1990s especially come to mind (Geddes 1999; Herbst 1994).

Civil Society

For the reasons mentioned above, the second internal factor under consideration, civil society, is closely related to economic development. Diamond (1999, 221) defines civil society as

> the realm of organized social life that is open, voluntary, self generating, at least partially self-supporting, autonomous from the state, and bound by a legal order or set of shared rules. It is distinct from "society" in general in that it involves citizens acting collectively in a public sphere to express their interests, passions, preferences, and ideas, to exchange information, to achieve collective goals, to make demands on the state, to improve the structure and functioning of the state, and to hold state officials accountable. Civil society is an intermediary phenomenon, standing between the private sphere and the state.

In this "intermediate space," as defined by Diamond, or "arena," as Linz and Stepan (1996) term it, various actors are involved in developing relationships based in networks: social movements (women's groups, religious groups, neighborhood associations, organizations of intellectuals), civic associations, unions, groups promoting particular interests. The public sphere includes this dense network of groups that, while based in the non-political interests of their members, sometimes have to take those interests into the political sphere. Political parties in turn are the principal agents for bringing these interests into the political sphere.[5] This is a peaceful process in the democratic context, but not so in an authoritarian context, where, even if there is a certain level of tolerance towards political parties and groups, their activity is in fact extremely restricted and closely monitored. If the interests of members of groups cannot be politically defended, it is difficult to characterize civil society as free (Gill 2000).

Non-democratic regimes can bridle and monitor associations, relationships, and communication via the creation of organizations able to structure and contain popular participation, in order to depoliticize public life and avoid independent mobilization.[6] The regime also can guarantee the passivity and acquiescence of the populace via the adoption of policies that guarantee relative economic wellbeing, even in the presence of notable inequality in favor of certain groups. This situation of relative wellbeing contributes to the formation of a civil society that can remain passive until such time as the condition of its members begins to slip, and a crisis manifests itself. It then can mobilize to challenge the regime. The formation of associations and their consolidation[7] can be essential in generating an opposition that initially may be weak, but later can grow until it forces the regime to take repressive actions or to liberalize (Linz and Stepan 1996).

More generally, as the possibilities for participation and protest increase, the number of interests whose preferences have to be taken into consideration grows (Dahl 1971). That creates conflicts of interests that often involve social unrest.[8] From country to country, mobilization of the citizenry can assume many different forms, depending on the kind of authoritarian regime, the civil society organizations involved, the size of membership, their territorial distribution, and their ability to connect with other organizations and movements both on the internal and international levels. Mobilization can employ peaceful or violent actions. In the first case, widespread and continuous non-violent protests (demonstrations, uprisings, strikes, etc.) can amount to "unarmed insurrections" in which citizens are the principal actors, rather than merely supporters of an armed vanguard (Schock 2005, xviff.). In the second case, violent mobilization can lead to divisions within the opposition forces and alienate sectors of civil society that fear a collapse of public order and security, in effect reinforcing the regime (Grilli di Cortona 2014, 24).

Naturally, even in the case of unarmed insurrection, a certain level of violence can always be present (Zunes 1994; Schock 2005), and regimes often respond to both violent *and* nonviolent mobilizations with forceful repression. When the costs of tolerance appear to exceed those of repression, there is a higher probability that the regime will use force. The ties regimes have forged with civil society, or parts thereof, have a bearing on their cost/benefits analysis. These ties vary according to the kind of authoritarian regime. Those that are purely military, being based on closed structures with a distinctive and exclusive esprit de corps, have limited contact with society. Civilian and civilian-military regimes can have different channels for contact with society or specific sectors thereof. Exclusionary regimes can try to guarantee their survival by massive use of repression that gives them control over the demands of civil society. Inclusionary and partially inclusionary regimes, however, use variable levels of repression, attempting to rein in civil society or forge special ties with specific sections of it, co-opting them into government or assuring them of benefits.

In any case, under certain conditions (persistent economic crises), regimes can come under pressure, not only from social groups that are out of favor, but from members of normally supportive groups, which in some cases could include the middle class, entrepreneurs, or landowning oligarchs, who nonetheless support a transformation (Dahl 1971; O'Donnell and Schmitter 1986). Despite this, even when the regime's repressive apparatus is particularly effective, under certain circumstances (for example, persistent economic crises) the wide use of violence can accelerate the regime's collapse, because of the interaction of internal and international factors. Isolation of the regime due to the condemnation of its repressive actions by international public opinion is an element that can energize civil society and unite its component organizations[9] in opposing the regime and forcing it either to capitulate or to negotiate a compromise that legitimizes the opposition.

Civil society organizations can become crucial actors during a regime transition by representing the interests of the masses and influencing the government's decisions, while transmitting the governing elite's decisions and facilitating their implementation, but also because actors within civil society can enter political society by forming political parties or other political institutions. In addition, the political leaders of new democracies can be recruited from civil society organizations (Uhlin 2006, 32). Finally, the participation of strong and effective civil society organizations in political decision-making during transitions can help reduce uncertainty, playing a fundamental mediating role between the masses and the state (Hamman 1998).

Case Studies

Concentrating on the crisis-transformation/collapse phase of nondemocratic regimes, we must ascertain to what degree economic development or crisis and civil society actions contribute, and how they intertwine. To allow for in-depth analysis, we will focus here on three paired cases: Spain and Portugal; South Korea and the Philippines; South Africa and Ghana. These cases fit into three different phases of the Third Wave. Each pair features strongly contrasting development indicators: high in Spain, South Korea, and South Africa; low in Portugal, the Philippines, and Ghana (Table 1). These differences in development, naturally, had effects on the growth of civil society, which took paths specific to each country, with repercussions for the transformation process. Finally, each country at the outset had an authoritarian regime of a different type, and ways of transitioning varied.[10] The latter reflected the relative strength of civil society.

Civil society plays a different role in pre-transitional, transitional and post-transitional contexts. It is evident that, in a nondemocratic regime, civil society is virtually absent from the public sphere until the start of crisis and transition. Then civil society actors can mobilize in opposition to the regime, as well as providing a reservoir for the recruitment of a future democratic leadership.

Table 1. Indicators of socio-economic development

	Portugal	Spain	South Korea	Philippines	South Africa	Ghana
GDP per capita USD	1,690 USD (1976)	2,920 USD (1976)	2,690 USD (1987)	590 USD (1987)	2,560 USD (1991)	400 USD (1991)
Distribution of GDP (%)	Agriculture: 18 Industry: 43 Services: 39 (1976)	Agriculture: 9 Industry: 39 Services: 52 (1976)	Agriculture: 11 Industry: 43 Services: 46 (1987)	Agriculture: 24 Industry: 33 Services: 43 (1987)	Agriculture: 5 Industry: 44 Services: 51 (1991)	Agriculture: 53 Industry: 17 Services: 29 (1991)
Percentage of urban population	29 (1975)	70 (1975)	69 (1987)	41 (1987)	60 (1991)	33 (1991)
Percentage of population enrolled in education	Primary: 96 Secondary: 81 Tertiary: 9 (1975)	Primary:115 Secondary: 78 Tertiary: 18 (1975)	Primary: 96 Secondary: 94 Tertiary: 32 (1987)	Primary:106 Secondary: 65 Tertiary: 38 (1987)	Primary: n/a Secondary: n/a Tertiary: n/a (1991)	Primary: 75 Secondary: 39 Tertiary: 2 (1991)

Source: World Bank, *World Development Report*, Various Years, available at:
http://elibrary.worldbank.org/action/showPublications?startPage=&target=browse&sortBy=Ppub_asc. For countries with universal primary education, gross enrollment ratios may exceed 100 percent, because some pupils may be below or above the official primary school age.

The presence of civil society during the pre-transitional phase depends on the kind of non-democratic regime, the degree of its repressiveness, and the historic strength or weakness of associations in each country. On the basis of these factors, we can therefore identify a civil society with greater or lesser potential impact on the outcome of regime change. To that end, as far as possible we must first examine the density of civil society, i.e. the number of organizations and citizens that take part in them, and, if they are present, their degree of institutionalization during the regime's crisis and transition phases. Then we must look at the degree of organization and the organizations' level of consensus or discord during the regime crisis and, finally, their contribution—active or secondary—in establishing the new institutional framework in the transition phase.

Our final objective is to verify if the variables under consideration can be considered crucial in producing regime change, have a complementary role with other internal and international variables, or only have a marginal, background role as compared to other variables that can be considered the true causes of change.

Spain and Portugal

According to Huntington (1991, 68ff.), the Mediterranean countries of the Third Wave present three exemplary cases of how extremely rapid economic growth can contribute markedly to destabilizing authoritarian regimes. Actually, in the twenty year period before the beginning of the regime transition process, Greece, Portugal, and Spain all experienced economic development, although at different levels and with different outcomes (Maravall 1997; Przeworski et al. 2000). The average annual growth rate between 1950 and 1973 was around 5.8% in Portugal, 5.9% in Spain and 6.7% in Greece, compared to a European average of around 4.7% (Gibson 2001, 3) and had a positive effect on citizens' standard of living. However, this development was due to the creation of economies predominantly based on tourism, remittances from immigrants, importation of energy sources, and the 1960s boom (Sapelli 1995, 66ff.). This made all three Mediterranean countries vulnerable to the 1973 energy crisis (Huntington 1991).

Economic development and improvements in the standard of living and in the level of education contributed to social change, especially in Greece and Spain, much less in Portugal. These traditional rural societies were progressively transforming into urban societies, where working class and student populations were newly emerging. The concentration of these two important civil society forces in the cities made mobilization of their members in anti-regime actions easier than in the more dispersed rural society of the past (Gill 2000).

In **Spain**, development in the 1950s and 60s fostered enormous social transformation: the underprivileged rural classes shrank, while the working class was strengthened and the university population increased. In the mid-1970s Spain was an industrialized and urbanized country with the 9th or 10th largest economy in the world (Bosco 2005, 17). It had a much higher standard of living, with more money and resources, but also more freedom of movement, opportunities for growth and wealth, less subservience to the authorities, and more learning (Pérez-Díaz 1993, 13). This transformation brought unexpected consequences for the Franco regime, forcing it to deal with opposition from civil society forces such as labor organizations, student movements, and even from what might have seemed the most improbable of opposition groups, the Catholic Church and its ancillary organizations. Strengthened at the end of the 1950s thanks to the law on collective bargaining (1958) that also facilitated strike actions, labor unions were dissolved in 1967, but reemerged clandestinely immediately after, both those that were leftist and those linked with Catholic Action.[11] Student movements were in constant development from the 1960s on, thanks to the rising number of students registering at the universities, which grew 500% between 1970 and 1974. In the Catholic Church there was a massive generational change, with young priests receptive to international liberal trends and the impact of Vatican II (Payne 1987, 487, 499).

The regime's problems worsened with the 1973 Oil Crisis, in a context where there already were serious public dissatisfaction, continuous strikes, and university shut-downs, as well as the rise of terrorism by ETA (*Euskadi Ta Askatasuna-Basque*, Basque Homeland and Freedom). The regime's attempts to adopt more open policies failed, because they were too limited and because of the simultaneous adoption of extremely repressive measures aimed at dividing the opposition forces (Maravall and Santamaria 1986). The increase in repression in the first few months of 1975, just before Franco's death, was counterproductive, because strikes[12] and student demonstrations intensified, revealing a regime that was increasingly isolated and abandoned by its traditional social base of legitimacy. The Catholic Church, which had already distanced itself from the regime in the mid-1960s, openly broke relations, led by the Archbishop of Madrid Enrique y Tarancón. Disappointment with immobility and the perpetuation of repression was palpable not only in the middle classes, who were a source of great pride for Franco (Pastor 1992, 41), but also among the administrative elite and the business community. Because of low productivity, a product of the corporatist system, the business community looked favorably on legalization of the unions, which would make it possible to negotiate new kinds of contracts that would promote profit growth (Gunther, Sani, and Shabad 1988, 26-27). Generally speaking, it was clear that the regime was worn out, and after Franco's death the transition accelerated.

In the Spanish case, it seems clear that socio-economic development was an important variable but that it acted only indirectly on the transition. If development had been the factor that triggered the transition, it would have occurred at least five to ten years earlier (Linz, 1992, 437). Instead, the economic crisis appears to have been the principal catalyst for change in a context ready for democracy. This was thanks to the role of civil society, which was already developed and active before the regime's crisis, and then active in the transition guided by elites that, in turn, had to respond to the multiple demands and pressures of the masses (Hamman 1998, Pérez Díaz 1993). In addition to political party organizations, which revived or were quickly re-created after Franco's death, the unions, also because of their links to political parties, played an essential role in channeling, uniting and communicating the masses' demands, as well as in implementing the decisions made by the elites.

Prior to regime change, **Portugal** benefited the least from the modernization process, remaining the poorest country in Western Europe, with the lowest level of education (Cuzán 1999, 128). Hence it is not surprising that "even on 23 July 1976, when Portugal instituted a democratic system, the country did not 'measure' up on any of the modernization 'democratic' indicators in education, literacy, attitudes and industrialization" (Manuel 1995, 3). This was also the result of an economy still largely based on agriculture (Table 1) and a limited and disorganized industrial middle class (Bermeo 1987, 220-21). Also, economic development in the 1960s and 70s did not contribute to the formation of a modern middle class, as it had in Spain (Bermeo 1987, 222), due to a large asymmetry in income distribution[13] and significant emigration.[14] The corporatist and anti-modern structure of Salazar's authoritarian *Estado Novo* was intended to depoliticize civil society, which during the First Republic (1910 -1926) already was weak and marginalized. The 1933 corporatist constitution further restricted the action of independent organizations, introducing institutions to control civil society: the secret police, propaganda and censorship structures, an education system that aimed at transmitting corporatist values, obligatory enrollment in the student youth organization (*mocidade portuguesa*), and obligatory profession of personal and professional loyalty to the regime by all public employees (Hamman and Manuel 1999, 75).

Maintaining institutions with liberal origins, such as parliamentary elections, was intended only to give the impression of popular legitimacy for the regime (Schmitter 1977). Political parties played no role whatsoever in organizing or representing interests, a role which fell to the Corporative Chamber, which represented the principal sectors of society (agriculture, industry, commerce, fisheries, the Catholic Church, the military) (Wiarda 1977). The Communist (PCP) and Socialist (PSP) parties, forced to operate clandestinely, had a completely negligible role in promoting regime change (Maxwell 1986, 109), and only reemerged, like other civil society organizations, after the 1974 coup organized by young, low-ranking military officers that put an end to the regime (Linz, Stepan, and Gunther 1995; Manuel 1998; Hamann and Manuel 1999).

The other principal civil society organizations—unions, employers' associations, and organizations linked with the Catholic Church—also had an insignificant role in transforming the regime. Independent unions and business associations did not exist at all, as corporatism included such groups within the system of state control. Joining unions was exclusively for workers belonging to the few companies that had more than 100 employees. In a country that became industrialized only in the mid-1970s, that meant excluding the majority of the work force, which in any case was denied the right to strike (Manuel 1998, 143).

Business interests constituted the support base of the Salazar regime, and their acquiescence was guaranteed by the political and economic stability the Salazar regime offered after the instability of the First Republic (Wheeler 1978). This support lasted until the explosion of the colonial war in 1961 (Barreto 1996), when Salazar decided to open the Portuguese economy to finance the war, changing the economic development model, which until then had favored the country's seven principal economic groups, which controlled 3/4 of the GDP (Manuel 1998). Although they were profiting from this opening to sign agreements with foreign companies, the industrialists' criticisms progressively grew, especially in the regime's last decade. They accused the regime of perpetuating a costly colonial war with no end in sight, depriving the country of internal investment and workforce and making it highly dependent on foreign financing (Maxwell 1982, 233). The influx of foreign capital, largely foreign investment attracted by low wages and the absence of free unions, as well as tourism and remittances from the numerous emigrants (Hamman and Manuel 1999; Sapelli 1995), generated a period of development, then halted by recession following the 1973 Oil Crisis. This economic crisis contributed to further weakening the regime, which, following its decision to change development path, involuntarily weakened its own corporatist structure by facilitating outside penetration of the internal market, the increase in foreign investments, and more generally, the impact of modern Western values introduced by returning emigrants (Manuel 1998).

The Catholic Church and its ancillary organizations were the exception to the absence of independent associations in Portugal and occupied a privileged position at the beginning of the Salazar regime. Their aim was to make Catholicism the state religion, and they used Catholic theories of corporatism to justify the *Estado Novo* (Hamman and Manuel 1999). With the 1940 Concordat, the Catholic Church reacquired the privileges it enjoyed under the monarchy, such as financial support and authority over education, de facto reversing the anti-clerical trend of the First Republic (Maxwell 2000, 148). Despite the good relations between the Catholic hierarchy and the regime, its largest organization, Catholic Action, was chomping at the bit to convey to the regime the economic and social problems of youth and the working classes, given the lack of other organizations to which citizens, even those less fervent in a population where 90% declared themselves to be Catholic, could turn (de Meneses 2009, 442ff.). This created a growing fracture with the regime. Catholic opposition to the colonial wars marked the definitive break.

In the Portuguese experience, socio-economic development and civil society action were background variables that acted in a very indirect manner on regime change. In this case, regime change was generated by the regime's inability to win the colonial wars (Huntington 1991, 54), the consequent end of the colonial era, and the economic disarray that followed the 1973 Oil Crisis. Unable to develop organizations to channel popular demands, civil society never took on a central role, neither during the regime crisis nor during the transition, led instead by military and political elites. Although in 1973, with the acceleration of the economic crisis, there was an increase in protests and strikes (even if both were illegal), popular mobilization was not the cause of the military intervention that ended the regime. Instead, there was an increase immediately following the coup and a rapid decrease soon afterword. As Manuel (1998, 144) observed: "The suddenness of the 25 April coup caught civil society off guard, organized interests were neither well organized nor well prepared for the dramatic changes that would occur after 1974."

South Korea and the Philippines

The remarkable economic development of **South Korea** can be attributed to the modernization policies of the authoritarian regimes that followed World War II (until the 1980s), its peculiar colonial legacy, and the serious threat from North Korea, which provided an impetus for growth (Kang 2002). The Japanese colonial legacy contributed to the adoption of a state-led developmental model which, entrusting economic decisions to a technocratic elite isolated from social and union pressures, engineered a sudden and impressive process of industrialization, despite high levels of corruption (Haynes 2001; Kang 2002). One need only look at the average annual growth rate, which between 1965 and 1987, for example, reached 6.4% (World Bank 1989, table 1, 165). Especially from the 1970s on, economic development transformed the country's social structure, greatly expanding the urban working and middle classes. In little more than 20 years, the urban population more than doubled, going from 32% in 1965 to 69% in 1987[15] and creating a small but important industrial middle class. Education also expanded: between 1965 and 1986, those with secondary education went from 35% to 95%, and those with post-secondary education from 6% to 33% (World Bank 1989, table 29, 221), signifying a large increase in the student body (Gill 2000). In 1987, the year when regime change began, the per capita GDP had reached 2,690 USD (World Bank 1989, table 1, 165).

The development policies pursued by the authoritarian regimes from the end of World War II to the end of the 1980s were successful in modernizing the country,[16] but at the same time fostered discontent among a population that was increasingly aware, educated, and unwilling to accept authoritarian restrictions. The growing unhappiness of the middle class with the regime translated into strong support for the pro-democratic student movement. At the opening of the 1960s, that movement had been the protagonist of powerful protests that made a fundamental contribution to the overthrow of the authoritarian, repressive, and corrupt regime of Syngman Rhee (Sik Lee 1994; Kim 2004). The suppression of civil society, including student, labor, professional and religious associations, was the hallmark, however, of the later authoritarian regimes that succeeded one another beginning in 1961. The objective was a "purification" of society and of forces opposed to the regime, to the point that, according to Koo (2002), one could not speak of the existence of civil society, in the sense of a variety of legal autonomous associations and civic activities. Rather, there was a network of student organizations, intellectual dissidents, union activists, and pro-democratic circles that existed outside a legal framework. Therefore, in the Korean case we cannot speak of a particularly dense civil society in the pre-democratic phase, because of regime repression.

However, there was an inheritance, dating to the era of Japanese colonialism (1910-1945) and the period following the Japanese surrender in 1945 (Kim 2004), which facilitated the "resurrection of civil society in the mid-1980s" (O'Donnell and Schmitter 1986, 48-56). Despite severe repression, especially in 1980-1983 by the Chun Doo Hwan regime, clandestine opposition groups were able to continue coordination and collaboration that enabled them to put pressure on the regime, especially via mobilization of student, labor, and religious groups (Kim 2000; Adesnik and Kim 2013). And the government also had to deal with growing dissatisfaction in the world of business, which began to feel the effect of government restrictions, while many in the financial sector became convinced that the state should have a less important role in economic affairs (White 1996, 196). Under these pressures, the regime decided to adopt some liberalizing policies, with the intention of fragmenting the opposition, even creating pseudo-opposition parties that were in reality controlled by the regime (Kim 2004, 145). Rather than fragmenting the opposition, however, this policy of moderate liberalization permitted the rapid reconstitution of groups that had been decimated by repression in the preceding years (Kim 2000).

Despite strong authoritarian repression, the student movement was one of the most important groups that constantly maintained its commitment to, and continued to play a crucial role in, the democratization process. The lifting of the ban on access to campuses led to the 1984 founding of the National Student Coalition for Prodemocracy Struggle, the first large student organization since the 1966 revolt (Kim 2004, 144). Also in 1984, the Korean Council for Labor Welfare was founded, a group that coordinated various union movements. These two groups formed a close alliance, which in 1985 enlarged to include religious associations, Catholic, Protestant, and Buddhist, creating an umbrella organization called the People's Movement Coalition for Democracy and Reunification (PMCDR). This facilitated the expansion of a real and increasingly solid opposition to the regime that, thanks to the drive of civil society, was transmitted to political society (Stepan 1988) with the formation of the New Korea Democratic Party (NKDP).

Ever more pressing pro-democracy demands by civil society organizations, and the progressive growth of the NKDP, along with a massive popular mobilization, were at the root of the change that took place in June 1987, when Chun Doo Hwan was forced to pass the baton to Roh Tae Woo, who in turn was forced to negotiate a democratization plan with the opposition, incorporating most of the demands of the opposition movements and political parties. From this moment on, civil society continued to advance, acquiring ever more negotiating power and becoming a protagonist in the transition toward a new democratic regime, and in its subsequent rapid consolidation. In sum, civil society established its absolutely central role not only in the authoritarian regime's crisis and fall, but also in South Korea's entire process of democratization.

From the end of World War II to the mid-1970s, the **Philippines** had economic performance similar to South Korea's, but were unable to achieve the levels of socio-economic development that South Korea achieved, especially from the 1980s on (Kang 2002). A long colonial history, first under Spain and then under the US until 1946, contributed to this outcome, and also to the seizure of power by an economic and political elite formed by a few powerful families of landowners and industrialists. Via alliances through marriage and business ties they held power for generations (Hutchcroft, 1991; Hedman and Sidel 2000; Haynes 2001; Abinales and Amoroso 2005). State control enabled the oligarchs and their political friends to enrich themselves and to buy the support of those, e.g. the military, who were necessary to maintain the elite in power and to promote the specific interests of its component groups (Paul 2010, 83). This patronage structure, active in both the political and economic system, was both the principal source of conflict within the elite and the reason for the country's failure to develop economically (Haynes 2001).

The results of this system can be seen in the economic data, showing from 1965 to 1987 an average annual growth rate of barely 1.7% and a very low per capita GDP of only $590 in 1987, the year after the beginning of the transition. This produced a serious delay in the country's modernization. It remained essentially agrarian, with only modest growth in the urban population. Between 1965 and 1987, the urban population went from 32% to 41%, an increase of barely 9% (World Bank 1989, table 29, 220). The absence of agrarian reform was one of the elements that contributed to the perpetuation of economic and political power in the hands of a few large landowners, who then diversified into the banking and industrial sectors. This made them the principal agents for continuation of the patronage system, and the key impediment to political change (Rueschmeyer, Stephens, and Stephens 1992).

Education is a particularly interesting indicator, however, as it runs counter to the other major indicators. At the end of the 1950s, the Philippines already had a literacy rate higher than most Asian countries. This is explained by the legacy of the US colonial administration (1898-1946), which invested around 25% of public spending in education (Kang 2002, 58). By 1960, more than 70% of the Philippine population was literate. Despite the country's generally low level of development, education continued to rise: in 1986, the year the transition began, secondary education was guaranteed to 68% of the population and higher education to 38% (World Bank 1989, table 29, 220). In spite of the very positive data on education, however, the other parameters indicated a situation of persistent underdevelopment.

The democratic phase (1946-1972) was characterized by weak governments controlled by the big oligarchic families and their political friends, who loaded down the state with demands for their particular interests, leading to incoherent policy making. In 1972, the pivot to authoritarianism came when Marcos (democratically elected in 1968) declared martial law, justifying it as necessary to reform a state controlled by oligarchic interests, but this quickly resulted in a predatory state that sacked the society from on high (Thompson 1995; Kang 2002).

The restructuring and centralization of the police and armed forces, carried out inter alia with US assistance, supported martial law as well as control over legislative and judicial power. With populist, anti-oligarch rhetoric and a strong military, Marcos steamrolled his opposition. The dictator's potential rivals, the most prominent oligarchs, were arrested, and their patronage networks dismantled. Their private armies were demobilized and their wealth expropriated.

Marcos's modernization strategy was based on the expansion of public spending, the creation of executive agencies led by technocrats who, on paper at least, were apolitical, and use of the armed forces to implement development programs (Abinales and Amoroso 2005, 194-5). After a first phase in which development programs actually went forward, guaranteeing a certain amount of growth, the fragility of reforms financed by public debt soon emerged. The public debt went from $2.6 billion in 1975 to $10.5 billion in 1980. Without the ability to generate income, by 1986 the Philippines had a debt of nearly $30 billion, making it one of the most indebted countries in the world.[17] The reason for this inability to generate income was the peculiar form of Philippine capitalism, not based on competition and the market, but rather on monopolies and income from jobs derived from the preferential treatment reserved for oligarchs and their friends who were loyal to Marcos (Kang 2002; Abinales and Amoroso, 2005). This system, clearly reflecting the "economic policy of patrimonialism" (Wurfel 1988, 258; de Dios 1990), damaged the country's economic performance.

Years of government under Marcos and his friends dragged the country into bankruptcy, creating even more marked inequality and exacerbating the already grave financial crisis that began in the mid-1970s. By 1980 real wages had fallen to less than half of what they were in 1962 (Abinales and Amoroso 2005, 215).

In this situation, ever more in ferment, aggravated by the war against the Muslim separatists in southern Mindanao, and with the strengthening of the National People's Army, military arm of the Communist Party of the Philippines (CPP), conditions in rural areas were ripe for the Marcos regime's replacement, which took place in 1986. Despite the presence of armed insurrectionary movements, the regime's overthrow came thanks to a peaceful popular revolution, led by the large, transverse, and interclass "People Power" movement, able to mobilize millions of people in a "moral crusade" against Marcos. The enormous demonstrations found the support also of dissident military factions, unhappy with corruption in the higher ranks of the armed forces (Abinales and Amoroso 2005, 223).

Philippine civil society had roots in the country's particular colonial past and in a long democratic tradition (Thompson 2004). Despite the brutal repression after the 1972 declaration of martial law, which effected not only the oligarchs who opposed Marcos, but also students, academics, businessmen and union leaders, the regime was unable to dismember civil society completely. Though very active, civil society was divided ideologically between the anti-Communist and Catholic-oriented social democrats (mostly concentrated in the cities) and the CPP (widespread even in rural areas).[18] Many organizations, especially those of the Catholic and anti-Communist urban middle class, survived by adopting a low profile or, in certain cases, by giving tacit support to the regime (Franco 2004). Other organizations, principally those linked to the CPP, worked clandestinely and their leaders were forced into exile.

The economy's rapid deterioration, the worsening in the standard of living even for the middle class, the obvious injustice, the brutal methods employed by the regime and the continuous violations of human rights[19] led to ever more frequent demonstrations, prayer meetings, and other forms of protest.

Civil society forces united in 1983, following the assassination of Benigno Aquino, Marcos's principal opponent. This event convinced even those in the middle class, who until then had been reluctant to demonstrate, to join in the non-violent initiatives organized by a new association called "Justice for Aquino, Justice for All" (JAJA). Important business and military sectors also began to take action. In the first case, the business and professional elite launched the Congress of Filipino Citizens (KOMPIL), with the aim of unifying the opposition around a political alternative to Marcos. In the second case, low-ranking officers formed a group called the Reform the Armed Forces Movement (RAM) (Diokno 1988, 150–51; Abinales and Amoroso 2005).

The "sham" elections for the national assembly in 1984 actually accelerated the regime's erosion. In an attempt to revive confidence, Marcos called early presidential elections in 1986. Marcos's attempt to declare victory over Corazon Aquino, widow of Benigno and massively supported by all the forces of civil society, was denounced by the National Citizen's Movement for Free Elections (NAMFREL), an election monitoring organization that documented the election fraud in 1986 and estimated that Aquino had won with 52% of the vote (Thompson 2004, 25). Aquino called on civil society to mobilize and organize civil disobedience to "bring down the usurper." Marcos was forced into exile on February 25, 1986 and Corazon Aquino and her supporters proclaimed the victory of the non-violent "People Power" revolutions (Elwood 1986). An alliance with the military officers in RAM led to a provisional government that managed a delicate and tortuous transition in which civil society organizations played an absolutely central role. However, the state's weakness partially thwarted the democratic conquests of the "People Power" movement, creating strong and persistent instability (Racelis 2000; Constantino-David 1997; Franco 2004; Paul 2010).

If there was a "golden age of political reform" during the 1992-8 Fidel Ramos presidency (Thompson 2010, 166), some noted a return of 1986-style "People Power" in the January 2001 popular overthrow of Joseph Estrada, accused of corruption and cronyism. Civil society again played an important role, with students and teachers at Catholic schools and universities the first to mobilize, followed by other students, trade unionists, and nongovernmental organizations across the political spectrum, as well as businesspeople. Estrada's mismanagement of the economy in fact was the crucial concern of the business sector (Landé 2001). The subsequent long presidency of Gloria Macapagal-Arroyo, who served from 2001 to 2010, though a relative economic success, also lapsed into "electoral manipulations, corruption scandals, human-rights abuses, and the undermining of institutions" (Thompson 2010, 166). The Philippine economy remains fundamentally weak, with about a third of the population impoverished outright, and only about 10% clearly in the upper and middle class. With the 2016 presidential elections approaching, it seemed likely the choice between populism and more avowedly "reformist" leadership could present itself again.

South Africa and Ghana

With respect to other African nations, **South Africa** has at least two peculiarities: its unique ethnic composition and its relatively high level of economic development. The Whites, of European origin, are about 9% of the population, Black Africans are about 76%, Coloured (mixed race) 9% and Indians and Asians, 2.5%. The high level of urbanization is evidence of an industrialized economy that makes South Africa the most developed country on the continent. For the World Bank, it is in the category of countries with "medium-high" income. In 1991, a year after the beginning of the transition, the per capita GNP was $2,560, compared to the Sub-Saharan Africa average of $350. In 1989-1991, it had an average annual growth rate of 0.7% compared to negative 1.2% growth for Sub-Saharan Africa (World Bank 1993). There traditionally has been a marked disparity in the distribution of wealth between the well-off White minority and the poor Black majority. These disparities were legitimized by the apartheid regime inaugurated in 1948 (Bratton and van de Walle 1994). During the 1950s and 60s, apartheid consolidated a regime of dominance of the White minority over the Black majority, with a democratic political order that was only valid for Whites. However, while that kind of regime could be compatible with a relatively poor rural economy, it was not compatible with a rich and complex urban, commercial, and industrial economy.

Economic development generated the need for skilled labor, improved education for the non-White population, and legalized union representation for them, along with freedom of movement and expanded purchasing power. In combination with the economic crisis, these elements led to the collapse of the apartheid system (Huntington 1991). In a situation that was already very tense, the deepening of the economic crisis in the mid-1970s acted as a catalyst for the transformation that followed. The low level of economic growth in the 1980s led to a general decline in the standard of living. From 1980 to 1990, the per capita GDP actually fell more than 10%, with the result that per capita wealth was no higher than in 1970. Poverty reached record levels among Blacks, with more than 16 million people living below the poverty level. This stagnation continued throughout the 1990s, and only after the fall of the apartheid regime was a program for reconstruction and development inaugurated (Clark 1997).

The actions of civil society were certainly central to bringing about regime change. The distinctive trait of South African civil society was its racial profile and its progressive transformation beginning in the early 1980s. Until that time, the dominant organizations were pro-apartheid and pro-business White groups that constituted the support base of the country's governing elite. Among the principal organizations were the *Afrikaner Broederbond* and the Afrikaner Trade Institute, while, on the labor union side, the main pro-apartheid organizations formed by the government to support discriminatory labor practices were the White Workers' Protection Association, the Mineworkers Union, and the South African Confederation of Labour (Sinai 1997). Even though they had a tradition dating to the 1950s,[20] Black civil society's student, women's and union organizations had no official recognition, and were systematically repressed, or, like political parties such as the African National Congress (ANC) and the Pan Africanist Congress (PAC), banned outright.[21]

Continuous protests, exacerbated by the grave economic crisis, and apartheid's condemnation by the international community led to a partial liberalization of the political system in the early 1980s. That allowed a tremendous growth in Black organizations that previously had been banned or prevented from working in public.[22] Labor organizations that already in the 1970s had organized anti-apartheid protests were legalized and saw their membership grow. New, independent labor confederations were born, and in 1983 the United Democratic Front (UDF) was formed, an umbrella organization, allied with the ANC in exile,[23] that coordinated the activities of various anti-apartheid student and labor groups, such as the Congress of South African Trade Unions (COSATU), the South African National Student Congress (SANSCO), the National Union of South African Students (NUSAS), and the Congress of South African Students (COSAS).[24] Despite liberalization, in 1988 the UDF was outlawed because of its activities but was replaced by an informal organization coordinating anti-apartheid groups, the Mass Democratic Movement (MDM). This organization was already active in the 1970s and early 1980s as an underground network. The MDM had no charter, nor did it have any legal status, but it was essential for maintaining unity among the different opposition groups, as well as for organizing protests, demonstrations, strikes, and civil disobedience campaigns.

The destruction of the apartheid regime was, therefore, principally due to internal causes, the economic crisis and the mobilization of socially and economically marginalized citizens, even if the acceleration of the process of change was attributable to the impact of the economic sanctions that from the mid-1980s on isolated the White segregationist regime (Huntington 1991, 98; Wood 2001; Sisk 2013). Economic crisis and continuous and sustained popular mobilization underpinned the destabilization of the authoritarian regime, also under pressure from some of its principal sources of support, the White economic elites, many of whom were convinced that a transition would preserve their interests better than the regime's continuation.[25] The mobilization of civil society, however, was not only central to the process of destabilizing/extricating the regime (Collier 1999), but was equally central in bringing the elites who were at the helm of civil society organizations to sit at the negotiation table that led the way to democracy.

Ghana's modernization intensified after its independence from Britain in 1957. Communications and infrastructure improved, there was growth in urbanization, an increase in agricultural exports (especially cocoa) and although free and obligatory education was instituted only in 1960, a relative expansion of education, especially for girls.[26] Despite all this development, as well as Ghana's wealth in raw materials and minerals (gold, diamonds, bauxite, and manganese), in the 1990s, during the regime transition, it was still largely an agricultural country and substantially undeveloped (Table 1).

Widespread corruption and the ineptitude of the alternating military and civilian governments that ruled after independence were at the bottom of the grave institutional and economic crisis in which the country found itself. Beginning in the mid-1960s, Ghana was in a vicious circle of high debt, a drop in the demand for raw materials, an overvalued currency, and a fall in production. The resort to further loans to guarantee the economy's survival only fueled a self-destructive cycle. Between 1965 and 1983 the average annual growth rate was -2.3% (World Bank 1985, table 1, 174). Along with the production of raw materials, the Ghanaian economy collapsed at the end of the 1970s (Chazan 1991). Between 1973 and 1983 inflation shot up to an average of 52%, reaching 116% in 1981 (World Bank 1985; IMF 2015). This naturally had an impact on real income and the standard of living.

It was in this climate that the 1981 military coup occurred, orchestrated by the middle ranks of the armed forces and led by Lt. Jerry Rawlings. This was billed as an intervention to eradicate corruption and launch a plan for economic restructuring that would facilitate a return to democracy. Rawlings gave rise to a populist regime based on the rule of the Provisional National Defence Council (PNDC), which combined legislative and executive functions. It was composed primarily of civilians, with a small military component, although, in reality, it was Rawlings who made the laws. In line with populist principles, Rawlings fostered the formation of civic committees,[27] instruments of popular power beyond the state's control, with the aim of using them as a counterweight to the existing power structures. These groups effectively operated independently of the political leadership (Hansen 1987, 178-79). The 1982 attempted coup against the PNDC led to a harsh response by the regime, which executed the conspirators, exiled dissidents, silenced the media, and abolished political parties, considered the true guilty parties responsible for corruption and the abuses of the regimes of Kwame Nkrumah (1957-66), Kofi Abrefa Busia (1969-72), and Hilla Limann (1979-81).

At the end of 1982, further deterioration in the country's economic condition led Rawlings to inaugurate the Economic Recovery Programme (ERP), supported by the International Monetary Fund (IMF) and the World Bank (WB). These institutions provided financial resources and expertise to promote stabilization and re-launch the economy, in return for adoption of a long-term austerity plan (Hansen 1987, 197-98; Herbst 1993, 36). The IMF and WB conditions in fact changed the government's orientation at the economic, political, and social levels. Contrary to the desiderata of the IMF and WB, Rawlings decided to silence the progressive wing within the regime. Popular groups were therefore excluded from the decision-making process, which was concentrated in a small circle within the government, assisted by foreign consultants. Simultaneously, violence increased and dissidence was repressed (Hutchful 2002).

The ERP was meant to put the country in a position to repay its foreign debt, emphasizing exports, and included a rigorous fiscal policy that later was geared towards privatization of state-owned property (Nimako 1996). The Rawlings regime strictly followed the directives that were imposed, so much so that in the mid-1980s the IMF considered Ghana its best student. Although this plan achieved significant macroeconomic results, these were not reflected in any improvement in the standard of living for most of Ghana's population. In 1993, ten years after the ERP launch, the minimum daily wage was barely 33 cents (Haynes 1995, 94).

This situation was reflected in widespread discontent among citizens, deeply affected by the crisis, and in growing criticism from various directions, which previously had been contained by repression. Most of the workers included in the various unions within the Trade Union Congress[28] no longer felt represented by the Worker's Defence Committees, considered unable to influence government policy. The unions abandoned their previous support for the regime, transforming into an opposition, also stimulated by their aversion to the PNDC's brutal methods and violations of human rights (Ninsin 1998; Herbst 1993). The same thing happened with the National Union of Ghanaian Students (NUGS),[29] which had supported Rawlings until his decision to adopt policies inspired by the WB and IMF, seen as damaging for the university and the country.

Resistance also came from other organizations within Ghana's rich fabric of civil society, which were more elitist, but historically had exercised strong influence on national policy, given their role as a substitute for a weak and corrupt political party system and a structurally unstable political system. The Ghana Bar Association (GBA), the Association of Recognized Professional Bodies (ARPB), the Christian Council of Ghana (CCG), the Catholic Bishops Conference (CBC), and the Ghana Journalists Association all played a central role (Owusu 1995, 203-206). The GBA was a professional organization that had as its objectives the defense of all the legal professions, maintaining the independence of the magistracy, the protection of human rights, and fundamental liberties. It played a role as critic and opponent of the Rawlings regime,[30] as it had with previous regimes (Adjetey 1996, 72). The same was true for the ARPB, founded in 1977, which included all professional associations. The ARPB was systematically repressed and its leadership arrested. The organization only resumed its activities in 1991 (Okudzeto 1996: 128). The CCG, born in 1929, worked via consultation among member churches, and was very involved in educational issues and the defense of human rights. The same was true for the CBC, founded in 1950, which collaborated closely with the CCG. Another group, based in London but associated with internal organizations, was the Ghana Democratic Movement. It was an active force against the Rawlings regime and included many elite professionals in exile, including lawyers, physicians, university professors, business people and politicians.

Given the large number of organizations that comprised it, the panorama of Ghanaian civil society seemed extremely rich[31], but it was a varied universe (Ninsin 1998), and it was unable to coordinate and act in a unified manner because of the regime's repression and Rawlings's constant attempts to coopt important sectors[32] (Ibrahim 2003; Whitfield 2003).

This situation changed at the end of the 1980s, when a new international scenario made it more difficult for the Ghanaian regime to evade ever more pressing demands for a multiparty democracy (Haynes 1995, 95). Many Ghanaian organizations became more vocal and, at the beginning of the 1990s, coordination among the various components of civil society increased. This enabled them to put continuous pressure on the government. A good example of this trend was the development of the Movement for Freedom and Justice (MFJ), led by the noted academic Adu Bohaden, who was the first to denounce the "culture of silence" (Haynes 1995; Ninsin 1996). The MFJ functioned as an umbrella organization, coordinating the activities of other associations critical of the regime, and was a force for democratic reform. Faced with growing pressures and in order to weaken opposition groups and steer the transition in the direction he wanted, Rawlings nominated a committee of experts, all allies of the government, to draft a new constitution and form a constituent assembly (Nugent 1995; Ninsin 1996; Gyimah-Boadi 1991a, 1991b; Handley 2013). Despite its origins, the Constituent Assembly showed a great deal of independence and rejected some of the PNDC's most important proposals, including for a French-style presidential system and for presence of the military in the president's advisory body (Haynes 1995, 98).

The new constitution was approved in 1992. In the same year Rawlings transformed the PNCD into the National Democratic Congress (NDC). He won the presidential elections, which were characterized by fraud and intimidation, and installed a competitive authoritarian regime (Levitsky and Way, 2010) that lasted 8 years. In this phase, civil society more clearly emerged as a force able to influence the choices that led towards complete democratization,[33] which became manifest with the turnover in the 2004 elections, then repeated in the presidential elections in 2008. In Freedom House's *Freedom in the World 2015* report[34] Ghana, like South Africa, figured as "free" (actually with a somewhat better score than South Africa's), despite the rather different paths the two countries had traveled to that result.

Conclusions

This chapter focuses on the roles of economic development/crisis and of civil society during the Third Wave of democratization, concentrating on a limited number of particularly interesting and contrasting cases, in different periods and different geographical areas, and in countries with different social/cultural profiles. The intent was to verify whether the impact of the economic and civil society variables could be considered crucial, complementary, or marginal in bringing about regime change. Table 2 presents a summary of the results, including the incidence of the variables in each national case, as well as when the transition started, the initial and outcome regimes, and the type of transition.

Given the complexity of civil society and the need to render it clearly, in Table 3 the civil society variable for each country is broken down into four dimensions: its density, i.e. the number of organizations present in the country immediately prior to the start of regime change (whether collapse or transformation); the links and the level of cooperation among organizations, which gives a measure of civil society's capacity to create a critical mass for exerting pressure on the regime; the ability to mobilize in the regime's crisis phase; civil society's importance during the transition phase (i.e. its capacity for mediation between the masses and the state).

In the Southern European cases (Portugal and Spain), socio-economic development was not uniform but created conditions favorable to future democratic development. However, the economic and social crisis resulting from the 1973 Oil Crisis was the major force behind the erosion of the authoritarian regimes. In other words, in these two countries, and in Greece as well, there was, even with notable differences, a sequence of unexpected socio-economic development, followed by recession, and then economic crisis, which helped destabilize the political regimes. In this situation of shared

Table 2. National cases compared

	Portugal	Spain	South Korea	Philippines	South Africa	Ghana
Start of regime change	1974	1975	1987	1986	1990	1991
Starting regime	Personal tyranny	Personal tyranny	Military oligarchy	Sultanism	Racial oligarchy	Single-party regime
Type of transition	Transition through replacement	Transition through transaction	Transition through extrication	Transition through replacement	Transition through extrication	Transition through transaction
Final regime	Consolidated democracy	Consolidated democracy	Consolidated democracy	Unstable democracy	Stable democracy	Stable democracy
Impact of economic development/crisis on regime change	Prevalent impact of economic crisis, in presence of limited development.	Combined effect of development and crisis. Development precedes transition; crisis is catalyst for change.	High impact of economic development.	Prevalence of economic crisis in context of limited development.	Combined effect of economic development and crisis in context of great racial inequality. Crisis is catalyst	Prevalence of economic crisis in context of limited development.
Role of civil society in regime change	Negligible	Very significant	Very significant	Crucial	Very significant	Limited until1992, then gradually increasing.

Table 3. Selected dimensions of civil society

	Density	Ties/cooperation among organizations	Mobilization capacity during regime crisis	Importance in the transition
		Civil Society		
Portugal	Low	Cooperation, but weak ties	Almost none	Moderate
Spain	Medium-high	Cooperation and strong ties	High	High
South Korea	Medium-high	Cooperation and strong ties	High	Gradually increasing
Philippines	High	Strong and cooperative ties, despite ideological differences	Very high	Very high
S. Africa	Medium-high	Cooperation and strong ties	High	High
Ghana	High	Strong ties among opposition associations, presence of pro-government associations	Low	Low until 1992, then gradually increasing.

economic crisis, however, civil society played distinctly different roles. In Spain there was a large middle class and a strong fabric of closely linked civil society organizations. In Portugal, on the other hand, civil society was traditionally very weak and unable to exert pressure or mobilize the masses, nor could it contribute to the political transition in a crucial way.

The Philippines and South Korea also presented very different economic situations, with the latter developing much more strongly. Generally speaking, socio-economic development favors creation of a population that is increasingly conscious, educated, and desirous of liberty and change. In South Korea, civil society culture had deep historic roots. It survived clandestinely and, thanks to a wide network and a high degree of mutual cooperation, organized anti-regime protests and mobilizations. After the regime fell, the ties among the various currents within civil society did not break down, and assumed growing importance in building the new democratic regime.

In the Philippines as well, civil society played an important role in the political transition. The country's civil society was very lively, even if persecuted by the Marcos regime. This phenomenon is explained in part by the heritage of a long democratic experience before the rise of the authoritarian regime. This also explains the presence of numerous urban organizations, predominantly Catholic in inspiration, and of rural organizations with Communist roots. The Philippines case is particularly striking, however, because regime change happened despite a low level of economic development, mostly because crony capitalism guaranteed the oligarchs' enrichment, rather than modernizing or generally developing the country. But economic *crisis* also played a concurrent and important role in regime change. It greatly affected the business and middle class, and gave a final push to change.

Turning to South Africa and Ghana, pre-transition economic development was significant in the former and weak in the latter. In South Africa, economic development, mostly the work of the White minority, ultimately demonstrated the incompatibility of the apartheid regime with an advanced economy. It was no longer possible to exclude the Black majority from the benefits (not only economic) of development. Racial segregation promoted recession and stagnation. The long-running economic crisis played a central role in creating conditions for liberalizing the system. The crisis led to the mobilization of a wide network of Black organizations, first coordinated underground, but later in the open. Civil society would play an important role in the negotiations that led to regime change.

Ghana, like the Philippines, had limited economic development, thanks to a series of corrupt regimes. Although it had a strong impact on civilians, economic crisis did not create problems for the Rawlings regime. It remained solid, coopting important sectors of civil society, and incorporating both pro-government and pro-democracy groups (Ninsin 1996). Despite this, pro-democratic groups were able to consolidate in the 1990s and exert pressure on Rawlings, forcing him to launch a transformation process. Still, persistent divisions in civil society enabled Rawlings to steer the transition, marginalizing pro-democratic groups. Only after 1992 were these organizations able to become more significant and have their voices heard in the process of completing democratization.

These six cases illustrate that internal factors, such as economic development and civil society, can vary greatly within the same time frame and geographical region. Even with all the differences found in comparing these cases, it is evident that factors like economic crisis and civil society have considerable, if not always crucial, explanatory value.

From a macro point of view, looking at other world regions as well, economic crisis and civil society often emerge as crucial or at least important variables, unlike economic development, which is often a background variable that does not directly cause regime change. In Latin America, for example, with its notable and complex history of regime transitions, the positive correlation between economic development and democracy postulated by theorists of modernization is debatable, especially in the Third Wave. Looking at the Southern Cone, for example, in the 1970s, some of the most repressive bureaucratic-authoritarian regimes were found in countries with long democratic traditions (especially Chile and Uruguay) and after 20 years of sustained socio-economic development (O'Donnell 1978, 1979; Collier 1979; Seligson, 1988; Smith 2005). Nun (1976) showed that, contrary to the theory of modernization, which posits the middle class as the principal base of support for democracy, support for the military regimes arrived precisely from the middle class of those countries, the most modern in the region. The fact that these countries had high levels of education and income, plus well-organized civil societies, did not impede the rise of repressive regimes.[35] In these cases, it is difficult to identify a positive correlation between economic development and democracy. Although an essential pre-condition for the later transition, socio-economic development in Latin American countries up to the end of the 1970s was prevalently a background variable, only indirectly influencing the transformation of Latin American regimes.

Analyses by Remmer (1991), Mainwaring and Pérez-Liñán (2003; 2005) and Smith (2005) provide additional empirical confirmation that changes in the authoritarian trend, and regime crises from the 1980s on, occurred independently of a country's level of socio-economic development. In many cases, rather than in a period of development, it occurred in a period of economic decline, deindustrialization and a sudden drop in regional standards of living (Remmer; 1992-93, 10). Internal economic crises, due to structural changes in the international economy, and in particular, the impact of the 1973 Oil Crisis, are the most convincing explanations for the crisis/collapse of Latin American non-democratic regimes, although the timing, pace, importance and results vary from country to country (Remmer 1990). This confirms that it is the development-recession-crisis sequence that leads to destabilization of non-democratic regimes, in which authoritarian governments, already lacking popular legitimacy and unable to confront economic crises, also lose their ability to hold on to their fragile base of social support, because they are unable to redistribute resources. In addition, the partnership among authoritarian government, the military, and economic elites is often weakened. Rifts develop within the political class and the political crisis accelerates.

In other words, if the failure to resolve economic crises is one of the principal justifications for military interventions in politics in Latin America (and elsewhere) it is also one of the principal motivations for substituting one authoritarian regime with another, and in the majority of cases where an authoritarian regime falls and a democratic transition occurs (Wiking 1983, 116). Therefore, the Latin American democratizations show that social and economic development is a necessary but not a sufficient condition for the development of democracy, reinforcing the idea that economic crisis is the variable that explains the weakening and fall of authoritarian regimes (Huntington 1991). Poor economic performance and the failure of centralized planning also were the impetus for anti-regime protests in the Communist world (East Germany in 1953; Poland between 1956 and 1988), attempts at reform (Czechoslovakia and Hungary in the 1960s and 70s), and its final crisis (Grilli di Cortona 1989).

Civil society is another internal factor of great importance, especially in conjunction with economic crisis. Crises and non-democratic regimes' inability to deal with them are the cause of more or less intense popular mobilization/protest and/or the erosion of social support for the regimes, and consequent legitimacy crises. Transformation processes are not linear and meet different levels of resistance on the part of the regimes, which frequently respond with repression that tends to perpetuate itself (Smith 2005). Civil society organizations' ability to mobilize, and their importance during the transition process, differs from one national context to another. Civil society is easily recognizable as the central factor in the processes of change in Latin America (Argentina, Bolivia, Chile, Mexico, Nicaragua, Paraguay, Peru, Uruguay, Suriname), East-Central Europe, (in particular Poland, Czechoslovakia, East Germany, Romania, and the Baltic countries) but also in Africa (South Africa, Benin, the Comoros Islands, Lesotho, Mali, Malawi, Niger, Tanzania, Togo, Zambia) and in Asia (Indonesia, Mongolia, Thailand, East Timor, the Philippines, and South Korea).

The Arab Spring in some ways confirms the importance of civil society in democratic transitions. Tunisia, which remains the one clear success story, had a strong and well-developed trade union movement before the transition, which played an important role in the process of change. In the protests that led to Mubarak's fall, Egyptians showed a remarkable degree of social solidarity and ability to cooperate (Anderson 2011), but the 2012 presidential election outcome suggested that only the Islamist Muslim Brotherhood really had a cohesive and effective *political* organization.

In the crucial case of Indonesia, a young democracy survived a challenge in the 2014 elections, with grassroots voluntarism playing a crucial role in the victory of Joko Widodo (Mietzner 2014). In fact, one of the striking aspects of Indonesian political life is the extraordinary level of civic engagement and participation in organizations. Indonesia confirms the lesson from the Third Wave that civic engagement promotes democracy (Lussier and Fish 2012). Also, the fact that Indonesia is a lower-middle income country confirms the finding here that the presence and efficacy of civil society is not necessarily a function of relatively high economic development.

Endnotes

[*] A preliminary version of this chapter was presented at the 29th Conference of the Italian Political Science Association (University of Calabria, September 10-12, 2015). I would like to thank the discussant, Giampiero Cama, and the participants in the conference panel for their useful comments.

[1] For example, India is a competitive regime, although historically it has not had a high level of economic development, while East Germany and the Soviet Union, although having a good level of economic development, were not competitive regimes (Dahl 1971, chap. 5).

[2] Brazil's case is particularly interesting in this regard, see Cardoso (1986), but similar situations can be found in other Latin American countries as well (Remmer 1992-1993).

[3] Frequently governments of non-democratic regimes are made up of coalitions with military, civilian, technocratic, and in some cases religious components. In addition, even in cases where the governing elite is exclusively military, there can be different factions with different interests, even linked with external groups, which can fuel divisions and increase the risk of rifts.

[4] On economic crises and bureaucratic-authoritarian regimes, see Collier (1979). More generally, Huntington (1991, 51) underlines that: "With rare exceptions, the policies adopted by authoritarian governments to deal with the oil and debt crises often made the economic situation worse, producing stagnation, depression, inflation, low or negative growth rates, expanded debt, or some combination of these conditions, and hence further undermining the regime's legitimacy."

[5] Although connected to it, civil society remains separate from political society, identified as "encompassing all those organized actors (in a democracy, primarily political parties and campaign organizations) whose

primarily goal is to win control of the state or at least some position for themselves within it" (Diamond 1999, 221).

[6] According to the type of authoritarian regime, social support bases can be identified in the business community and the traditional sectors of landowning oligarchies, but also in the broad popular sector (workers and farmers) thanks to financing of youth and cultural associations, unions (more often obligatory associations controlled by the state), and in certain cases, even political parties, designed to monitor participation and prevent forms of mobilization that are anti-regime.

[7] The development of organizations, especially unions, can be promoted by rural immigration towards the cities following industrialization. In the city, workers can be more easily organized because they are more concentrated than in the country and can be called by the leadership to participate in actions such as demonstrations and strikes.

[8] The regime is forced to come up against not only the working class, which is more active and able to be mobilized because of the deterioration in living conditions brought on by the economic crisis, but also the business community, who, no longer seeing their interests protected, can react by opposing the regime.

[9] It has already been shown that a regime can lose its social support base because of its inability to deal with a crisis or because it choses solutions disliked by its supporters.

[10] We will use the distinctions made by Ruth Berins Collier (1999): transition through transaction, in which the regime elites drive negotiations with opposition forces and civil society and are much stronger than the former; transition through extrication/destabilization, in which civil society forces, in particular the working class, destabilize the authoritarian regime via lockouts and strikes, beginning the process that leads to transition; transition through replacement, in which civil society's position of strength progressively grows in relation to a delegitimized regime that quickly weakens.

[11] The two major unions were the Unión General de Trabajadores, founded in 1888 and closely affiliated with the Spanish Socialist Workers' Party (PSOE), and the Communist-inspired Comisiones Obreras. A third anti-Franco union that continued to operate in the 1980s was the Catholic-inspired Unión Sindical Obrera.

[12] Between 1966 and 1975, man hours lost to strikes rose from 1.5 to 14.5 million. In 1976 the number rose to 150 million (Maravall and Santamaria 1986, 77, 82).

[13] The bottom 50% of households received merely 14% of total national income before 1974, while the top 5% received 40% (Maxwell 1982, 235).

[14] In 1974 more than a million Portuguese lived abroad, about 1/8 of the

country's population (Manuel 1988, 143).

[15] World Bank (1989, table 31, 225).

[16] This also was supported by an extremely high level of US assistance, which between 1946 and 1980 amounted to more than 12.7 billion dollars, compared to the 2.8 billion given to the Philippines. This enormous gap was due to South Korea's strategic importance (Kang 2002, 43).

[17] To give an idea of how difficult this period was, it is not difficult to pay the interest on a debt that is less than 60% of GDP. Above this threshold it becomes much more difficult. The Philippines debt in 1986 was equal to 98.8% of GDP.

[18] Two clear examples of this division were the labor and student organizations: the Federation of Free Farmers (FFF) and the Federation of Free Workers (FFW), founded by the Jesuits (Racelis 2000) and the Communist-inspired umbrella federation *Kilusang Mayo Uno* (May First Labor Movement) (West 1997; Thompson 1995). Analogous divisions also were found in the student movement, with the social democratic Lakasdiwa and the Catholic youth organizations Khi Ro and the National Union of Students of the Philippines (NUSP) on one side, and the *Kabataang Makabayan* (KM—Patriotic Youth) and *Samahang Demokratikong Kabataan* (SDK—Democratic Youth Organization) on the other (Franco 2004, 106n17).

[19] Among the organizations that conducted a campaign to sensitize international public opinion to human rights violations were the following Catholic-oriented groups: Association of Major Religious Superiors of the Philippines (AMRSP) and Task Force Detainees of the Philippines (TFDP). In addition to sensitizing international public opinion, the Free Legal Assistance Group (FLAG) provided free legal aid (Franco 2004, 108n22).

[20] The Federation of South African Women dates from 1954, and the South African Congress of Trade Unions from 1955.

[21] The South African Students' Organization, part of the larger Black Consciousness Movement, was dissolved after the bloody suppression of the 1976 Soweto uprising. Its leader, Steven Biko, was killed after his arrest.

[22] The Fundraising Act of 1978, for example, prohibited Black NGOs from collecting funds to finance themselves and was abrogated only after the end of apartheid (Habib 2003).

[23] On this point see Lodge and Nasson (1991).

[24] The important role of the South African Council of Churches also deserves mention (Sisk 2013).

[25] After the Soweto uprising, capital flight and a sharp curtailment of new investment began to have real costs for the capacity of the state to oversee sufficient economic growth to meet the needs of the growing population.

Policies of import substitution and state-financed parastatal corporate spending did little to quell the growing dissatisfaction among leading industrialists and other business leaders (Sisk 2013, 177).

[26] Only 28% of girls were enrolled in secondary school in 1993 compared to 44% of boys (World Bank, 1997, table 7, 226).

[27] Among the most important were the Workers' Defence Committees (WDCs), People's Defence Committees (PDCs), Citizens' Vetting Committees (CVCs), and National Defence Committees (NDCs)

[28] The TUC always had a big following, with more than 500,000 registered members in 16 affiliated unions. Because of this, all governments beginning with independence tried to control it, also the case for the pro-government Ghana Private Road Transport Union (Gyimah-Boadi 1994a, 132-135).

[29] The NUGS represented more than 8,000 students from the country's three major universities. Since Ghana's independence, it had always been one of the most politically active groups.

[30] The GBA was particularly active in condemning the creation of special tribunals outside the normal legal system to prosecute opponents of the government. However, GBA criticisms of the anti-democratic nature of the special tribunals and demands for their closure went unheeded.

[31] Ghanaian civil society grew despite the lack of economic development and related factors, such as high levels of education. The result was the birth of groups primarily composed of members of the small middle class. (Ninsin 1993).

[32] Among the multiple pro-government groups were several evangelical Christian organizations, the 31st December Women's Movement, ethnic/regional associations such as the Volta Region Development Corporation, and the Ghana Private Road Transport Union within the TUC. These groups received government financing and other resources, unlike other groups that maintained their autonomy and suffered systematic regime persecution and repression (Gyimah-Boadi 1994a).

[33] As Levitsky and Way (2010, 303) observe, while Rawlings could have reconsolidated the authoritarian regime, he invested instead in a democratic project, strengthening the constitution and institutions.

[34] See https://freedomhouse.org/report/freedom-world/freedom-world-2015#.VkE0SISdL0s.

[35] It must be underlined that, from the 1960s and 1970s, the middle classes, not adequately represented in the democratic arena, gave their support to coups rather than to governments supported by the working class.

Reference List

Abdulai, David. 1992. "Rawlings 'Wins' Ghana's Presidential Elections: Establishing a New Constitutional Order." *Africa Today* 39 (4): 66–71.

Abinales, Patricio N., and Donna J. Amoroso, 2005. *State and Society in the Philippines.* Lanham,MD: Rowman & Littlefield.

Adesnik, David A., and Sunhyuk, Kim. 2013. "South Korea: The Puzzle of Two Transitions." In *Transitions to Democracy: A Comparative Perspective,* edited by Kathryn Stoner and Michael McFaul, 266-89. Baltimore. Johns Hopkins University Press.

Adjetey, Peter A., 1996. "The Role of Ghana Bar Association in Ghana's Democratisation Process." In *Civil Society in Ghana,* edited by F. K. Drah, and Mike Oquaye, 61-5. Accra: Friedrich Ebert.

Anderson, Lisa. 2011. "Demystifying the Arab Spring: Parsing the Differences Between Tunisia, Egypt, and Libya." *Foreign Affairs* 90 (2): 2-7.

Barreto, Antonio, ed. 1996. *A situacão social em Portugal, 1960-1995.* Lisbon: Instituto de Ciencias Sociais, Universidade de Lisboa.

Bermeo, Nancy. 1987. "Redemocratization and Transition Elections: A Comparison of Spain and Portugal." *Comparative Politics* 19 (2): 213-31.

Bosco, Anna. 2005. *Da Franco a Zapatero: La Spagna dalla periferia al cuore dell'Europa.* Bologna: Il Mulino.

Bratton, Michael, and Nicholas van de Walle. 1997. *Democratic Experiments in Africa: Regime Transitions in Comparative Perspective.* Cambridge: Cambridge University Press.

Byun, Chonghyun Christie, and Ethan J. Hollander. 2015. "Explaining the Intensity of the Arab Spring." *Digest of Middle East Studies* 24 (1): 26-46.

Cardoso, Fernando H. 1986, "Entrepreneurs and the Transition Process: The Brazilian Case." In *Transitions from Authoritarian Rule,* edited by Guillermo O'Donnell, Philippe C. Schmitter, and Laurence Whitehead, 137-53. Baltimore: Johns Hopkins University Press.

Chazan, Naomi, 1988, "Problems of Governance and the Emerging Civil Society." In *Democracy in the Developing Countries, Vol. II,* edited by Larry Diamond, Juan J. Linz, and Seymour M. Lipset, 93-139. Boulder, CO: Lynne Rienner.

_____. 1991, "The Political Transformation of Ghana under the PNDC." In *Ghana: The Political Economy of Recovery,* edited by D. Rotchild, 21-47. Boulder, CO: Lynne Rienner.

Clark, Nancy L. 1997. "The Economy." In *South Africa: A Country Study,* edited by Rita M. Byrnes, 171-246. Washington, DC: Federal Research Division, Library of Congress.

Collier, David, ed. 1979. *The New Authoritarianism in Latin America.* Princeton, NJ: Princeton University Press.

Collier, Ruth Berins. 1999. *Paths toward Democracy: The Working Class and Elites in Western Europe and South America*. Cambridge: Cambridge University Press.

Constantino-David, Karina. 1997. "Intra-Civil Society Relations." In *Philippine Democracy Agenda: Civil Society Making Civil Society*, edited by Miriam Coronel Ferrer. Quezon City, Philippines: Third World Studies Center.

Cutright, Phillips. 1963. "National Political Development: Measurement and Analysis." *American Sociological Review* 28 (April): 253-64.

Cuzán, Alfred G. 1999. "Democratic Transitions: The Portuguese Case." In *Comparative Democratization and Peaceful Change in Single-Party-Dominant Countries*, edited by Marco Rimanelli, 119-36. New York: St Martins Press.

Dahl, Robert A. 1971. *Polyarchy: Participation and Opposition*. New Haven, CT: Yale University Press.

de Dios, Emmanuel. 1990. "A Political Economy of Philippine Policy-Making." In *Economic Policy-Making in the Asia-Pacific Region*, edited by John W. Langord and K. Lorne Brownsey, 109-47. Halifax, Nova Scotia: Institute for Research on Public Policy.

de Meneses, Filipe. 2009. *Salazar: A Political Biography*. New York: Enigma Books.

Diamond, Larry. 1992. "Economic Development and Democracy Reconsidered." In *Reexamining Democracy: Essays in Honor of Seymour Martin Lipset*, edited by Larry Diamond and Gary Marks, 91-139. London: Sage.

———. 1999. *Developing Democracy: Toward Consolidation*. Baltimore: Johns Hopkins University Press.

Diokno, Serena I. 1988. "Unity and Struggle." In *Dictatorship and Revolution: Roots of People Power*, edited by Aurora Javate de Dios, Petronilo Bn Daroy, and Lorna Kalaw-Tirol, 136-7. Manila: Conspectus Foundation.

Elwood, Douglas J. 1986. *Philippine Revolution 1986: Model of Nonviolent Change*. Quezon City, Philippines: New Day Publishers.

Franco, Jennifer C. 2004. "The Philippines: Fractious Civil Society and Competing Visions of Democracy." In *Civil Society and Political Change in Asia: Expanding and Contracting Democratic Space*, edited by Muthiah Alagappa, 97-137. Stanford, CA: Stanford University Press.

Geddes, Barbara. 1999. "What Do We Know About Democratization After Twenty Years?" *Annual Review of Political Science*, 2 (June): 115-44.

Gibson, Heather D. 2001. "Economic Change in Southern Europe." In *Economic Transformation, Democratization and Integration into the European Union: Southern Europe in Comparative Perspective*, edited by Heather D. Gibson, 1-29. London: Palgrave Macmillan.

Gill, Graham. 2000. *The Dynamics of Democratization: Elites, Civil Society and the Transition Process.* Basingstoke, UK: Palgrave.

Gonzalez, Francisco E. 2008. *Dual Transitions From Authoritarian Rule: Institutionalized Regimes in Chile and Mexico, 1970-2000.* Baltimore: Johns Hopkins University Press.

Grilli di Cortona, Pietro. 1989. *Le crisi politiche nei regimi comunisti.* Milano: Franco Angeli.

_____. 2014. "Crisi e crollo dei regimi non democratici. Condizioni e tendenze nella terza ondata." In *Come cadono i regimi non democratici: Primi passi verso la democrazia nei paesi della "terza ondata,"* edited by Luca Germano, Pietro Grilli di Cortona, and Orazio Lanza, 1-36. Naples: Editoriale Scientifica.

Gunther, Richard, Giacomo Sani, and Goldie Shabad. 1988. *Spain after Franco: The Making of a Competitive Party System.* Berkeley, CA: University of California Press.

Gyimah-Boadi, Emmanuel. 1991a. "Tensions in Ghana's Transition to Constitutional Rule." In *Ghana's Transition to Constitutional Rule,* edited by Kwame A. Ninsin and Francis K. Drah, 35-40. Accra: Ghana University Press.

_____. 1991b. "Notes on Ghana's Current Transition to Constitutional Rule." *Africa Today* 38 (4): 5–17.

_____. 1994a. "Associational Life, Civil Society, and Democratization in Ghana." In *Civil Society and the State in Africa,* edited by John W. Harbeson, Donald Rothchild, and Naomi Chazan, 125-48. Boulder, CO: Lynne Rienner Publishers.

_____. 1994b. "Ghana's Uncertain Political Opening." *Journal of Democracy* 5 (2): 75–86.

Habib, Adam. 2003. "State-Civil Society Relations in Post-Apartheid South Africa." In *State of the Nation: South Africa 2003–2004,* edited by John Daniel, Adam Habib, and Roger Southall. 227-41. Cape Town: HSRC Press.

Haggard, Stephan, and Robert R. Kaufmann. 1995. *The Political Economy of Democratic Transitions.* Princeton, NJ: Princeton University Press.

Hamann, Kerstin. 1998. "Spanish Unions: Institutional Legacy and Responsiveness to Economic and Industrial Change." *Industrial and Labor Relations Review* 51 (3): 424–44.

Hamann, Kerstin, and Paul C. Manuel. 1999. "Regime Changes and Civil Society in Twentieth-Century Portugal." *South European Society and Politics* 4 (1): 71-96.

Handley, Antoinette. 2013. "Ghana: Democratic Transition, Presidential Power, and the World Bank." In *Transitions to Democracy: A Comparative Perspective,* edited by Kathryn Stoner and Michael McFaul, 221-43. Baltimore: Johns Hopkins University Press.

Hansen, Emmanuel. 1987. "The State and Popular Struggles in Ghana, 1982–86." In *Popular Struggles for Democracy in Africa*, edited by Peter Anyang Nyong'o, 170–208. London: Zed Books

Haynes, Jeffrey. 1993. "Sustainable Democracy in Ghana: Problems and Prospects." *Third World Quarterly* 14 (3): 451–67.

_____. 1995. "Ghana: From Personalist to Democratic Rule." In *Democracy and Political Change in Sub-Saharan Africa*, edited by John A. Wiseman, 92-115. London: Routledge.

_____. 2001. *Democracy in the Developing World: Africa, Asia, Latin America and the Middle East*. Cambridge: Polity Press.

Hedman, Eva-Lotta, and John Sidel. 2000. *Philippines Politics and Society in the Twentieth Century*. London: Routledge.

Herbst, Jeffrey. 1993. *The Politics of Reform in Ghana, 1982-91*. Oxford: University of California Press.

_____. 1994. "The Dilemmas of Explaining Political Upheaval: Ghana in Comparative Perspective." In *Economic Change and Political Liberalization in Sub-Saharan Africa*, edited by J. Widner, 182-98. Baltimore: Johns Hopkins University Press.

Huntington, Samuel. 1991. *The Third Wave of Democratization in the Late Twentieth Century*. Norman, OK: University of Oklahoma Press.

Hutchcroft, Paul. 1991. "Oligarchs and Cronies in the Philippines State: The Power of Patrimonial Plunder." *World Politics* 43 (3): 414-50.

Hutchful, Eboe. 2002. *Ghana's Adjustment Experience: The Paradox of Reform*. Oxford: James Currey

Ibrahim, Jibrin. 2003. *Democratic Transitions in Anglophone West Africa*. Dakar: CODESIRA.

International Monetary Fund. 2015. *World Economic Database 2015*. https://www.imf.org/external/pubs/ft/weo/2015/01/weodata/index.aspx.

Kang, David C. 2002. *Crony Capitalism: Corruption and Development in South Korea and the Philippines*. Cambridge: Cambridge University Press.

Kim, Sunhyuk. 2000. *The Politics of Democratization in Korea: The Role of Civil Society*. Pittsburgh: University of Pittsburgh Press.

_____. 2004. "South Korea Confrontational Legacy and Democratic Contributions." In *Civil Society and Political Change in Asia: Expanding and Contracting Democratic Space*, edited by Muthiah Alagappa, 138-64. Stanford, CA: Stanford University Press.

Koo, Hagen. 2002."Civil Society and Democracy in South Korea." *The Good Society* 11 (2): 40-45.

Landé, Carl H. 2001. "The Return of 'People Power' in the Philippines." *Journal of Democracy* 12 (2): 88-102.

Landman, Todd. 1999. "Economic Development and Democracy: The View from Latin America." *Political Studies* 47: 607-625.

Levitsky, Steven, and Lucan A. Way. 2010. *Competitive Authoritarianism: Hybrid Regimes After the Cold War.* Cambridge: Cambridge University Press.

Linz, Juan J. 1992. "La transición democrática en España en perspectiva comparada." In *Transición política y consolidación democrática: España (1975-1986)*, edited by Ramon Cotarelo, 431-57. Madrid: Centro de Investigaciones Sociológicas.

Linz, Juan J., and Alfred Stepan. 1996. *Problems of Democratic Transitions and Consolidation: Southern Europe, South America, and Post-Communist Countries.* Baltimore: Johns Hopkins University Press.

Linz, Juan J., Alfred Stepan, and Richard Gunther. 1995. "Democratic Transition and Consolidation in Southern Europe, with Reflections on Latin America and Eastern Europe." In *The Politics of Democratic Consolidation: Southern Europe in Comparative Perspective*, edited by Richard Gunther, Nikiforos Diamandouros and Hans-Jürgen Puhle, 77-123. Baltimore: Johns Hopkins University Press.

Lipset, Seymour M. 1959. "Some Social Requisites of Democracy: Economic Development and Political Legitimacy." *American Political Science Review* 53 (1): 69-105.

_____ 1960. *The Political Man: The Social Basis of Politics.* Garden City, NY: Doubleday.

Lodge, Tom, and Bill Nasson. 1991. *All, Here, and How: Back Politics in South Africa in the 1980s.* New York: Ford Foundation and Foreign Policy Association.

Londregan, John B., and Keith T. Poole. 1990. "Poverty, the Coup Trap, and the Seizure of Executive Power." *World Politics* 42 (2): 151-83.

_____. 1996. "Does High Income Promote Democracy?" *World Politics* 49 (1): 1-30.

Lussier, Danielle N., and M. Steven Fish. 2012. "Indonesia: The Benefits of Civic Engagement." *Journal of Democracy* 23 (1): 70-84.

Mainwaring, Scott, and Aníbal Pérez-Liñán. 2003. "Levels of Development and Democracy: Latin American Exceptionalism, 1945-1996." *Comparative Political Studies* 36 (9): 1031-67.

_____. 2005. "Latin American Democratization since 1978: Democratic Transitions, Breakdowns, and Erosions." In *The Third Wave of Democratization in Latin America: Advances and Setbacks*, edited by Frances Hagopian and Scott P. Mainwaring, 14-59. Cambridge: Cambridge University Press.

Manuel, Paul C. 1995. *Uncertain Outcome: The Politics of the Portuguese Transition to Democracy.* Lanham, MD: University Press of America.

_____. 1998. "Portuguese Civil Society under Dictatorship and Democracy, 1910–1996." *Perspectives on Political Science* 27 (3): 142-7.

Maravall, José M. 1997. *Regimes, Politics, and Markets: Democratization and Economic Change in Southern and Eastern Europe.* Oxford: Oxford University Press.

Maravall, José M., and Julian Santamaria. 1986. "Political Change in Spain." in *Transitions from Authoritarian Rule: Southern Europe, Vol.1,* edited by Guillermo O'Donnell, Philippe C. Schmitter, and Laurence Whitehead. 71-108. Baltimore: Johns Hopkins University Press.

Maxwell, Anderson J. 2000. *History of Portugal.* Westport, CT: Greenwood Press,

Maxwell, Kenneth. 1982. "The Emergence of Portuguese Democracy." In *From Dictatorship to Democracy: Coping With the Legacies of Authoritarianism and Totalitarianism,* edited by John Herz, 231-50. Westport, CT: Greenwood.

_____. 1986. "Regime Overthrow and the Prospect for Democratic Transition in Portugal." In *Transitions from Authoritarian Rule: Southern Europe, Vol.1,* edited by Guillermo O'Donnell, Philippe C. Schmitter, and Laurence Whitehead, 109-37. Baltimore: Johns Hopkins University Press.

McLaughlin, James, L. and David Owusu-Ansah. 1995. "Historical Setting." In *Ghana: A Country Study,* 3rd ed., edited by LaVerle Barry, 1-58. Washington, DC: Federal Research Division, Library of Congress.

Mietzner, Marcus. 2014. "How Jokowi Won and Democracy Survived." *Journal of Democracy* 25 (4): 111-25.

Nimako, Kwame. 1996. "Power Struggle and Economic Liberalization in Ghana." In *Liberalization in the Developing World: Institutional and Economic Changes in Latin America, Africa and Asia,* edited by Alex E. Fernandez Jilberto and Andre Mommen, 266-84. London: Routledge.

Ninsin, Kwame A. 1993. "Some Problems in Ghana's Transition to Democratic Governance." *Africa Development* 18 (2): 5-22.

_____. 1996. *Ghana's Political Transition 1990–1993.* Accra: Freedom Publications.

_____. 1998. "Civil Associations and the Transition to Democracy." In *Ghana: Transition to Democracy,* edited by Kwame A. Ninsin, 49-81. Dakar: CODESRIA.

Nugent, Paul. 1995. *Big Men, Small Boys and Politics in Ghana: Power, Ideology and the Burden of History, 1982–1994.* London: Pinter Publishing.

Nun, José. 1976. "The Middle-Class Military Coup Revisited." In *Armies and Politics in Latin America.* edited by Abraham F. Lowenthal, 49-86. New York: Holmes & Meier.

Nyoagbe, J. K. 1996, "Teacher Activism in Ghana: The Past and Present Scenarios." In *Civil Society in Ghana,* edited by F. K. Drah and Mike Oquaye, 77-91. Accra: Friedrich Ebert.

O'Donnell, Guillermo. 1978. "Reflections on the Patterns of Change in the Bureaucratic-Authoritarian State" *Latin American Research Review* 12 (1): 3-38.

———. 1979. *Modernization and Bureaucratic-Authoritarianism: Studies in South American Politics*, 2nd ed. Berkeley, CA: Institute of International Studies, University of California.

O'Donnell, Guillermo, and Philippe C. Schmitter. 1986. "Tentative Conclusions about Uncertain Democracies" in *Transitions from Authoritarian Rule*, edited by Guillermo O'Donnell, Philippe C. Schmitter, and Laurence Whitehead, 37-47. Baltimore: Johns Hopkins University Press.

Okudzeto, Sam, 1996, "The Role of the Association of Recognised Professional Bodies in the Political Struggles of Ghana." In *Civil Society in Ghana*, edited by F. K. Drah and Mike Oquaye, 109-28. Accra: Friedrich Ebert.

Orvis, Stephen. 2001. "Civil Society in Africa or African Civil Society?" In *A Decade of Democracy in Africa*, edited by Stephen N. Ndegwa, 17-38. Leiden: Brill.

Owusu, Maxwell. 1995. "Government and Politics." In *Ghana: A Country Study*, 3rd ed., edited by Berry LaVerle, 191-254. Washington, DC: Federal Research Division, Library of Congress.

Pastor, Manuel. 1992. "Las postrimerías del franquismo." In *Transición política y consolidación democrática: España (1975-1986)*, edited by Ramón Cotarelo, 31-46. Madrid: Centro de Investigaciones Sociológicas.

Paul, Erik. 2010. *Obstacles to Democratization in Southeast Asia: A Study of the Nation State, Regional and Global Order*. Houndmills, Basingstoke, UK: Palgrave Macmillan.

Payne, Stanley G., 1987. *The Franco Regime 1936-1975*. Madison, WI: University of Wisconsin Press.

Pepinsky, Thomas B. 2009. *Economic Crises and the Breakdown of the Authoritarian Regimes: Indonesia and Malaysia in Comparative Perspective*. New York: Cambridge University Press.

Pérez-Díaz, Victor. 1993. *The Return of Civil Society: The Emergence of Democratic Spain*. Cambridge, MA: Harvard University Press.

Przeworski, Adam, and Fernando Limongi. 1997. "Modernization: Theories and Facts." *World Politics* 49 (2): 155-83.

Przeworski, Adam, Michael E. Alvarez, José A. Cheibub, and Fernando Limongi. 2000.*Democracy and Development: Political Institutions and Well-Being in the World, 1950-1990*. Cambridge: Cambridge University Press.

Racelis, Mary. 2000. "New Visions and Strong Actions: Civil Society in the Philippines." In *Funding Virtue: Civil Society Aid and Democracy Promotion*, edited by M. Ottaway and T. Carothers. Washington, DC: Carnegie.

Remmer, Karen. 1990. "Democracy and Economic Crisis: The Latin American Experience." *World Politics* 42 (3): 315-35.

_____. 1991. "The Political Impact of Economic Crisis in Latin America in the 1980s." *American Political Science Review* 85: 777-800.

_____. 1992-1993. "The Process of Democratization in Latin America." *Studies in Comparative International Development* 27 (4): 3-24.

Rueschmeyer, Dietrich, Eveline H. Stephens, and John D. Stephens. 1992. *Capitalist Development and Democracy.* Cambridge: Polity Press.

Russett, Bruce M. 1965. *Trends in World Politics.* New York: Macmillan.

Sapelli, Giulio. 1995. *Southern Europe since 1945. Tradition and Modernity in Portugal, Spain, Italy, Greece and Turkey.* London: Longman.

Schmitter, Philippe C. 1977. "Portée et signification des élections dans le Portugal autoritaire." *Revue Française de Science Politique* 27 (1): 92-122.

Schock, Kurt. 2005. *Unarmed Insurrections: People Power Movements in Nondemocracies.* Minneapolis: University of Minnesota Press.

Seligson, Mitchell A. 1988. "Democratization in Latin America. The Current Cycle." In *Authoritarians and Democrats: Regime Transition in Latin America*, edited by James M. Malloy and Mitchell A. Seligson, 3-12. Pittsburgh: University of Pittsburgh Press.

_____. 1997. "The Vanhanen Thesis and the Prospects for Democracy in Latin America". In *Prospects for Democracy: A Study of 172 Countries*, edited by Tatu Vanhanen, 277-83. London: Routledge.

Sik Lee, Chong. 1992."Historical Settings." In *South Korea: A Country Study*, 4th ed., edited by Andrea Matles Savada and William Shaw, 1-65. Washington DC: Federal Research Division, Library of Congress.

Sinai, Joshua. 1997. "Government and Politics." In *South Africa: A Country Study*, 3rd ed., edited by Rita M. Byrnes, 247-327. Washington, DC: Federal Research Division, Library of Congress.

Sisk, Timothy D. 2013. "South Africa: Enabling Liberation." In *Transitions to Democracy: A Comparative Perspective*, edited by Kathryn Stoner and Michael McFaul, 168-91. Baltimore: Johns Hopkins University Press.

Smith, Peter H. 2005. *Democracy in Latin America: Political Change in Comparative Perspective.* New York: Oxford University Press.

Stepan, Alfred. 1988. *Rethinking Military Politics: Brazil and the Southern Cone.* Princeton, NJ: Princeton University Press.

Thompson, Marc R. 1995. *The Anti-Marcos Struggle: Personalistic Rule and Democratic Transition in the Philippines.* Quezon City, Philippines: New Day Publishers.

_____. 2004. "The Puzzles of Philippine 'People Power.'" In *Democratic Revolution: Asia and Eastern Europe*, edited by M. R. Thompson, 18-34. London: Routledge.

_____. 2010. "Reformism vs. Populism in the Philippines." *Journal of Democracy* 21 (4): 154-68.

Uhlin, Anders. 2006. *Post-Soviet Civil Society: Democratization in Russia and the Baltic States*. London: Routledge.

Vanhanen, Tatu. 1997. *Prospects of Democracy: A Study of 172 Countries*. Washington, DC: Carnegie Endowment for International Peace.

West, Lois. 1997. *Militant Labor in the Philippines*. Philadelphia: Temple University Press.

Wheeler, Douglas L. 1978. *Republican Portugal: A Political History, 1910-1926*. Madison, WI: The University of Wisconsin Press.

White G. 1996. "Civil Society, Democratization and Development." In *Democratization in the South: The Jagged Wave*, edited by Robin Luckham and Gordon White, 178-220. Manchester: Manchester University Press.

Whitfield, Lindsay. 2003. "Civil Society as Idea and Civil Society as Process: The Case of Ghana." *Oxford Development Studies*, 31(3): 379-400.

Wiarda, Howard. 1977. *Corporatism and Development: The Portuguese Experience*. Amherst, MA: University of Massachusetts Press.

Wiking, Staffan. 1983. *Military Coups in Sub-Saharan Africa*. Uppsala: Scandinavian Institute of African Studies.

Winckler, Onn. 2013. "The 'Arab Spring': Socioeconomic Aspects." *Middle East Policy* 20 (4): 68-87.

Wood, Elisabeth Jean. 2001. "An Insurgent Path to Democracy: Popular Mobilization, Economic Interests, and Regime Transition in South Africa and El Salvador." *Comparative Political Studies* 34 (8): 862-88.

World Bank. 1985. *World Development Report 1985*. Oxford: Oxford University Press.

_____. 1989. *World Development Report 1989*. Oxford: Oxford University Press.

_____. 1993. *World Development Report 1993*. Oxford: Oxford University Press.

_____. 1997. *World Development Report 1997*. Oxford: Oxford University Press.

Wurfel, David. 1988. *Filipino Politics: Development and Decay*. Ithaca, NY: Cornell University Press.

Xiao Zhou, Kate, Shelley Rigger, and Lynn T. White III, eds. 2014, *Democratization in China, Korea and Southeast Asia? Local and National Perspectives*. New York: Routledge.

Zunes, Stephen. 1994. "Unarmed Insurrections Against Authoritarian Governments in the Third World: A New Kind of Revolution." *Third World Quarterly* 15 (3): 403-26.

Weak Stateness and Political Change in Non-Democratic Regimes in the Third Wave

by Nicoletta Di Sotto and Pietro Grilli di Cortona[1]

The *weakness* of certain states most commonly receives high-profile attention when it creates serious challenges to the security and stability of the international order (Zartman 1995; Carment 2003; Clapham 2004; Iqbal and Starr 2008). Especially since September 11, 2001 a belief has taken hold that fragile states (or the so-called "failed states" that are objects of particular concern) offer fertile ground for the proliferation of terrorist movements, criminal organizations, and armed conflicts, as well as problems like poverty, the spread of illness and drug trafficking, and various humanitarian emergencies (Fukuyama 2004; Krasner and Pascual 2005). The strength of the Islamic State in Iraqi and Syrian territory at the beginning of 2016, despite the efforts of the international community, illustrated the continuing danger that weak and/or crumbling states could pose. This is not a new problem, in fact. Between 1989 and 2001, for example, many international crises were the product of fragile or failed states (Somalia, Haiti, Cambodia, Bosnia, Kosovo, Rwanda, Liberia, Sierra Leone, Congo, East Timor). The international community had to intervene in many states in crisis (with various forms and levels of invasiveness, and not always successfully) to take on the functions of the failed state. At the same time, research in the field has thrived, including the creation of data banks to help better recognize and prevent state crises (King and Zeng 2001).

Stateness and Its Political Implications: Theoretical Perspectives

But *stateness* is not important solely because its absence or weakness can have international ramifications. Indeed, in the first instance, it relates to characteristics one might readily consider "internal." Unlike *statehood*, which signifies an attachment (even emotional) to the state, the term *stateness* refers to the existence of a coercive power (Tilly 1990, 28) exercised in exclusive fashion over a given territory, i.e. consistent with Weber's classic definition of the state. In its widest meaning, stateness concerns the level of development and perception of the state, especially referring to the relationship between political community and territorial borders (Linz and Stepan 1996; Stepan, Linz, and Yadav 2011).[2] Stateness can have varying degrees of strength. Melville, Stukal, and Mironyuk (2013), for example, based on examination of differing development paths in post-Communist countries, developed a typology of stateness that identified three levels: *full, thin, or average.*

The primary focus of this chapter is the connection between weak stateness and political change, specifically the crisis and collapse of non-democratic regimes during the Third Wave of democratization, which began with the April 1974 Carnation Revolution in Portugal, and subsequent democratic transitions, more or less successful. In many countries, the crisis of non-democratic regimes was intertwined with profound differences concerning what the political community should effectively be, and what people or peoples should belong to that political community (Linz and Stepan 1996). A classic challenge to "stateness" arises, in fact, when citizens do not recognize a state as legitimate (Elkins and Sides 2008), creating problems of territorial organization and management that lead to the rise of actors that threaten the state's integrity. Precisely such challenges to stateness are at the center of the following analysis.

The political science literature has devoted little attention so far to the connection between stateness and democratization. Beginning with Lipset (1959), Moore (1966), Rustow (1970), and Dahl (1971), the literature has featured an often rich and stimulating debate concerning the historic, cultural, and socio-economic conditions for democratization. Despite an evident awareness of the issue (the expression *no state, no democracy* is repeated in some works), the subject of the state's importance is on the whole ignored.

There is also an issue of what is the cause and what is the effect. Carbone and Memoli (2015), for example, note the established view in the political science field that a sound and functioning state is a necessary precursor to democracy, but argue that democratization in turn can play a role in consolidating the state. Many democratization processes, in fact, have ended up fomenting state crises and reorganizations that in turn then conditioned democratization. This understandably shifts attention to the relationship between state stability and the outcome of democratization and on possible reciprocal interference between regime and state transformation. The latter can involve the crisis, failure, and disintegration of old state institutions, as well as the birth of new ones, perhaps even from the ashes of those that had died out.

Without exaggerating potential causal linkages, it is interesting to juxtapose the historical waves of democratization and of change in the organization of states. As is well known, Huntington (1991) identified three waves of democratization: a first wave beginning in the 1820s and continuing until Mussolini's rise to power in 1922; a wave following the Second World War and lasting until 1962; the aforementioned Third Wave. After the 1648 Treaty of Westphalia (Carment 2003) there also were numerous waves of transformation of state organization. These were the effect of great events such as: 1) large scale conflicts (the Napoleonic Wars, World Wars I and II) ending with important treaties (1815, 1919, 1945); 2) the end of the European empires and the emergence of national states; 3) the decline of colonial empires (for example, Spain in the 19th century and the United Kingdom in the 20th); 4) the end of the USSR's ideological empire after 1989. Also accompanying these moments of state system reorganization in some regions were processes that produced incremental changes, with various targets, and that perhaps paved the way for later and more dramatic transformations. Changes that did not necessarily impact the number of states but that certainly changed their physiognomy and function included: globalization of economic and social processes with consequent appropriation of state sovereignty in certain areas; aggregation phenomena (the European Union, for example); forms of disintegration due to the fact that, unlike in the past, territorial extension was no longer a source of state enrichment (Herbst 2004); the break-up of internal sovereignty and decentralization (federalization processes). In any case, it seems possible to discern significant overlaps between periods of democratization and periods that saw extensive change in the characteristics of states.

Before testing the hypothesis of a relationship between conditions of stateness and the results of democratization processes via an empirical examination of the Third Wave democratizations after 1974, however, it is necessary to clarify the empirical dimensions of state fragility. Then, we will turn to an analysis of the influence of stateness on political change in various areas of the world and, finally, compare the factors cited for the various regions.

The concept of state fragility is multi-faceted (Meierhenrich 2004; Rotberg 2004; Herbst 2004; Townshend 2007) and attempts to define it present problems. With the intent to amplify Weber's minimalist definition of the state, many more current definitions focus on a state's functional inabilities, ending up confusing the state with the political regime. The fact that a state is not efficiently providing certain services to citizens can be more a regime problem than a state problem. This issue is evident in the Organization for Economic Cooperation and Development's (OECD) *Principles for Good International Engagement in Fragile States and Situations*, which define states as fragile when their structures lack an adequate ability and/or political will to perform the basic functions necessary to reduce poverty, promote development, and safeguard the security and human rights of their populations (OECD 2007, 2).

In choosing indicators of state fragility, not infrequently the cause (weak stateness) is confused with its own manifestations,[3] e.g. inability of the state to implement specific *policy* objectives (perhaps broadly acceptable ones), beyond the responsibilities traditionally attributed to the state (maintaining order, the rule of law, security, defense, extraction of resources, social services, territorial administration, currency management). It is evident that inability to fulfill important roles can undermine legitimacy, but there is a risk of failing to distinguish between the responsibilities of the state and of the political sphere, and consequently failing to distinguish between state and regime fragility. It risks confusing every regime crisis with a state crisis. (The distinction, however, is crucial.)

We believe that the principal manifestations of a state's fragility are the ones that directly concern the defining elements of the state: control over territory, the exercise of sovereignty, the ability to administer, and a common identity. Variations or degeneration in these dimensions can undermine stateness, indeed the very legitimacy of the state, and influence political processes, including democratization. This decline of legitimacy can be the fruit of a genetic crisis (incomplete state-building and nation-building, e.g. in the USSR and Yugoslavia) or a functional crisis (the state as such in crisis or called into question, e.g. with the current rise of secessionism in a country like Belgium). The most frequent crises that can strike a state's configuration are uncertainty regarding state borders, limits on its internal sovereignty, failure of the state bureaucracy, and the disintegration of cultural identity. Each of these indicators can be linked to their most frequent and probable causes, among which the lack of correspondence between political-administrative borders and those of the political community's cultural identity is particularly important. In this case, if cultural identities become politicized, challenges and demands can arise that directly impact the form and stability of the state, provoking the decline of state identity and encouraging internal conflict. (See Table 1 below.)

Fragility should not be interpreted in a binary fashion (absent or present), but rather as a *continuum*, a property measured on a scale indicating differences in degree. At one extreme are strong states capable of exercising control (even if not total and homogeneous) over their territory. At the other extreme are failed states and, in the center, varying degrees of state weakness. In this vein, Rotberg (2004, 4-10) makes a distinction among *weak, failed,* and *collapsed states*. States that have conflictual internal situations, though not yet to the point of exploding, are weak. In failed states there is a situation of enduring and extensive civil war, with institutions unable to guarantee control over parts of state territory. Once it has collapsed, the state is reduced to being a mere geographic expression. Institutions cease to function and power vacuums are created that private military groups attempt to fill. But fragility is not a property that only concerns developing countries with incomplete state building. In fact, symptoms of state fragility can be found even in states governed by consolidated democracies. Hence an optimal fragility index must be able to assign comparable scores to countries in very different situations (Mata and Ziaja 2009, 5).

Table 1. State Fragility and Crisis, Dimensions, Causes, and Effects

Dimensions	Causes	Effects
1) Territorial dimension: border uncertainties and challenges	Presence of irredentist populations Claims of neighboring states Growing permeability of borders that influences the perception of collective security Massive and uncontrollable phenomena of clandestine immigration	Territorial claims and development of different ideas of the state (Greater Germany, Greater Romania, pan-Slavic ambitions, etc.) Difficulty in guaranteeing border security Possible armed conflicts Effects on the concept of citizenship
2) Power dimension: exercising limited internal sovereignty	Intense conflicts between center and periphery Internal sovereignty limited by an external power	Competing nationalisms Rise of internal violence, up to civil war
3) Functional dimension: disintegrating state; failing armed forces and administration; compromised functionality; lack of rule of law; inter-institutional conflict	Disconnect between political-administrative and cultural-identity borders Parts of territory controlled by adversarial forces (multiple sovereignty)	Proliferation of armed groups and militias Spread of illegality Collapse of the state's ability to perform normal functions
4) Cultural dimension: decline of a common identity vis-à-vis the state and proliferation of non-complementary identities	Growing localizing and regionalizing of politics. Development of the principle of self-determination at each level	Heightened localism Various forms of decentralization in an attempt to hold the state together. Decline of the state's central authority and secessionist challenges

Source: Di Sotto and Grilli di Cortona (2012), 65.

We (Di Sotto and Grilli di Cortona 2012) examined the relationship between state fragility and democracy in 86 countries touched to some degree by the Third Wave of democratization, using a modification of the *Failed States Index* of Mata and Ziaja (2009), intended to make the index more congruent with the priority dimensions of state fragility laid out in Table 1. While Mata and Ziaja had given equal weighting to all factors they considered, we doubled the weighting of demographic pressure, presence of refugees, dissatisfaction of ethnic groups, migration phenomena, delegitimation of the state, security issues, fragmentation of elites, and possible external interventions, i.e. phenomena that directly weaken the structure of the state, more than the regime. As a measure of democracy, we used the *Freedom House* 2011 democracy indices for each country in question. Among the 18 states with what we considered "very high" indices of fragility, four were "Not Free" and 14 were only "Partly Free" by 2011. Of the 46 states with high fragility 9 nine were not free, 17 were partly free, and 20 were free. States with low fragility, on the other hand were overwhelmingly free by 2011 (22 out of 24), with all the remainder partly free. This large-N approach broadly speaking confirms an inverse relationship between state fragility and democracy, but of course is not focused on the *mechanisms* whereby weak stateness can impact on non-democratic regime change and/or democratic transition in specific national cases.

Weak Stateness and Political Regime Change: Regional Perspectives

A regional approach is common in studies of non-democratic regime change and democratization, and regional commonalities are by no mean inconsiderable, as illustrated in other chapters in this collection. Given the limited degree of investigation so far into the stateness/regime change connection, or at least the possible connection, it seems appropriate to ask whether commonalities within regions, and differences between regions, are identifiable.

Early studies of regime transition concentrated on Western Europe, where some stateness crises were successfully resolved (Spain), or on Latin America (Linz and Stepan 1996, Vasilache 2007), where threats to the integrity of the states and their functionality were not frequent and not especially clamorous. Today, however, given the continuing challenges to democracy deriving from the stateness crises and collapse of the former USSR and the former Yugoslavia, or from state weakness/failure/collapse in countries such as Afghanistan, Iraq, and Syria, along with the continuing precarious conditions of state-building in Africa, it is urgent to consider how problems of stateness constitute an obstacle to the success of democratization.

It is also true that challenges to stateness, even when it comes to the crucial relationship between political community and territorial borders, an important source of state fragility, do not always represent a primary cause for a regime's crisis or possible collapse. As the contributions to this collection illustrate, non-democratic regime change and democratization require multi-causal explanations. By itself, the presence of an ethnic minority in a state (or across political borders) does not represent the minimum sufficient condition for the crisis and/or collapse of a non-democratic regime. The agency of political actors, for example, remains crucial, and in many cases dissidence is silent and not politically organized. In Latin America, for example, ethnic differences, though present, have had limited impact on the political party system and on the crisis or collapse of authoritarian regimes. On the other hand, ethnic differences have been decidedly more important, and in some cases decisive, in Eastern Europe and countries of the former Soviet Union.

Europe and Eurasia

The Third Wave of democratization is considered to have begun in Southern Europe with the April 25, 1974 Carnation Revolution in Portugal, moving rapidly to Greece and Spain.[4] Portugal in fact did not have major problems of stateness, given its ethnically homogenous population and border stability, and no major challenges to the exercise of sovereignty in Portugal itself. The revolution derived from a *regime* problem, specifically the costly and unsuccessful war to preserve Portugal's colonial possessions in Africa. Greece as well did not present *politically significant* ethnic diversity, despite the presence of ethnic Albanians and Turks. The Colonels' regime in a sense created a problem for itself, by expanding its definition of the Greek polity that should be within Greece's borders so as to include the ethnic Greeks of Cyprus. The July 1974 Athens-led coup intended to assassinate Cyprus president Makarios and unite Cyprus with Greece triggered a successful Turkish military intervention, and rapidly led to the fall of the Greek military junta. As in Portugal, this was a *regime* problem, rather than a stateness problem. The stateness challenge really would fall to the Greek Cypriot government in Nicosia, but, while scholars may lament problems with governance and democratic deficits in Cyprus (Varnava and Yakinthou 2010), the political difficulties stemming from the island's division have not blocked democratic development. Northern Cyprus as well ranks as politically free.[5]

In Spain, on the other hand, ethnic and cultural diversity was very marked, and did create some challenges in the transition to democracy. The Franco regime in essence had continued a centuries-long tradition of Spanish governments in building and maintaining strong central authority, and undermining the historic autonomy of the numerous political entities that had acquired distinctive identities during the long process of pushing back Arab control. Despite some ETA terrorist attacks, Franco had established a strong centralized system able to control from above any form of autonomist demands. Following Franco's death, however, latent stateness challenges had to be addressed in the course of the democratic transition, even though demands for autonomy of ethnic and cultural groups do not appear to have had a role in triggering the collapse of the Franco regime following his death. Although Spain is today one of the most decentralized states in democratic Europe, the 1978 Spanish constitution did not resolve the question of territorial distribution of power to the satisfaction of all groups. There remains the difficult coexistence of different nationalisms, in particular Basque (Basque terrorism has claimed 800 victims in the past 40 years) and Catalan (frequent and persistent demands for independence) (Lanza 2011). But democratic politics serve as a means of addressing these issues, and it is hard to discern fundamental threats to democracy from such stateness challenges.

The situation has been perhaps more challenging on the far

southeastern end of Europe, in Turkey. Renewed conflict in 2015 between the Kurdistan Workers' Party (PKK) and government forces highlighted the continued salience of demands for Kurdish autonomy, although the year also saw considerable electoral successes for the Kurdish-oriented People's Democratic Party (HDP), which operates within the mainstream political system. Concern about the ability of civilian political leaders to address threats to security, including Kurdish separatism, is an influential consideration in Turkish politics, and helped precipitate, for example, the bloodless and widely popular 1980 military coup that opened the way to the 1982 constitution, modeled on France's Fifth Republic constitution. Aydin-Düzgit and Gürsoy (2013) treat the 1983 Turkish democratic transition as a successful case of "incremental transition," but one can argue that the state of Turkish democracy is currently problematic. Freedom House in 2016 identified a downward trend and categorized the country as only partly free, citing harassment of the political opposition and the media as a key consideration, along with heightened conflict with Kurdish militants. In other words, while challenges to Turkish stateness historically and currently seem connected with the condition of democracy, they are not the only relevant considerations.

Within Europe, it is in the eastern parts (the former Soviet sphere and Yugoslavia) and in countries of the former Soviet Union where challenges to stateness and their implications for regime change and democratic transition have been most evident. In some cases, such challenges may have represented the principle variable in the crisis and/or collapse of regimes. The politicization of the stateness variable via the formation of nationalist and/or ethno-regional parties and movements allows us to examine the behavior of such political actors and their influence in the successive phase of democratic consolidation. A second order of problem is how difficulties in defining state borders or populations slowed down or even impeded completion of democratic transitions. This may be taken as evidence that the solution to the problem of stateness should precede democratization (Huntington 1991; Linz and Stepan 1996).

Of course, international and economic dimensions also had particular importance in the European context, especially for the countries of the ex-Soviet Union. Their fragile and economically backward situations as they achieved independence in 1991 left a heavy legacy that conditioned the democratization phase. From an international point of view, the end of bipolarism was certainly critical for launching the process of regime change, long awaited in some countries.

Among the post-Soviet states, Ukraine recently has been a particular focus of attention, for understandable reasons. Soviet Ukraine was an epicenter of challenges to the stateness of the USSR in the period leading up to dissolution of the Soviet Union, with aspirations for independence in effect driving the process of regime change in Ukraine. However, the fault line that for centuries divided the Ukrainian lands between Catholicism and Orthodoxy, and between control by Catholic powers such as Poland or the House of Habsburg, on the one hand, or Russia on the other, is still reflected in an east/west demographic and political divide, with a strong and relatively concentrated Russian and pro-Russian population in the eastern part of Ukraine. This internal divide, in turn, has become a constant issue in internal politics, reflected for example in the Orange Revolution (2004), ushering in what was depicted by Moscow and its supporters in Ukraine as an anti-Russia regime, followed by a pro-Russian turn with Yanukovych's election to the presidency in 2010, and then by his 2014 overthrow, perceived as an anti-Russian action. In addition to prompting separatism among the ethnic Russians and Russophile Ukrainians in the easternmost parts of the country, Yanukovich's ouster prompted Russia to annex the Crimea. Despite this, however, the October 2014 Ukrainian parliamentary elections were more of a success for pro-European moderates than for extreme Ukrainian nationalists.

A perhaps even more dramatic case of unresolved stateness issues in the former Soviet republics is Georgia, where Soviet control left the heavy legacy of a majority Georgian population alongside almost 80 different nationalities, promoting regional secessionist initiatives. As elsewhere in the collapsing Soviet Union, the independence aspirations of the majority population prevailed, helping undermine the USSR's stateness. It took some time after independence for the stateness challenges to Georgia to emerge fully. Disaffection with Shevardnadze's long and increasingly ineffectual and corrupt tenure was the main driver of the November 2003 Rose

Revolution that brought reformist Mikheil Saakashvili to power. But the de facto breakaway of Abkhazia and South Ossetia in 2008, with Russian military and political backing, illustrated the weakness of Georgia's independence from Russian control, and the relationship with Russia is a central question in Georgian politics.

Armenia had not been particularly restive under Soviet rule, and nationalistic aspirations in the late Soviet period were heavily irredentist in character, focused on unification with ethnic Armenians in Nagorno-Karabakh, an enclave in neighboring Azerbaijan. Inter-ethnic violence in Nagorno-Karabakh began in 1988, and the Armenian National Movement, focused on claims to the enclave, won a majority in the Armenian parliament in 1990.[6] In the 1990s, Armenia conducted an outright war to secure Nagorno-Karabakh. Differences over how to obtain the enclave have continued to dog Armenian politics, and the area continues to be heavily disputed. But many of the persistent democracy shortfalls in Armenia may have more to do with corruption and the desire to conserve political power than with perceived failures to unite all Armenians under one flag.

While it is questionable whether Nagorno-Karabakh truly represents a stateness challenge for Armenia, it unquestionably does for Azerbaijan, since the enclave is internationally recognized as Azerbaijani territory. The 1988 outbreak of fighting in Nagorno-Karabakh actually led to anti-Armenian pogroms in Azerbaijan, and Moscow intervened militarily against Azerbaijan in January 1990. In a sense, this made for a fusion of anti-Soviet and anti-Armenian nationalism in the emerging Azeri political leadership, whether Communist or not. When Heydar Aliyev, leader of the Communist Party, overthrew president Abulfez Elchibey (from the Azerbaijan Popular Front) in 1993, he too adopted a nationalist platform. But the Aliyev regime's persistence also has a great deal to do with control over distribution of oil revenues, and exploitation of clan ties and cronyism. In sum, while the challenge to Azerbaijan stateness in Nagorno-Karabakh helped promote short-term regime change, i.e. the downfall of the Soviet Communist regime, it has been something of an obstacle, along with many others, to democratic transition in a country that Freedom House routinely ranks among the least democratic in the world.

The nexus between stateness challenges and regime change/democratization in several countries of former Yugoslavia—Bosnia-Herzegovina, Croatia, Kosovo, Macedonia, and Serbia—also is important. In the Tito era, the larger ethnic groups, notably the Serbs, but also the Croats, often complained that their interests were sacrificed to buy off smaller groups, e.g. the Kosovar Albanians. Tito's departure from the scene helped open the door to demands by the various ethnic groups. This rivalry ultimately was expressed at the political level with the formation of ethnic parties and the creation of paramilitary forces that led to war, the international community's intervention in Bosnia, the 1995 Dayton Accords, and ultimately the 1999 NATO intervention against Milošević-led Serbia over Kosovo.

Note that it was almost ten years after Tito's death in 1980 before ethnic conflicts started, a situation we find often in the literature: the non-democratic regime creates a kind of "cork" in an area with latent infighting (Grilli di Cortona 2003) that explodes with particular vigor when the cork pops. Facing large challenges like defining borders and the rights of peoples, emerging leaders in the new self-proclaimed republics emerging from Yugoslavia devoted little attention to democratic transition, which resumed only when states assumed a defined and stable character. (Slovenia, where fighting against the federal army lasted a matter of days and was primarily a matter of political symbolism, was the major exception.)

Bosnia continues to exhibit all the problems that are created when the democratization process coincides with the creation of the state. The geographic and ethnic divisions among the Bosnian (48%), Serbian (37.1%) and Croatian (14.3%) populations, enshrined in the two separate republics that compose the state, so far have prevented the creation of an efficient democratic system. Ethnic polarization has exacerbated institutional conflicts, preventing strengthening of the state at the central level. Croatia's situation is different, in that the problem of stateness mostly concerned defining the country's borders, resolved by agreements in 1998 after two wars, peacekeeping operations and diplomatic efforts. But the death of independent Croatia's first president, the authoritarian nationalist Franjo Tuđman, was probably also a precondition for a complete democratic transition.

Kosovo's stateness problems were even more diverse. A borderland containing various cultures, by the 20th century Kosovo had an overwhelming majority Albanian population and a Serbian minority that was not content. In Tito's Yugoslavia, Kosovar Albanians de facto had a privileged position as the lead nationality in an autonomous province within Serbia. As central control weakened in the post-Tito era, Milošević used the Albanian question to stoke Serbian nationalism, in effect portraying Kosovo autonomy as an insult to Serbian stateness and profiting politically from that resentment, to the point of de facto breaking the power of the Yugoslav federal government over Serbia. On the Kosovar Albanian side, the emerging nationalist leadership defended Kosovo's autonomy (and hence in a sense its stateness), and won the support of much of the international community when Milošević stepped up repression. It was almost nine years after the 1999 NATO intervention before Kosovo declared independence, however, and only 108 countries have recognized it. The ethnic Serb minority (perhaps one tenth of the population) remains restive, and Kosovo's transition to democracy is not yet complete, primarily due to de facto constraints on freedom of the press.[7]

For Macedonia, the refusal of Greece to recognize the country by its chosen name is a continuing aggravation, viewed as an attack on Macedonian stateness. On the positive side, Macedonia and Kosovo completed demarcation of their border in 2008. This is the third country of the former Yugoslavia where regime transition overlaps with the state's consolidation. Tensions between ethnic Macedonians and Albanians remain a problem, and the country's democratic transition is far from complete, as shortcomings in the conduct of the April 2014 general elections indicated.

In Serbia, the 1999 NATO intervention dealt a strong blow to Milošević's nationalist and centralizing ambitions. He left power a year later, after an electoral defeat. Progress in terms of respect for human rights and minorities, confirmed by European Union reports and the Freedom House Index, seems to show that the quality of leadership can be more important than perceived challenges to stateness, e.g. Kosovo.

The case of the former Czechoslovakia also is worth mentioning. The collapse of the Communist regime in 1989 inter alia opened the way for emerging political forces in Slovakia to adopt autonomist, if not outright independentist, platforms. The authoritarian nationalist Slovak leader Vladimir Mečiar perhaps went further than intended, and in effect started the process leading to the bloodless separation of the Czech and Slovak republics as of January 1, 1993. In the short term, at least, Mečiar benefited politically, as did his free market conservative counterpart in the Czech Republic, Václav Klaus, whose decision *not* to make the defense of *Czechoslovak* stateness a priority was in fact popular. The democratic transition, which already was well advanced in the Czech Republic, proceeded calmly. Mečiar continued to play the nationalist card, directing animus against Slovakia's ethnic Hungarian minority, but this faded after Mečiar's defeat in 1998, and Slovakia, like the Czech Republic, now receives the highest possible Freedom House rating.

Slovakia's situation compares favorably with that of erstwhile rival Hungary, which has a much longer history as an independent state. In the 2016 Freedom House ratings Hungary remained among the free countries, though its score was not as good as Slovakia's, and the trend was negative, due to anti-migrant legislation, a worsening situation for the media, and corruption. Indeed, this could be a case in which political actors construct perceived threats to stateness to generate support for programs that represent backsliding on democracy.

Latin America and the Caribbean

The Latin American countries, i.e. Central and South America and Mexico, have relatively long histories as independent states, stretching back in many cases to the early 19ᵗʰ century, though political regimes in many cases have been unstable. They have experienced some threats to territorial sovereignty, notably in the US-Mexico war of 1846-48, in which Mexico lost over a million square kilometers of territory. In the 1879-84 War of the Pacific, Chile annexed Bolivia's coastal region, and in the Chaco War of 1932-35, Bolivia sought an outlet to the sea by trying to seize the Chaco region, controlled by Paraguay, in order to connect with the Rio de la Plata river system. Before the Second World War, Nicaragua, Haiti, and the Dominican Republic all experienced years-long US occupations. But in the period of the Third Wave of democratization, threats to territorial integrity were modest, and there were no major modifications of the map that had emerged from the Latin American revolutions of the 19th century and British decolonization in the Caribbean region after World War II.

In fairness, the Latin American and Caribbean region is not entirely devoid of the challenges to stateness discussed above. Disaffected population groups are present in most countries. Colonization created large waves of European immigration, resulting in racial and social stratification, with indigenous peoples experiencing chronically low socio-economic status. The dominance of the Catholic Church in the Latin American countries in theory could provide some cultural commonality between in-groups and out-groups, but class differences, regardless of religion, have been primary drivers of political developments, with issues of wealth distribution at the forefront of concern. Protests against the state, which included acts of terrorism, especially from the 1960s to the 1980s, were primarily ideological in nature, with ethnic/racial differences superimposed on ideological differences. The non-democratic military regimes that were common in Latin America prior to the Third Wave often served to maintain the privileged position of existing, European-origin elites. Identity politics did gain traction in Latin America in the 1980s and 1990s, with indigenous movements taking the lead role, and as a result Latin American countries undertook very significant reforms to integrate ethnic diversity. Indigenous presidents such as Evo Morales in Bolivia (since 2006), and Alejandro Toledo (elected 2001) and Ollanta Humala in Peru (since 2011) would have been unimaginable not so long ago. But populations of African origin often lag behind (Yashar 2015).

The Bolivian case is especially interesting. Morales has used his continuing strong support, which in the 2014 election even included increased support in the wealthier regions of the country, to redefine the country as the Plurinational State of Bolivia. In Peru, ethnic-racial divisions between the elites, composed of *criollos* and *mestizos*, concentrated on the coast, and the vast Native American majority, located in the Andean highlands and the forests, have been politically important. The Shining Path and the Túpac Amaru terrorist organizations active in the 1980s and 90s, for example, sought support among indigenous peoples, as well as other economically disenfranchised groups. Interestingly, the military junta that ruled Peru from 1968 to 1975 also had perceived the need for concessions to indigenous interests, opening up use of the Quechua and Aymara languages in schools in parts of the country. In Ecuador, indigenous groups were successful in securing land reform and land rights at the beginning of the 1990s, and participated in the 2000 overthrow of president Mahuad, who had adopted the US dollar as Ecuador's currency.

Broadly speaking, therefore, in the Andean states, the presence of relatively poor Indian populations has been a prominent issue in the political process, but not a fundamental or unmanageable challenge to stateness. In Guatemala, with its poor democracy record, violence between government forces and indigenous groups reached more dramatic levels, and former president Rios Montt was convicted of crimes against humanity in 1982-1983, including the killing of over 1700 members of the Maya Ixil people. (The Constitutional Court, however, ordered a retrial, which never took place.) The conflict has been more of an obstacle to democratization than a stimulus to it.

Guyana differs from other South American countries in having been a British possession, beginning in the early 19th century, after a period of Dutch control. The primary ethnic divide is between people of African origin, linked to the Dutch colonial period and now constituting roughly a third of the population, and those of South Asian origin, linked to British rule, currently about 40% of the population. (Indigenous peoples constitute less than 10%.) This divide is expressed via two main opposing political parties: the *People's Progressive Party* (PPP, a left-wing party mainly supported by the Indian-origin community) and the *People's National Congress* (PNC, socialist and supported by the African-origin community). Both ideological and ethnic components have had considerable weight, and the 2001 presidential elections, for example, were marked by strong inter-ethnic tensions, which persisted despite efforts to reduce ethnic strife in the 2006 local elections (Chaubey, Mawson, and Kuris, 2013). That said, the ethnic divide has not translated into a true threat to stateness, since neither ethno-nationalist party has sought autonomy from the state. The Guyanese case is one of contention for power and control, not a failure to recognize the legitimacy of the state. The process of democratic transition, though hardly problem-free, reflected successful pressure in the 1980s from the PPP on the then-ruling PNC for a greater political role, rather than a challenge to Guyanese stateness.

Neighboring Suriname, which remained under Dutch control until independence in 1975, is more ethnically diverse than Guyana. The South Asian ethnic group is the most numerous, comprising over a quarter of the population, and other large groups include the Creoles, descendants of Javanese contract laborers, and the Maroons, descendants of escaped African slaves. This diversity has been reflected in the political party system as well. A breakdown in the long-standing cooperation between the Suriname National Party (Creole) and the party representing the South Asian population opened the way for a military coup in 1980, led by Dési Bouterse. Initially non-ideological and focused on military corporate interests, the junta tilted increasingly to the left and became highly repressive, executing 15 leaders of civilian protests in 1982. A challenge to stateness came from the Surinamese Liberation Army, consisting primarily of Maroons, which staged raids threatening bauxite production, countered with force by the government. The military regime persisted until 1991, when Dutch and US pressure helped pave the way for government by a coalition of parties representing the Creole, South Asian, and Javanese populations. Despite serious problems with corruption and organized crime, Freedom House currently assigns Suriname a "Free" rating, although maintaining cooperation among the ethnic parties is a continuing challenge. The country also lost a long-standing maritime border dispute with Guyana, losing rights to potentially oil-rich areas. In sum, stateness challenges have abounded for Suriname, but have been primarily part of the context of regime change and democratic transition, rather than causative factors.

Recent events have recalled Haiti's long and troubled history of attempts at democratic transition since the fall of the repressive Duvalier regime, which led to the first free elections in 1990. Haiti certainly has weak stateness, i.e. the inability to fulfill effectively the characteristic functions of the state. On the other hand, it has a long history as an independent state (since 1804) and its territorial integrity is not at issue. (The neighboring Dominican Republic, on the other hand, complains of the threat of uncontrolled Haitian migration.) The population is homogeneous, almost entirely of African origin, apart from a small mulatto elite. François "Papa Doc" Duvalier came to power in 1957 on a platform of transferring full power to the Black majority, and social class-based power struggles have continued to dominate Haitian politics since the collapse of Duvalier rule, certainly hampering democratic transition. But there is little basis on which to posit an ethnically rooted threat to Haitian stateness.

In sum, while this review is far from encyclopedic, it suggests that, in Latin America and the Caribbean, stateness problems, specifically challenges to territorial integrity, or from dissident ethnic groups, have not been a primary factor in the crisis of authoritarian regimes. In some countries, however, challenges to stateness have created difficulties in the process of democratic transition.

Asia

In Asia, challenges to territorial integrity and national unity have had varying connections to the downfall of democratic regimes and to democratic transitions, but broadly speaking seem to have been significant primarily as challenges in the transition process. Perhaps the most politically important ethnic minority in parts of East and Southeast Asia has been the ethnic Chinese diaspora, which now makes up about three fourths of the population of Singapore, dominating a political system that remains authoritarian, had only a "Partly Free" rating from Freedom House in 2015, and seeks to repress racial/ethnic self-expression. Neighboring Malaysia has retained a large Chinese minority (about 25%) since the 1965 split with Singapore, but since independence (1963) the Malay majority has been politically dominant, and non-Malays at times have felt under pressure to assimilate. The political party structure remains ethnically based, with non-Malay parties both allied to the main Malay governing party and in opposition. Malaysia's democratic transition remains incomplete, and it is only partly free according to Freedom House. Indeed, neither Malaysia nor Singapore is considered to have participated in the Third Wave of democratization.

In Taiwan, ethnic Chinese immigrants from southern China were present in large numbers well before the influx of Mandarin-speaking Nationalists (Kuomintang) who fled China after the 1949 Communist victory in the civil war, and currently compose about 15% of the population. The Taiwanese people, who constitute the bulk of the island's population, are descendants of the pre-1949 Chinese immigration. Aboriginal populations of Malayo-Polynesian origin are present and have been able to organize politically in recent years, but only constitute around 2% of the population.

Taiwan has faced two main stateness challenges, with important political implications. The Nationalists, who initially wanted to use Taiwan as a base for retaking control of China, antagonized the local populace, and for decades used force to maintain their hold over the Taiwanese. The death of historic Kuomintang leader Chiang Kai-shek in 1975 (the same year as Franco's death in Spain), however, inaugurated a phase of reform and democratic transition under continued Kuomintang leadership (until 2000). Whether governed by the Kuomintang or by the Democratic Progressive Party, which triumphed, for example, in the January 2016 elections, Taiwan has to face a major stateness challenge: its non-recognition by most other countries and Beijing's insistence that Taiwan is in fact part of China. The issue of how to deal with the People's Republic of China is naturally central to politics in Taiwan, but it has not posed challenges to democracy.[8]

A number of other Asian countries featured prominently in the Third Wave of democratization, among them Bangladesh, Indonesia, Nepal, the Philippines, South Korea, and Thailand. Challenges to territorial integrity and national unity played varying roles in the process. The stateness challenge was perhaps especially acute for South Korea, locked in an unresolved conflict with North Korea, a threat that helped justify repressive military rule. Significantly, as reformist Roh Tae Woo, elected president in 1988, began the democratization process, he also sought to improve South Korea's international position, via openings to the USSR and China (the latter in particular considered close to North Korea). How to deal with Pyongyang understandably has remained a central issue in South Korean politics, but has not posed a challenge to the democratic process.

In some of these countries, challenges to territorial integrity and ethnic differences have played a modest role. For some time after Bangladesh's independence (1972), the government fought local paramilitaries that had remained loyal to Pakistan, and guerrillas mounted a twenty-year insurgency seeking autonomy for the indigenous population in the Chittagong Hill Tracts, settled by negotiation. But Bangladesh has a largely homogeneous Bengali population, and economic and demographic, rather than ethnic, challenges have been at the center of political contention.[9]

In the Philippines, Ferdinand Marcos justified his 1972 declaration of martial law in part by citing the threat from the Moro National Liberation Front, a Muslim separatist movement.[10] The Philippines also faces a Communist insurgency, which is not ethnically based. The main drivers, however, of the 1986 "People Power" revolution that toppled Marcos, were popular dissatisfaction with martial law, the corruption of the Marcos regime, and resulting poor economic performance. The Muslim and Communist insurgencies have not been the primary continuing challenges to the democratic process, while corruption and political cronyism tend to be major problems.[11]

Indonesia is highly diverse, with some 300 different ethnic groups. Most Indonesians are broadly speaking of Malay background and of Muslim religion. It was primarily economic discontent that triggered the popular demonstrations leading to Suharto's ouster in 1998, but subsequent leaders have had to grapple with interethnic violence, sometimes including a religious component, and outright ethnic separatist challenges, e.g. in the Aceh province and Irian Jaya, the part of Papua that Indonesia controls. Megawati, who succeeded to the presidency in 2001, granted autonomy and increased budgets for Aceh and Irian Jaya, and approved full sovereignty for East Timor, which Indonesia had seized in 1975-1976 from Portugal. While ethnic challenges remain, the main political issues over the last 15 years have focused on economics, concerns about corruption, and responses to natural disasters, and have not fundamentally hindered free elections and peaceful transfer of power.

Nepal also has a highly diverse population, with a primary division between people of Indo-Aryan origin and Hindu religion (the majority) and Tibeto-Nepalese groups (including the Sherpa) in the north and east. The monarchy established a multiparty parliamentary system in 1991, which faced challenges from ethnic and religious movements. The monarchy was dissolved in 2008, in favor of a democratic republic, at the negotiated conclusion of a decade-long Maoist insurgency, making Nepal a case in which a powerful threat to stateness actually contributed to democratic transition. Ethnic federalism and the rights of underprivileged ethnic groups have been central themes for the Nepali Maoists, and the multiparty negotiations over the federalism provisions in the new constitution, finally approved in 2015, were acrimonious.

The difficult situation of democracy in Thailand has garnered extensive media attention. The overwhelming majority of citizens identify as Thai (2% as Burmese), though there is separatist violence along the southern border with Malaysia, and the population includes members of the Karen people (concentrated in Burma). The first democratic transition in Thailand dates back to 1932, when a bloodless coup induced the king to initiate constitutional governance. By the end of 1938, however, a military regime was in place, which after the Second World War took actions against the ethnic Chinese of Thailand, suspected of Communist sympathies, and against suspected Lao and Malay separatists. Public demonstrations for constitutional government in 1973 led to the restoration of a direct political role for the monarchy, and what resulted by 1980 was a system in which the monarchy mediated power sharing between the military and the parliament. Among the stateness concerns Thailand faced was the Vietnamese occupation of Cambodia in 1979 and a flood of refugees. Tussles over the relative roles of the military and elected authorities continued until September 1992, the beginning of almost 14 years of government by civilian parliamentary majorities. The 1997 constitution reflected among other things the growing role of civil society groups advocating for the rights of ethnic and religious minorities. Thaksin Shinawatra, winner in the 2001 parliamentary election, was a Chinese-origin Thai from the northern part of the country, where he had his political base, notably among rural voters. Thaksin's decision to repress the Malay-Muslim insurgency in the south without first pursuing a negotiated solution contributed, however, to his growing unpopularity. He tried to neglect the protests of the urban-based "Yellow Shirt" opposition, and his political supporters, under a new party name, won the elections that followed an anti-Thaksin military coup in September 2006. Protests and counter-protests by the Yellow Shirts and the Red Shirts (Thaksin supporters) dominated Thai politics for the next several years, until yet another declaration of martial law in May 2014. In sum, political power struggles between the pro- and anti-Thaksin forces have overlaid on long-standing competition between civilian and military authorities to create the main current challenge to democracy in Thailand, although the insurgency in the south, and debate over how to deal with it, have added to the challenges. It is noteworthy that even a Human Rights Watch representative was ready to describe the insurgency as "brutal," though also criticizing abuses by the Thai military.[12]

Sub-Saharan Africa

The ethnic challenges to stateness in Africa, and their implications for the fate of non-democratic regimes and for the democratization processes in some countries, would merit a chapter unto themselves. Among the ten most fragile countries we identified (Di Sotto and Grilli 2012), six were in Sub-Saharan Africa, which was not surprising. The drawing of borders among the competing imperial powers in Africa in the 19th and early 20th centuries, which in effect established the borders that new states would have after decolonization, reflected the geopolitical convenience of the competing great powers, not any concerns about ethnic boundaries. African states have both large concentrated populations of different ethnic groups in the same country, and important ethnic groups divided by state borders, such as the Ewe in Ghana and Togo, or the Afars in Djibouti, Eritrea, and Ethiopia.[13]

In many countries of Sub-Saharan Africa, the process of state building has been difficult. Herbst underlined how, given the relative historical absence of inter-state warfare in post-colonial Africa, rulers had to contend with the geographical borders received at the time of decolonization, which determined the prospects for successful state-building, measured in terms of the ability of governments to collect taxes. (Thies 2009). Most ethnic conflict in fact has been *within* individual countries, although the presence of Hutus and Tutsis in Burundi, Democratic Republic of Congo, and Rwanda in effect internationalized their conflict. South Africa, often held up as the continent's success story, has suffered nether from challenges to territorial integrity nor from extensive interethnic conflict in the post-apartheid period, despite its considerable ethnic diversity. Bloodshed has come, however, from an internal split among the Zulus, the largest single ethnic group in the country, between members of the multiethnic African National Congress and of the ethnically specific Inkatha Freedom party.

Herbst developed a four-part, geographically based typology of stateness challenges (Thies 2009). The *difficult* countries are large, with dispersed areas of high population density, and tend to have high levels of ethno-linguistic fragmentation. Angola and Mozambique, the Democratic Republic of the Congo, and Nigeria are examples of difficult countries. Of these, only Mozambique and Nigeria are considered to have participated in the Third Wave of democratization, but with numerous problems and limits. The *hinterland* countries, to continue with Herbst's typology, also are large, but the urban areas are not dispersed. This makes it easier to exercise control over and extract taxes from most of the population, but creates the risk of weak state control over large swaths of territory. Examples of hinterland states are Mauritania, Mali, Chad, and Niger, not coincidentally states that have been facing problems with penetration of terrorist groups, e.g. Al Qaeda in the Islamic Maghreb. Of these countries, Mali and Niger can be considered as participants in the Third Wave of democratization, but the former has faced stateness challenges from both Islamist militants and ethnic Tuareg rebels. In Niger, disputes over the role of Islam and then-president Tanja's 2009 attempt to extend his time in office beyond the two-term limit, followed by a military coup and then return to civilian rule, have been more significant than ethnic differences, although dissatisfaction among the Tuareg population is an issue here as well.

Countries with *neutral* political geographies, in Herbst's typology, have population centers that are not very widely dispersed, and their hinterlands are small, as compared to the countries of the previous group. Cameroon, Cote d'Ivoire, Ghana, Kenya, and

Zambia are examples. The last three are considered to have participated in the Third Wave. Ethnic conflict has not been a prominent
feature of politics in either Ghana or Zambia, as compared to economic concerns. Ethnic politics have been more tense in Kenya,
as exemplified by violence following the 2007 elections, involving
the prominent Kikuyu, Kalenjin, and Luo peoples among others,
and resulting in perhaps 1000 deaths and the displacement of over
600,000 people. But the 2013 elections were relatively conflict-free,
thanks to a new constitution that decentralized authority, helping
meet concerns of some ethnic groups. A partially external threat to
Kenya has come from Somalia, specifically the Islamic militants of
al-Shabaab, and Kenya itself has a small Somali population, estimated at 1% of the total.

The African states with *favorable* political geographies for state
building, in Herbst's typology, are relatively small, with populations centered around the capital, and decreasing gradually as one
moves away from there. These include Botswana, Burkina Faso,
Lesotho, Togo, Gabon, Gambia, Guinea, and Swaziland. The first
four figure among participants in the Third Wave, albeit with quite
differing outcomes. While Botswana, Burkina Faso and Lesotho do
not have especially diverse populations by African standards, careful balancing of ethnic interests was a prominent feature of the long
rule of Togo strongman Gnassingbé Eyadéma. The Ewe people in
the southern part of the country were at the core of opposition to
Eyadéma, and politics have retained a significant regional dimension since Eyadéma's death and installation of a more free political
system.

All this suggests that in Africa the relationship between weak
stateness, the salience of ethnic tensions, and prospects for democratization is not simple. Despite situations of weak stateness and
ethnic rivalry, some progress toward democracy can occur. In turn,
relatively strong stateness and moderate ethnic tension are not in
themselves guarantees of democratization.

Middle East and North Africa

While neither the Arab Spring nor the virtual dissolution of Libya and Syria can reasonably figure as parts of the Third Wave of

democratization, such events, along with what followed from the 2003 invasion of Iraq and the ouster of Saddam Hussein, provide important insights into the relationship between stateness problems and autocratic regime change/democratic transition. It seems no accident, in fact, that the one true success story, Tunisia, has an ethnically homogeneous population, no border disputes, and no challenges to its territorial integrity. Syria, on the other hand, was a bomb waiting to explode. With almost all power in the hands of the Alawite minority, the majority Sunni Muslims, Islamist or not, had nothing to lose, and the ruling Assad family could not risk loosening the reins even a bit. In Iraq, the 2003 invasion in effect allowed for the majority Shiite Arabs to replace the minority Sunni Arabs as the politically dominant group, with Sunni discontent opening the way for the Islamic State to dominate a large part of the country. In the case of Iraq, religious affiliation has proved a more potent source of conflict than ethnic differences, since the ethnic Kurds of Iraq would have preferred to steer clear of inter-Arab Sunni/Shiite tensions. But the existential threat of the Islamic State has forced the Kurds into what is de facto an ethnic as well as religious confrontation. Of course, the case of ethnically quite homogeneous Egypt illustrates how factors other than ethnic discontent, again in this case a perceived existential threat from Islamic fundamentalism, can fuel tensions and block hoped-for democratic transitions.

Although Freedom House considers it an Asian country, Afghanistan is highly relevant to how international political leaders think about the Middle East. Since 2001, the numerous and powerful ethnic differences within Afghanistan have been a major obstacle to state building and to effective democratic transition. This case seems to offer strong support for the "no state, no democracy" formula, and to have fed the caution of foreign governments about further state building efforts in ethnically diverse countries. The collapse of Libya after the international intervention that helped remove Qaddafi from power, and was supposed to open the way to democracy, has turned into another cautionary tale, as the conflict between the eastern and western regions of the country has made governance extremely difficult.

Conclusions

It is common to speak of the dangers failed states pose to their citizens and to the international community. But *weak stateness*, not necessarily reaching the point of outright failure, can have major implication for states' internal political processes, including the crisis and collapse of non-democratic regimes and subsequent efforts at democratic transition. Weak stateness (or state fragility) can have multiple dimensions. Inability of the state to perform effectively its characteristic functions, such as administration, is certainly a major dimension of weakness, but may be more of a challenge to extant political regimes than to the state as such. This chapter, intended to bolster the relatively scarce literature on stateness problems and democratization, focuses instead on weakness stemming from challenges to states' control over their territory and/or from the presence of ethnic groups that are not reconciled to a broader national cultural identity or to membership in the state in which they reside.

The severity of such challenges to stateness can vary along a continuum, including not only weakness, but also failure, or outright collapse. The cases of collapse of otherwise reasonably functional states under the impact of ethnic differences over the last 30-40 years have come most notably in Eastern Europe. In the early 1990s, three multi-ethnic, federal states collapsed: the Soviet Union, Yugoslavia, and the Czech and Slovak Federal Republic. It is difficult to generalize, however, about the collapse of authoritarian regimes and democratic transitions in the new states that emerged from the break-up of the three federations. Both the extent and the pace of change have varied dramatically, and successor states with ethnically mixed populations sometimes have found the resulting political challenges hard to address. Ukraine, with its large Russian and Russophile population, is a case in point, while Slovakia, over time, found a modus vivendi with its ethnic Hungarian population. The democratic transitions in Southern Europe, on the other hand, were relatively unhampered by ethnic minority issues, with highly diverse Spain adopting a federal structure. Turkish governments have used force against Kurdish threats to territorial integrity, while moderate citizens of Kurdish ethnicity have found greater political representation in recent years.

Latin America and the Caribbean have seen few threats to the territorial integrity of states, most of which have long histories of independence reaching back into the 19ᵗʰ century, despite some inter-state conflict over border areas. Dissatisfaction among economically underprivileged indigenous groups has been a political challenge in many countries, and provided fuel for terrorist groups like Shining Path in Peru. But political regimes—democratic, democratizing, or not—generally have found ways over time to address indigenous concerns within regular political processes, and racial/ethnic tensions have on the whole diminished. In some countries, like Guyana and Suriname, the split between citizens of African and South Asian descent has been at the core of political confrontation, but without posing dramatic threats to the state.

Among Asian countries that participated in the Third Wave of democratization, which began in 1974, the political salience of ethnic differences has varied dramatically. Indonesian governments, for example, have worked at addressing minority issues (an important aspect of Nepal's transition as well). The main issues in Indonesia's democratic politics now seem to involve economics and good governance, which seems true in the Philippines as well, despite the continuing Muslim insurgency, and in Thailand, though democracy has been at serious risk there. For South Korea and Taiwan, external challenges to sovereignty have been important issues of internal political contention, but ultimately have not impeded thoroughgoing democratic transitions.

Sub-Saharan Africa faces major problems of weak stateness, not primarily because of inter-state conflict, but because of the remarkable ethnic diversity within states and the presence of large ethnic groups residing across state boundaries. A number of African countries participated, to varying degrees, in the Third Wave of democratization, including countries in conditions promoting weak stateness, and it is difficult to generalize about the stateness/democracy connection.

The Middle East and North Africa provide more unequivocal support for an association between weak stateness and difficulties in non-democratic regime change or democratic transition. Ethnically homogeneous Tunisia, which also has no external challenges to its territorial integrity, has been the success story of the Arab

Spring. In Iraq and Syria, on the other hand, dynamics between population majorities and minorities have opened the way for the Islamic State to seize large tracts of territory, creating huge stresses on the political systems.

In sum, the strength or weakness of stateness is a variable with potentially important impacts on change in non-democratic regimes and subsequent democratic transitions. Challenges to stateness, such as threats to territorial integrity or presence of discontented ethnic groups that do not identify with the state, can be relevant to either regime change or democratic transitions, or to both. To some degree, the effects have varied region by region, but are not especially consistent even within regions. It is difficult to generalize, therefore, regarding the impact of the stateness variable, beyond accepting the "no state, no democracy" nostrum, since democracy does need a meaningful "container." Stateness is a variable primarily suited to analysis of regime change and democratic transitions on a nuanced, case-by-case basis.

Endnotes

[1] Pietro Grilli di Cortona is the author of the section on "Stateness and Its Political Implications: Theoretical Perspectives." Nicoletta Di Sotto wrote the section on "Weak Stateness and Political Regime Change: Regional Perspectives."

[2] *State building* refers to the processes that lead to the formation and consolidation of the state via stabilization of borders, control and extraction of resources, and administrative centralization. *Nation building* is understood as the construction and reinforcement of national identity via cultural and sometimes linguistic homogenization.

[3] The Fund for Peace 2010 *Failed States Index* distinguishes among social, economic, and political indicators. While some are symptoms of state crisis (e.g. foreign military intervention), others are above all a cause of crisis (e.g. economic decline). http://www.fundforpeace.org/global/ library/cr-10-99-fs-failedstatesindex2010-1103g.pdf.

[4] The following discussions of specific national cases draw on: Luca Germano, Pietro Grilli di Cortona, and Orazio Lanza, eds., *Come cadono i regimi non democratici: Primi passi verso la democrazia nei paesi della "terza ondata"* (Naples: Editoriale Scientifica, 2014); the 2015 and (when available) 2016 country reports from Freedom House; the *CIA World Factbook*; standard reference works.

[5] According to the Freedom House 2016 ratings, https://freedomhouse. org/sites/default/files/FH_FITW_Report_2016.pdf.

[6] Armenian independence was declared in October 1991.

[7] Coverage of ethnic minority issues is not extensive.

[8] Taiwan had a Freedom House rating of "Free" in 2015.

[9] Bangladesh has had parliamentary government since 1991.

[10] The Filipino Muslims are concentrated in the south and constitute roughly 5% of the population of this heavily Catholic country.

[11] The country in fact had only a "Partly Free" rating from Freedom House in 2015.

[12] Associated Press Bangkok, "Report Charges Thai Government Ignores Torture Allegations," Feb. 10, 2016, http://abcnews.go.com/International/wireStory/report-charges-thai-government-ignores-torture-allegations-36833521.

[13] See the website of the University of Maryland's Minorities at Risk project, http://www.cidcm.umd.edu/mar/.

Reference List

Aydin-Düzgit, Senem, and Yaprak Gürsoy. 2013. "Turkey: The Counterintuitive Transition of 1983." In *Transitions to Democracy: A Comparative Perspective*, edited by Kathryn Stoner and Michael McFaul, 290-315. Baltimore: Johns Hopkins University Press.

Carbone, Giovanni, and Vincenzo Memoli. 2015. "Does Democratization Foster State Consolidation? Democratic Rule, Political Order, and Administrative Capacity." *Governance* 28 (1): 5-24.

Carment, David. 2003. "Assessing State Failure: Implications for Theory and Policy." *Third World Quarterly* 24 (3): 407–27.

Chaubey, Varanya, Amy Mawson, and Gabriel Kuris. 2013. "Cooling Ethnic Conflict in Guyana's Elections." *Foreign Policy* (blog), March 13. http://foreignpolicy.com/2013/03/13/cooling-ethnic-conflict-in-guyanas-elections/.

Clapham, Cristopher. 2004. "The Global-Local Politics of State Decay." In *When States Fail: Causes and Consequences*, edited by Robert I. Rotberg, 76-93. Princeton, NJ, Princeton University Press.

Dahl, Robert A. 1971. *Polyarchy: Participation and Opposition*. New Haven, CT: Yale University Press.

Di Sotto, Nicoletta, and Pietro Grilli di Cortona. 2012. "'No State, No Democracy': Fragilità statale e democratizzazioni nella terza ondata." *Rivista italiana di scienza politica* 62 (1): 59-92.

Elkins, Zachary, and John Sides. 2008. "Seeking Stateness." Department of Political Science, University of Illinois and Department of Political Science, George Washington University, April. http://home.gwu.edu/~jsides/stateness.pdf.

Fukuyama, Francis. 2004. *State-Building: Governance and World Order in the 21st Century*. New York: Cornell University Press

Grilli di Cortona, Pietro. 2003. *Stati, nazioni e nazionalismi in Europa*. Bologna: Il Mulino.

_____. 2009. *Come gli Stati diventano democratici* Rome: Laterza.

Herbst, Jeffrey. 2004. "Let Them Fail: State Failure in Theory and Practice." In *When States Fail: Causes and Consequences*, edited by Robert I. Rotberg, 302-18. Princeton, NJ: Princeton University Press.

Hirschman, Albert O. 1978. "Exit, Voice, and the State." *World Politics* 31 (1): 90-107.

Huntington, Samuel. 1991. *The Third Wave of Democratization in the Late Twentieth Century*. Norman, OK: University of Oklahoma Press.

Iqbal, Zaryab, and Harvey Starr. 2008. "Bad Neighbors: Failed States and Their Consequences." *Conflict Management and Peace Science* 25 (4): 315–31.

King, Gary, and Langche Zeng. 2001. "Improving Forecasts of State Failure." *World Politics* 53 (4): 623-58.

Krasner, Stephen D., and Carlos Pascual. 2005. "Addressing State Failure." *Foreign Affairs* 84 (4): 153–63.

Lanza, Orazio. 2011. "Eredità autoritarie, modalità della transizione, apprendimento politico e disegno istituzionale: Spagna e Portogallo." In *Tra vecchio e nuovo regime: Il peso del passato nella costruzione della democrazia*, edited by Pietro Grilli di Cortona and Orazio Lanza, 109-36. Bologna: Il Mulino.

Linz, Juan J., and Alfred Stepan. 1996, *Problems of Democratic Transitions and Consolidation: Southern Europe, South America, and Post-Communist Countries*. Baltimore: Johns Hopkins University Press.

Lipset, Seymour M. 1959. "Some Social Requisites of Democracy: Economic Development and Political Legitimacy." *American Political Science Review* 53 (1): 69-105.

Mata, Javier Fabra, and Sebastian Ziaja. 2009. *Users' Guide on Measuring Fragility*. The German Development Institute, Bonn, and United Nations Development Programme (UNDP), Oslo. http://www4.carleton.ca/cifp/app/serve.php/1245.pdf.

Meierhenrich, Jens 2004. "Forming States After Failure." In *When States Fail: Causes and Consequences*, edited by Robert I. Rotberg, 153-69. Princeton, NJ: Princeton University Press.

Melville, Andrei, Denis Stukal, and Mikhail Mironyuk. 2013. "Trajectories of Regime Transformation and Types of Stateness in Post-Communist Countries." *Perspectives on European Politics and Society* 14 (4): 431-59.

Moore, Barrington, Jr. 1966. *Social Origins of Dictatorship and Democracy: Lord and Peasant in the Making of the Modern World.* Boston: Beacon Press.

OECD (Organization for Economic Co-operation and Development). 2007. *Principles for Good International Engagement in Fragile States & Situations.* http://www.oecd.org/dacfragilestates/43463433.pdf.

Rose, Richard, and Doh Chull Shin. 2001. "Democratization Backwards: The Problem of Third-Wave Democracies." *British Journal of Political Science* 31 (2): 331-54.

Rotberg, Robert I. 2004. "The Failure and Collapse of Nation-States." In *When States Fail: Causes and Consequences,* edited by Robert I. Rotberg, 1-45. Princeton, NJ: Princeton University Press.

Rustow, Dankwart. 1970. "Transitions to Democracy: Toward a Dynamic Model." *Comparative Politics* 2 (3): 337-63.

Stepan, Alfred, Juan J. Linz, and Yogendra Yadav. 2011. *Crafting State-Nations: India and Other Multinational Democracies.* Baltimore: Johns Hopkins University Press.

Thies, Cameron. 2009. "National Design and State Building in Sub-Saharan Africa." *World Politics* 61 (4): 623-69.

Tilly, Charles. 1990. *Coercion, Capital, and European States, AD 990-1992.* Cambridge MA: Blackwell.

Townshend, Ashley 2007. *Anatomy of State Failure: Case Studies in Zaïre, Afghanistan and Yugoslavia.* Discipline of Government and International Relations, University of Sydney. http://ses.library.usyd.edu.au/bitstream/2123/2156/1/Ashley%20Townshend.pdf.

Varnava, Andrekos, and Christalla Yakinthou. 2011. "Cyprus: Political Modernity and the Structures of Democracy in a Divided Island." In *The Oxford Handbook of Local and Regional Democracy in Europe,* edited by Frank Hendriks, Anders Lidström, and John Loughlin, 455-76. New York: Oxford University Press.

Vasilache, Andreas. 2007. *Precarious Stateness and the Fleeting Boundaries of Sovereignty: Reflections on Transition Theory and the Indonesian Case.* GARNET Working Paper, n. 12/07. http://www2.warwick.ac.uk/fac/soc/pais/research/researchcentres/csgr/garnet/workingpapers/1207.pdf.

Yashar, Deborah J. 2015. "Does Race Matter in Latin America? How Racial and Ethnic Identities Shape the Region's Politics." *Foreign Affairs* (March/April). https://www.foreignaffairs.com/articles/south-america/2015-02-16/does-race-matter-latin-america

Zartman, William. 1995. "Introduction: Posing the Problem of State Collapse." In *Collapsed States: The Disintegration and Restoration of Legitimate Authority,* edited by William Zartman, 1-11. Boulder, CO. Lynne Rienner.

International Sources of Regime Change: A Framework for Analysis

Barbara Pisciotta

How to explain the start of a democratization process and its success, failure, or stagnation remains one of the major challenges facing political scientists (Grilli di Cortona 2009). This subject has particular importance as the nexus of two distinct issues: on one hand, the possible existence of internal prerequisites for a natural evolution of political regimes toward more democratic models, and, on the other hand, the influence of the international system on the spread of democracy on a global scale. The link between internal and external factors is central in important recent works such as Levitsky and Way (2010) or Stoner and McFaul (2013). But there is still solid ground for a focus on internal factors, underlining the specificity of individual countries and formulating "local" theories of democratization, *and* for careful attention to international factors, in the hope of identifying a common context for democratization and formulating more generalizable theories.

When it comes to international sources of regime change, one can make a useful distinction between structural (long-term) factors and conjunctural (short-term) ones. The former include the configuration of the international system, international economic trends, geopolitical position, and regional integration processes. The latter include military outcomes, the momentary international diplomatic setting, and what can be termed *Zeitgeist*, the spirit of a given historical moment. Voluntary international interventions to promote democracy can take multiple forms, either coercive or consensual, while democracy also can spread spontaneously, via contagion. In the current climate, whether looking at trends in the former Soviet area (notably the Russia/Ukraine crisis) or at the aftermath of the Arab Spring in North Africa and the Middle East, careful delineation of the international factors seems fundamental.

Background

The difficulty of addressing internal and external aspects together probably helps explain the delay in introducing the international variable into the study of democratization. And yet, international organizations and leading democracies have intervened repeatedly to promote the establishment and consolidation of democratic regimes since the First World War. Wilson's 14 Points and, later on, the Marshall Plan were examples of democracy promotion on very large scales (Pisciotta 2002).

Until 1989, however, the outcome of initiatives to promote democratization was often disappointing. In Southern Europe, for example, Greece, Spain, and Portugal preserved their authoritarian institutions until the mid-1970s. The countries of Latin America, except for Venezuela and Colombia, oscillated between military dictatorships and brief democratic interludes until the early 1980s. In the post-colonial countries of Asia and Africa, other than India, Western attempts to transfer democratic institutions were unable to halt the slide toward authoritarianism (Huntington 1991).

In the advanced democracies, political leaders and academic experts began to fear that democracy promotion could succeed only in the presence of certain prerequisites, and within specific cultural contexts. Up to the 1970s, a long series of political scientists also underlined a close connection between democracy and economic development: countries with high per capita incomes, high literacy, and an entrepreneurial middle class were the most democratic (Lipset 1960). US foreign policy in the Cold War era reflected this conviction, and in less wealthy countries opted to support "useful dictators" who would maintain the status quo, rather than launching democracy-building efforts with uncertain outcomes.

Portugal's Carnation Revolution in 1974 started a gradual change in thinking about democratization. The transition from authoritarianism to democracy in what appeared to be unfavorable cultural and institutional contexts, including also in Latin America, put a spotlight on the individuality of each new national political synthesis and on the importance of specific internal factors, e.g. the human factor or the type of compromise reached by national leaders and civil society (O'Donnell, Schmitter, and Whitehead 1986; Linz and Stepan 1996; Morlino 1998).

But it was the fall of the Berlin Wall that radically transformed our way of thinking about the international variable in democratization. Democracy appeared to emerge as the only legitimate political regime. This provided a humanitarian justification for spreading the Western model throughout the globe. In security policy, the theory of a "separate peace" (Russett 1993) posited a connection between the spread of democratic institutions and practices and a concomitant expansion of areas of peace. In the 1990s, the idea began to take hold that intervention in a country's internal affairs, based on humanitarian and/or security objectives, was not just permissible, but an actual duty. Western leaders finally could justify, before the international community and their own electorates (who had to bear the costs), interventions intended to promote stability by spreading democratic institutions and norms to other countries (Schmitter and Brouwer 2000).

The Search for an Interpretative Framework

The post-Cold War change in perspective on the international dimension of democratization can be seen as a late-maturing, but also ambitious, fruit of two distinct research strategies. The first of these, which has been the more prolific, recognizes democratic transition as a "macro phenomenon" and, while focusing primarily on internal political dynamics, considers that international factors can *activate* a process of institutional change (Whitehead 1996; Pridham 1997) or, in some cases, *condition* the subsequent stabilization of democracy (Schmitter 1996). The second research strategy, not especially widespread, but nonetheless significant, completely reverses the internal/external causal relationship, and explains the democratic transitions of the 1990s as a result primarily of international structural dynamics (Bonanate 2000).

Two other factors increasingly have highlighted the role of international dynamics in democratization. Scholars focused on internal dynamics have become more sensitive to the role of information media in spreading Western values, practices, and institutional models, even in non-democratic contexts, and promoting the idea of regime change among both civil society and the political class. They also have devoted increasing attention to the role of hegemonic international actors in fostering economic and political transformation within given geographical areas (the US in Latin America, the European Union in Eastern Europe).

Those focused on the international dimension, on the other hand, not only grasp the global impact of democratization processes (for believers in a "separate peace" a more democratic world is also a more peaceful one), but also see the need to explain a phenomenon which "cannot be divided among a thousand tiny streams" because it originated with a "singular and extremely important event" (Bonanate 2000, 19).

Both research strategies, however, while opening up some interesting avenues of analysis, also have demonstrated some notable limitations which merit examination. Without attempting an exhaustive review of the literature on regime transitions, it is nonetheless possible to identify a few key points.

It is entirely plausible, for example, that international factors can produce internal regime change via "contagion" from one neighboring country to another, imitation of a given institutional model within a region marked by shared culture and tradition, or Western media "bombardment" fueling rising expectations in non-democratic countries. The real question, though, is how do you *prove* it (Pridham 1997; Morlino 1998)? What channels facilitate contagion? Why should cultural similarities necessarily promote transmission of foreign models? How can you measure the impact of mass media on individual preferences?

At the empirical level, in fact, the international variable dissolves into a myriad of seemingly unconnected effects, hard to trace back to an original external cause. There is little doubt that, in Eastern Europe, a single external cause (the end of Cold War bipolarity) produced widespread institutional change. But why did the democratization process stop on the shores of the Black Sea and fail to involve Belarus or the Middle East? Because conditions at the outset were different? Or, more specifically, because national cultures, values, and institutions hindered the effects of the international variable and stopped the wave of democratization from producing a *uniform* effect?

It is true that, since 1974, most countries on the path toward democratization have been influenced by factors that have crossed national and regional frontiers. Democratization processes in different countries have influenced each other, overcoming distance and differences in languages and levels of development (Whitehead 1996). But it is also true that these processes have developed in different ways, in line with national political and cultural contexts, regardless of leadership decisions.

Structural International Factors

Even granted that the aforementioned theories raise more questions than they answer, it is still worth trying to widen the horizons of democratization research. The start of a regime transition always has multiple causes, usually both internal and international. To promote an orderly discussion, one may employ an interpretative grid (see Table 1), distinguishing whether factors influencing the crises of non-democratic regimes are structural or conjunctural, and classifying the international variable accordingly. Structural factors are those deriving from the structure of the international system itself, and tend to have a long-term influence on the evolution of internal political processes. Conjunctural international factors only influence internal dynamics temporarily and/or occasionally.[1]

In general, the influence of the international variable on internal politics is directly proportional to the importance of a specific event. As the international relevance of such an event increases, the international dimension cuts across the internal dimension (Bonanate 1986), genuinely conditioning politics within individual countries. Going into greater depth, it seems that most of the factors listed in Table 1 have produced significant effects across the world, although the intensity of the effects has varied from region to region, and the results have not been uniformly positive.

Table 1. International Factors: Structural and Conjunctural

Structural International Factors	*Conjunctural International Factors*
1.Configuration of the international system End of bipolarity and start of democratization in East Central Europe, Asia, and Africa	*1. Military defeat* Collapse of non-democratic regimes in Germany, Italy, and Argentina. Accelerates Soviet regime's crisis of legitimacy after intervention in Afghanistan
2. International economic trends Introduction of free markets and economic liberalization in Russia, China, and Southeast Asia	*2. International diplomatic setting* Climate during the 1990s favorable to international agreements and the global spread of democracy
3. Geopolitical position Political and cultural influences favorable to the spread of democracy in East Central Europe. Absence of solid democratic traditions in the Middle East, Africa, and Asia. Serbia's strategic position facilitates NATO military intervention against Milošević's nationalist expansionism	*3. Zeitgeist* Spread of democracy in Latin America (1980s), Eastern Europe (first half of 1990s), Asia and Africa (since the 1990s).
4. Regional integration processes EU influence on political and economic reform in East Central Europe. Western interventions in Kosovo, Afghanistan, Iraq, and Libya to destabilize non-democratic regimes.	

Configuration of the International System

If we define the international system based on the degree of concentration or diffusion of power among the component countries, it
follows almost automatically that democratization in East Central
Europe was linked to the end of the bipolar system of the Cold War
era. Despite previous efforts (in 1956, 1968, and 1980-81) to initiate transitions, this in fact only became possible for the countries
of East Central Europe when the configuration of the international
system allowed it. The dissolution of the old world order allowed
the satellite countries of the Soviet Union to reacquire autonomy in
both foreign and domestic policy, including the ability to manage
political and economic transformations. If, until 1989, the policies
of these states were a consequence of the bipolar international system, after the fall of the Berlin Wall the influence of the international system reached into the individual national contexts and opened
the way for the definitive crisis of the Communist regimes. (In some
cases, such as Romania, Bulgaria, and Czechoslovakia, even the Soviets pushed for reform.) In Southern Europe and Latin America,
on the other hand, conjunctural internal or external events, such as
the death of Franco, the military's anti-authoritarian coup in Portugal, popular demonstrations in Greece, and Argentina's defeat in
the Falklands/Malvinas war, speeded up the collapse of authoritarian regimes already devoid of legitimacy in the eyes of civil society.

The end of the bipolar system also was decisive for transformations of non-democratic regimes outside Europe, e.g.in Africa
(South Africa, Ghana, and Namibia) and in Asia (Mongolia, Taiwan, Thailand). In Latin America, on the other hand, the crisis and
collapse of most non-democratic regimes came before 1989, though
the non-democratic regime in Cuba persisted even following the
collapse of its Soviet patron, and has survived long enough to re-
ceive significant recognition from its long-time US adversary.

Despite exceptions, however, the conditioning role of the international system and its configuration remains important. During the
Cold War, for example, the US was concerned exclusively with containing the Soviet menace (see the interventions in Chile, Nicaragua,
and Grenada), but readily adopted a new strategy at the end of the
1980s, in a new international climate, intervening militarily in Panama to depose the authoritarian Manuel Noriega (December 1989).

International Economics

Studies in the field of international political economy have examined how economic interdependence shapes the decisions of national governments regarding political structures (Keohane and Nye 1977; Rogowski 1987; Cox 1987; Mansfield and Busch 1995; Keohane and Milner 1996; Strange 1996; Schwartz 2000; Frieden and Lake 2000; Gilpin 2001; Held and McGrew 2003). These studies share a macro-oriented approach, and are based on the conviction that it is impossible to understand internal politics without understanding links between national economies and the world economy. In this optic, the process of economic internationalization, not the political coloration of a governing coalition, is the real independent variable that shapes the attitudes of socio-economic actors in domestic politics. In the current situation of complex interdependence, all that national institutions can decide on is a country's degree of economic liberalization. This does help explain, however, how the external independent variable can produce different domestic impacts from one country to another.

From this point of view, the international economic structure seems to have played a significant role in the spread of market economics to regions with traditional economic structures (Africa, Southeast Asia) or socialist ones (Russia, Eastern Europe, China). Although in most of these countries economic liberalization has not been accompanied by determined efforts to transform non-democratic political regimes, one cannot rule out that, over time, economic development can have a positive impact at the political level (Miller-Adams 1999; Woods 2006; Williamson 2006; Collier 2007). Continuing growth in median pro-capita incomes, growing literacy, and increasing life expectancies in developing countries may facilitate the rise of a middle class and undermine non-democratic regimes. The stability in China and Singapore of the "markets without democracy" model may argue against such hopes, but other cases, especially Taiwan, Hong Kong, and South Korea, but also, to some degree, Thailand, Indonesia, and the Philippines, seem to confirm a link between free markets and democratization.

Geopolitical Context

Political, economic, resource, population, and cultural geography can either facilitate or hinder democratization, as amply discussed in the chapter by Eric Terzuolo. If we accept that all democracies are territorially based, the geopolitical context can influence internal political processes along at least three main lines: 1) facilitating the spread of democracy from one country to another; 2) influencing the domestic, national goals that democratizing leaderships set for their countries; 3) influencing the consolidation of democracy (Whitehead 1999).

While historical and cultural influences on the oil-rich Middle East have not favored the growth of democratic institutions (Grilli di Cortona 2009), countries like the Czech Republic, Hungary, Poland, Slovakia, and Slovenia found themselves in a geopolitical context that favored the spread of values such as constitutionalism, pluralism, and political competition (Diamandouros and Larrabee 2001). The geopolitical dimension has been vitally important in Eastern Europe. The geographical position of the Czech Republic, Hungary, and Poland exposed them to strong Western influence. To the southeast, Bulgaria and Romania are exposed to continuing repercussions from the Yugoslav crisis of the 1990s, still not entirely resolved in parts of the Western Balkans, and are not entirely insulated from latent conflict between Greece and Turkey. The Russia/Ukraine crisis that erupted in 2014 has illustrated once more the high risk of active intervention by Russia in the affairs of bordering countries, not only Ukraine.

This seems to confirm Rokkan's view that there is a strong connection between a country's geopolitical position and prospects for what he terms *exit* and *voice*. The historical focus of Continental countries on establishing and maintaining control over their borders promoted internal authoritarianism and hindered development of democratic/representative channels of *voice*, with the goal of avoiding the *exit* of territorial units. In the peripheral states of Northern Europe, on the other hand, maintaining borders was a less critical and resource-intensive enterprise. Channels of political representation developed gradually, without pressure from concerns about security and unity (Rokkan 1974).

Geopolitical context also can play a decisive role in destabilizing a non-democratic regime, if it finds itself surrounded by democratic states. Social and political pressure and the flow of information from outside can undermine a regime's base of support and activate a process of change. In Serbia and Croatia, for example, after Milošević and Tuđman had exited the scene, the geopolitical context played a very important role in the transition to democracy. Previously, Serbia's geopolitical position had created conditions for the 1999 NATO intervention in Kosovo, which aimed at reestablishing security in Europe, weakening Milošević's leadership, and blocking further nationalist expansionism in a very ethnically heterogeneous region.

Regional Integration Processes

The major regional organizations, the European Union (EU), Organization of American States (OAS), and the African Union (AU) always have emphasized democracy promotion, defense of human rights, economic development, and security. In Europe, regional integration has guaranteed peace, security, democracy, and the stability of borders among participating countries, and provided a model of wide-ranging relevance. The prospect of EU membership has stimulated the countries of Eastern Europe to speed up their institutional changes and bring themselves into line politically and economically with the more advanced European democracies.

Other regional organizations, e.g. for Latin America and Africa, have not had the same impact as the EU, given the greater heterogeneity of the member countries and the fact of operating in more challenging economic and social contexts. The impossibility of replicating the European model in other world regions has not hindered the drive toward regional economic integration: the Association of Southeast Asian Nations (ASEAN), for example, has opted to promote cooperation and mutual assistance in economic development and maintenance of regional stability, but without setting political or institutional prerequisites for participation. The absence of internal or regional conditions promoting the spread of democracy, as well as a markedly case-by-case US approach, did not stop the OAS from intervening several times, between 1991 and 2002, against coups in Haiti (1991-1994), Peru (1992), Paraguay (1996, 2000), and Venezuela (1992, 2002), though not always successfully. The OAS also imposed sanctions against Haiti in the 1990s, and in 2009 suspended Honduras's membership because of the military coup there. The role of the African Union (originally the Organization of African Unity) has been even more controversial. Although its efforts have not been effective in most cases of serious human rights violations (Rwanda, Sudan, Zimbabwe), the AU managed to overcome its internal divisions and sanction the dictatorial regime in Togo in 2005, suspend Mauritania's membership in 2008, and reverse a coup in the Comoros Islands that same year.

NATO's remarkable adaptation to new challenges and new missions underlines the importance of international structures for political and military, not just economic, cooperation (Colombo 2001, 2004; Barany 2006). The eastward expansion of NATO's membership has drawn a clear line between those countries that have successfully realigned with the Western democracies and those, like Belarus, Georgia, and Ukraine that have not managed to distance themselves fully from what Russia considers its sphere of influence. Furthermore, since 1989 NATO has proved itself an effective instrument of coercion against non-democratic regimes in Europe and elsewhere, e.g. in Kosovo, Afghanistan, and Libya.

Conjunctural International Factors

Three main conjunctural international factors have contributed to the collapse of authoritarian and totalitarian regimes: military outcomes, diplomatic action, and *Zeitgeist*.

Military Outcomes

Military victory long has been an effective way for external powers to delegitimize non-democratic governments (Thompson 1993). Italy and Germany in the Second World War, where military defeat led to regime change, are paradigmatic cases, as Antonino Castaldo recalls in his chapter. Argentina's defeat in the 1982 Falklands/Malvinas war was the last act in a gradual process of delegitimation, leading the military regime to initiate a democratic transition and call free elections. The Soviet defeat in Afghanistan was among several factors leading to the collapse of the USSR. It called into question the Red Army's invincibility, raising doubts that the USSR actually could control the borders of its far-flung empire. Simultaneously it fed the independence aspirations of Moscow's subject peoples and created new forms of political participation, e.g. via the sharing of news that veterans brought back from the Afghan front (Reuveny and Prakash 1999).

Diplomatic Action

For almost a decade, the end of the Cold War promoted international cooperation and peace efforts. It was no accident that this period saw the signing of the Oslo Accords (1993), which for over 20 years seemed the highpoint of the long and precarious negotiation between Israelis and Palestinians, along with the end of apartheid in South Africa. Already in November 1990, the UN Security Council had voted unanimously to sanction Iraq for invading Kuwait and to legitimize international military intervention.

From this point on, we see an increasingly expansive definition of UN jurisdiction, challenging the Westphalian principle of national sovereignty based on non-intervention in internal affairs. In the 1990s, the increased importance attributed to defense of human rights pushed the question of sovereignty somewhat into the background, legitimizing intervention within the borders of states that violated the rights of their own citizens. Although the results were sometimes problematic, the interventions in Namibia (1989), Angola (starting in 1989), ex-Yugoslavia (1992-1995), Cambodia (1992), Somalia (1992-1993), Rwanda (1993-96), Democratic Republic of the Congo (1999), and Kosovo (1999) focused international attention on the challenges of exporting democracy to areas where the minimum prerequisites seemed to be entirely lacking.

The international climate changed dramatically toward the end of the 1990s, as Russia's negative reaction to the NATO intervention in Kosovo and the Alliance's eastward expansion damaged a climate which had fueled hopes for the further advance of democracy throughout the world. The Chinese and Russian Security Council vetoes of coercive measures in Sudan, Zimbabwe, and Syria, as well as the US intervention in Iraq in 2003, confirmed that the trade-off between national sovereignty and human rights remained an open question.

Zeitgeist

According to Linz and Stepan (1996) a "spirit of the age" favorable to democracy can manifest itself and actually promote regime change. Starting with the "Third Wave," democracy began to spread in Southern Europe, then in Latin America, and subsequently in Eastern Europe and in some parts of Asia and Africa. In recent decades, democratization has had wide-ranging international support, which on the whole has facilitated its spread. The Chinese model, currently the only alternative to the Western one, faces a challenge from information technologies that have transmitted, documented, amplified, and disseminated democracy throughout the social fabric of non-democratic countries, and not just in the corridors of power. All that said, the Third Wave is widely considered to have ended in 2004, if not earlier, and the collapse in several countries of the so-called Arab Spring has raised concerns about prospects for future democratization.[2]

Interventions to Promote and Protect Democracy: Coercion and Consensus

Along with the demarcation between structural and conjunctural, one may categorize international factors in other useful ways. The human factor is certainly highly significant for regime change. Quite a number of studies have tried to reconstruct and delimit the impact of "voluntary interventions" by international actors (states or international organizations) that have contributed to democratization. Schmitter and Brouwer (2000) define such interventions as all visible and voluntary actions undertaken by external actors, public or private, with the explicit objective of promoting political liberalization or democratization of autocratic regimes, or the consolidation of democracy in a given country. Such interventions can be classified using three categories: recipients, objectives, and whether the interventions are consensual or coercive.

Schmitter and Brouwer identify four types of beneficiaries: individual citizens, civil society, political society, and the state. Interventions directed at individual citizens aim at influencing their values and behaviors, and building their confidence in democratic institutions. Activities directed toward civil society and political society seek to support, respectively, private associations and interest groups and the formation and consolidation of political parties. With respect to the state, reforms to create more efficient, responsible, and transparent administration are key.

When it comes to the objectives of voluntary interventions, one must distinguish between those intended to promote democracy and those intended to consolidate it, since they relate to different phases of a complex process. In the first case, outside intervention aims to destabilize the authoritarian regime and favor the establishment of democracy. In the second case, the goal is to increase the stability of a newly democratic system.

Both promotion and protection of democracy reflect the manifest intent of external actors, and can include a whole gamut of activities to put pressure on the target states: economic and military sanctions, diplomatic protests, threats to intervene, actions to protect human rights, education in civic democratic norms, transfer of institutional models. Aid to political parties or social movements to support mobilization for regime change is an example of democracy promotion. On the other hand, police training and civics education regarding democratic principles and practices are typical of Western initiatives to support newly established democratic regimes. It is possible, though, that activities for democracy promotion and for its protection increasingly will overlap in the middle and longer terms.

There is also a significant distinction between initiatives intended to promote the construction and consolidation of democratic systems and those focused on the effects of the transformation, generally on aspects of the consolidation process (Schmitter and Brouwer 2000). For example, electoral reform can both promote stable government by reducing political fragmentation and offer new opportunities to a single, specific political organization. Programs intended to promote economic liberalization can provide opportunities for donor countries to benefit from the opening of new markets or to favor the interest of specific organizations, e.g. associations of business leaders or trade unions, as long as this does not introduce distortions into the market.

Democracy promotion and protection activities not only reflect the interests of the donor countries, but also are conditioned by a series of internal factors specific to the beneficiary countries. These include economic conditions, the stability or instability of political parties, the actual willingness of national elites to democratize, and what instruments are at the disposal of political actors. In particular, the probability that external influences will influence internal policy-making processes depends on how intensely policy makers *perceive* those influences. If they demonstrate greater sensitivity to external influences than to the demands of internal political groups, the state's international policies inevitably will reflect that balance (Kozhemiakin 1998).

The third criterion for classifying external interventions is the degree to which they are consensual or coercive. They fall into three types: military intervention, conditionality, and democratic assistance (Schmitter 1996; Whitehead 1996). A fourth type, contagion or emulation, is not strictly speaking a voluntary activity by an external actor.

Military intervention is obviously the most coercive form of democracy promotion. The primary objective is to destabilize or overturn a non-democratic regime. The military occupations of Germany and Japan after the Second World War, which imposed Western-style democratic systems, were the first examples of this strategy. During the Cold War, US interventions in Latin America did not make democratization a key objective. Starting in the 1980s, democracy promotion became more explicitly an objective of military interventions, as the cases of Grenada and Panama demonstrated. Following the collapse of the Soviet empire, the United States and the international community (though the latter's commitment varied dramatically from case to case) explicitly sought to remove authoritarian governments in Serbia (1999), Afghanistan (2001), Iraq (2003), and Libya (2011). These military interventions were highly coercive, and focused exclusively on the territory of the target country.

Democracy assistance, on the other hand, is a consensual external intervention in a target country and entails the substantive cooperation of national political elites in implementing procedures and actions aimed primarily at stabilizing a newly established democratic regime, e.g. election monitoring, technical consultations, training of administrative and political personnel, infrastructure development, and support for "intermediate structures" mediating between individuals and elites. While military interventions are focused on national leaderships, democracy assistance is directed at all four target groups identified above. In most cases, it is managed by international actors, such as the UN, EU, IMF, or various non-governmental organizations, and it has been primarily directed at regions with newly established democracies, e.g. in Eastern Europe or Latin America.

Conditionality

Conditionality, in turn, is a *coercive* voluntary external intervention, based on the formula "credit in exchange for democratization." It can be defined as the ability of certain international actors, such as the IMF and EU, to: a) impose, or threaten to impose, sanctions for failure to implement and respect international standards; b) reward, or offer to reward, adaptation to international standards (Schmitter 1996). Before 1989, individual Western countries rarely resorted to conditionality. But since then it has been above all the international organizations, in particular the IMF in Latin America and the EU in East Central Europe,[3] that have taken on a critical role in promoting democratization.

One should bear in mind, however, that linkage between access to development assistance and respect for human rights has come out of a long and complex process, which only recently has produced results worthy of note. Despite US president Carter's efforts to introduce respect for human rights as a basic principle of political and economic relations with the countries of Latin America, US foreign policy remained, into the 1980s, highly flexible in applying conditionality and focused on the need to prevent Latin American countries from aligning with the Eastern Bloc (Fossati 2006).

After 1989, economic and strategic goals hindered any strict application of conditionality by the US government. Following the violent repression of protests at Tiananmen Square, for example, China was only briefly banned from negotiations on joining the General Agreement on Trades and Tariffs (GATT), and did join its successor, the World Trade Organization (WTO), in 2001. The view prevailed that precisely the prospect of WTO membership would provide a strong incentive for internal change in China. Demands for rigorous application of the 1974 Jackson-Vanik amendment, which would have blocked Chinese membership in the WTO because it prohibited preferential US trade agreements with non-free-market countries that barred the emigration of their own citizens, fell on deaf ears (Andreatta 2004).

In Thailand, on the other hand, the US suspended aid in February 1991 because of human rights violations by the Thai military. The US pursued the same strategy in Latin America and the Caribbean: in autumn of 1991, for example, the US suspended financial support to Haiti in order to force the military regime to hold free elections. The US also instituted economic sanctions against Fujimori in Peru (April 1992) and Serrano in Guatemala (May 1993).

The situation has been equally ambiguous among the Europeans.[4] In the 1980s, France and Great Britain decided to impose conditionality on development assistance to their former colonies in Africa. For both, the results were disappointing, if not outright counterproductive (see Nigeria, Sudan, Cameroon, and Democratic Republic of the Congo). In fact, in 1993 the Balladur government in France declared flatly that democratization could not be promoted from outside (Fossati 1999). Before 1989, the European Economic Community did not rigorously apply conditionality: the commercial agreements with countries in Africa, the Caribbean, and the Pacific region, based on the first of the Lomé conventions, did not yet make a strict connection between aid and respect for human rights. Even after the end of the Cold War, some European countries, such as Italy, Spain, and Austria, still avoided applying conditionality in relations with developing countries. The aid strategies of most Scandinavian governments, whether European Union members (Finland and Sweden) or not (Norway), have seemed to favor poor countries over those able to guarantee the strongest democratic performance.

There have been exceptions. In November 1991, the Netherlands cut funding to Indonesia following the East Timor massacre (Fossati 2006). In the 1990s, Belgium responded to the genocide involving Zaire, Rwanda, and Burundi by cutting off funding to those countries. Germany and Denmark, in turn, rigorously applied conditionality, respectively providing funds for democracy assistance (for example by sending election observers to Eastern Europe, but also to Togo and Cameroon) or suspending aid to countries that openly violated human rights (e.g. Rwanda, Burundi, Somalia, and Zaire).

In European Union enlargement, the "credit for democracy" approach has become firmly established, and the process of evaluating performance based on preconditions has become more objective and impartial. One contributing factor has been the adaptation of national rules and structures to the European democratic model, which began to emerge with the first agreements on cooperation and commerce and has developed further through the association agreements that are the last step before full EU membership.

The second factor that explains the nature of relations between the EU and the post-Communist states derives from the fact that convergence is not just a matter of the voluntary transfer or adoption of institutional arrangements developed and tested elsewhere. A process of standardization based exclusively on consensus could result in only partial acceptance of the Western democratic model, importing only those rules that do not challenge the national equilibrium of power. It follows that an element of coercion is necessary for full implementation of the convergence process.

At the formal level, coercion derives from constitutional requirements: the obligation to create stable democracies is a basic condition for membership in the EU. Legislative harmonization requires that all member states be able to guarantee the application of EU regulations and directives throughout their national territory.

At the substantive level, coercion foresees the explicit resort to sanctions. In Eastern Europe, for example, the then-European Economic Community (EEC) imposed sanctions on states guilty of serious human rights violations. In 1989, for example, the commercial and cooperation agreements with Bulgaria were suspended for roughly a year, in response to the government's abuse of the rights of the Turkish minority. The following year, the EEC suspended economic and technical assistance in response to violent repression in Romania. Soviet military action in the Baltic republics resulted in immediate interruption of financing and commercial relations. In the former Yugoslavia, economic sanctions against violations of human rights began in 1992, admittedly later than may have been appropriate.

The rigorously hierarchical relationship between the EU and the states of East Central Europe demonstrates the central role of coercion in the adaptation of new member states to EU criteria. The transfer from above (from the EU) of norms, administrative techniques, paradigms of public policy, individual policies, or constitutional arrangements has been the result of pressure, both formal and informal, by a central organization on the political systems of nations economically and culturally dependent on it (DiMaggio and Powell 1991). It is true that, especially in cases like Bulgaria, Romania, and Slovakia, external pressure from the EU significantly helped accelerate the process of institutional adaptation, reducing the risk of backsliding into authoritarianism. But it is also true that this top-down process, based on conditionality, required the beneficiary states to accept outside direction (Bonanate 2000).

Spontaneous International Factors: Contagion

Unlike the voluntary interventions discussed above (military intervention, democracy assistance, conditionality), contagion or emulation is a spontaneous form of the spread of democracy. As Huntington (1991) underlined, contagion implies a chain reaction spreading from one country to another, like a virus, thanks to geographical proximity. It is a substantially neutral form of transmission, in which the democratic model, once it is successful in a given country, triggers a process of emulation in bordering countries. The underlying mechanism involves the spread of a perception of the feasibility of democracy as the best possible political system. If what works in one country can work in others, it is logical to import not only that particular set of procedures, but also the political and institutional process that led to it.

Although contagion is the most difficult to analyze of all the processes that can spread democracy, its importance during the

Third Wave can be traced to the simultaneous presence of three conditions: the growth of communication systems; the spread of a *Zeitgeist*, a spirit of the age, favorable to democracy; the presence of relatively homogeneous cultural contexts linking democratizing states. The increasing difficulty that non-democratic regimes encountered in controlling the flow of information facilitated the outbreak of demonstration effects, giving life to a process of institutional change that spread like wildfire, reaching all continents. With respect to the second and third conditions, a favorable international situation linked up, as we have seen, with geographical and cultural proximity, creating a process of emulation on regional scale. The anti-authoritarian coup in Portugal spread first in Southern Europe and then in Latin America. The fall of Marcos in the Philippines contributed to democratic tendencies in South Korea and Taiwan. Gorbachev's advent had better results in the satellite countries than in Russia. The "bulldozer revolution" in Serbia turned into a model for all the "color" revolutions that spread through Georgia, Ukraine, and Kyrgyzstan, even briefly reaching Iran. In North Africa, the process of internal change that began in Tunisia in December 2010 did spread to Egypt and Libya, although matters evolved differently in the three countries.

One of the most important characteristics of democratic contagion is that it does not occur only in the presence of favorable conditions for democratization. While contagion cannot even penetrate into countries where governments still have effective control over information media, e.g. China and North Korea, where contagion does penetrate, the absence of the prerequisites for democratization still can put a reform process at risk before it really gets going (Carothers 2006; 2013). Events in Belarus, Ukraine, and Georgia at various points have confirmed this hypothesis.

Conclusions

The connection between internal and international factors in regime transitions has been a matter of vigorous debate, with some scholars emphasizing the former, and others the latter. Despite some notable exceptions,[5] a truly global vision of political phenomena only starts to become evident after the fall of the Berlin Wall. Said vision has allowed us to frame the "contamination" between internal and international politics along three main theoretical lines:

1. Regime transitions have multiple causes, in most cases with both internal and international dimensions.

2. International factors can be structural or conjunctural, and either voluntary or spontaneous, and their impact is directly proportional to the importance of the external events from which they stem.

3. Internal factors (political culture, leadership quality, the type of non-democratic regime in question, level of economic development, previous experience with democracy) tend to "filter" the impact of international factors, shaping the democratization process and accounting for differences from one region to another (e.g. between Eastern Europe and Africa) and between individual countries in the same region.

If one frames the link between internal and international factors in terms of *constraints* and *opportunities*, it follows that the international system can limit the range of options for national governments, blocking pursuit of certain paths, as was richly demonstrated during the Cold War era. On the other hand, a radical change in the structure of the international system can trigger a process of democratization, providing national leaders with once-in-a-lifetime opportunities, as the collapse of the Soviet Union and its sphere of control demonstrated.

International factors can produce different effects in different countries, and their influence can vary according to the exact phase of the transition in a given country. We still may view transition from one regime to another as a *reversible* phenomenon (Morlino 1998) according to the schema: *crisis, possible collapse, transition, establishment,* and *consolidation*. Still, it is worth underlining how the presence or absence of a given international factor can be influential in one period, but may give way to a different international factor in a subsequent period.

The configuration of the international system, the diplomatic situation, and military defeat all can make important contributions to democratization, as one notes in the countries of Eastern Europe (end of the bipolar Cold War system and favorable diplomatic context) or with military defeats such as the USSR experienced in Afghanistan and Argentina encountered in the Falklands/Malvinas conflict. The voluntary military interventions in Serbia, Iraq, and Libya have aimed explicitly at destabilizing non-democratic regimes. Geopolitical context is influential primarily in the early phases of democratization. In Southern Europe, Latin America, and Eastern Europe, for example, geographical proximity facilitated democratic contagion and spread of a *Zeitgeist* favorable to democracy.

International economic trends, on the other hand, seem to influence all the different phases of the democratization process. In Russia and Southeast Asia, for example, economic factors were especially important in the early phases of transition, while in Hungary, Poland, and the Czech Republic the economic dimension was more visible in later phases of transition, promoting both the introduction of a market economy and democratic consolidation. Regional integration efforts also have influenced democratic transitions, to varying degrees and in varying ways from one area to another. The conditionality imposed by the EU was especially significant for institutional change in East Central Europe during the establishment and consolidation of democracy. In Latin America, on the other hand, the International Monetary Fund played a crucial role in the earlier phases of democratization. In their regions, the Organization of American States and the African Union often have intervened against efforts to restore authoritarianism.

Recent events in Europe (notably the conflict in Ukraine) have led to a crisis in relations between Russia and the West, while escalations of unprecedented violence in North Africa and the Middle East (e.g. the rise of the Islamic State) have revived fears of a "clash of civilizations." In such cases, analysis of the diverse international factors at play both helps us understand their role in stimulating regime change and prompts an in-depth reflection on the complex dynamics deriving from the permeability of national borders. The perverse effects of the Syrian crisis, for example, highlight the risks that the phenomenon of democratic contagion can pose in regions that are profoundly unstable and characterized by multiple dividing lines (religious, ethnic, cultural, economic). It is no accident that many recent studies highlight how frequently democratization efforts in the post-Soviet area, the Middle East, and North Africa have ended in failure and authoritarian backsliding, while also pointing to the frequently negative effects of military interventions (Afghanistan, Iraq, Libya) on attempts at democratic transformation in the target countries (McFaul, Magen, and Stoner-Weiss 2007; Diamond, Fukuyama, Horowitz, and Plattner 2014).

In conclusion, regime transition remains a complex phenomenon, at the center of an intense but fruitful debate. The literature has become increasingly cautious about the feasibility of a general theory of democratization, favoring local theories (Schmitter and Karl 1994; O'Donnell 1996; Morlino 1998, 2011; Grilli di Cortona 2009). It also underlines the risk of attempts at democratization in the absence of fundamental preconditions (Linz and Stepan 1996; Carothers 2002, 2006; Bunce and McFaul 2009; O'Donnell 2010; Carothers and de Gramont 2013). This has helped avoid an exclusive focus on the spread of the Western democratic model, and has promoted study of comparatively neglected regions that have been resistant to the establishment and consolidation of democracy (Zakaria 1997; Morlino, Dressel, and Pelizzo 2011; Schmitter 2012; Carothers 2013).

Endnotes

[1] On structural factors see also Tolstrup (2010).

[2] The very "transition paradigm" has been under challenge, notably from Carothers (2002), but also in recent panel deliberations at the National Endowment for Democracy's International Forum for Democratic Studies (Diamond et al. 2014).

[3] For further details see Pisciotta (2010).

[4] Just look at the different strategies adopted in Sudan, where the failure of the Islamic fundamentalist regime to respect human rights elicited international sanctions that included a military dimension, and in Algeria, where neither France nor the rest of the international community intervened after Islamists won the first round of parliamentary voting in December 1991 and looked poised to win the second round, until the Algerian military took control.

[5] See Hintze ([1929] 1990), Deutsch (1966), and Rosenau (1969).

Reference List

Andreatta, F. 2004. *Alla ricerca dell'ordine mondiale*. Bologna: Il Mulino.

Barany, Zoltan. 2006. "NATO's Post-Cold War Metamorphosis: From Sixteen to Twenty-Six and Counting." *International Studies Review* 8 (1): 165-78.

Batt, Judy. 1997. "The International Dimension of Democratization in Hungary, Slovakia and Czech Republic." In *Building Democracy? The International Dimension of Democratization in Eastern Europe*, edited by G. Pridham, E. Herring and G. Sanford, 154-69. Leicester: Leicester University Press.

Bonanate, Luigi. 1986. "Sistema politico internazionale." In *Teoria e analisi delle relazioni internazionali*, edited by L. Bonanate and C. M. Santoro, 119-30. Bologna: Il Mulino.

_____. 2000. *Transizioni democratiche, 1989-1999*. Milan: Franco Angeli.

Bunce, Valerie J., and Michael McFaul, eds. 2009. *Democracy and Authoritarianism in the Postcommunist World*. Cambridge: Cambridge University Press.

Carothers, Thomas. 2002. "The End of the Transition Paradigm." *Journal of Democracy* 13 (1): 5-21.

_____, ed. 2006. *Promoting the Rule of Law Abroad: In Search of Knowledge*. Washington, DC: Carnegie Endowment for International Peace.

_____. 2013. "Egypt's Dismal Opposition: A Second Look" [Web site post]. Carnegie Endowment for International Peace, May 14. http://carnegieendowment.org/2013/05/14/egypt-s-dismal-opposition-second-look/g3cf.

Carothers, Thomas, and Diane de Gramont. 2013. "Development Aid Confronts Politics: The Almost Revolution." *The Guardian*, May 9. Posted to Web log of Carnegie Endowment for International Peace. http://carnegieendowment.org/2013/05/09/development-aid-confronts-politics/g3a4.

Collier, Paul. 2007. *The Bottom Billion: Why the Poorest Countries Are Failing and What Can Be Done About It*. New York: Oxford University Press.

Colombo, Alessandro. 2001. *La lunga alleanza: La Nato tra consolidamento, supremazia e crisi*. Milan: Franco Angeli.

_____. 2004. "L'alleanza atlantica tra globalizzazione e marginalizzazione." In *L'Occidente diviso: La politica e le armi*, edited by Alessandro Colombo, 3-32. Milan: Bocconi Editore.

Cox, Robert.W. 1987. *Production, Power and World Order*. New York: Columbia University Press.

Deudney, Daniel, and G. John Ikenberry. 1992. "The International Sources of Soviet Change." *International Security* 16 (3): 74-118.

Deutsch, Karl. 1966. "External Influences on the Internal Behavior of States." In *Approaches to Comparative and International Politics*, edited by R. Barry Farrell, 5-26. Evanston, IL: Northwestern University Press.

Diamandouros, P. Nikiforos, and F. Stephen Larrabee. 2001. "La democratizzazione nell'Europa sud-orientale." *Rivista italiana di scienza politica* 31 (1): 31-72.

Diamond, Larry, Francis Fukuyama , Donald L. Horowitz, and Marc F. Plattner. 2014. "Reconsidering the Transition Paradigm." *Journal of Democracy* 25 (1): 86-100.

DiMaggio, Paul J., and Walter W. Powell. 1991. "The Iron Cage Revisited: Institutional Isomorphism and Collective Rationality in Organizational Fields." In *The New Institutionalism in Organizational Analysis*, edited by Paul J. DiMaggio and Walter W. Powell, 63-82. Chicago: University of Chicago Press.

Fossati, Fabio. 1999. "Cooperazione allo sviluppo: la condizionalità politica." *Politica internazionale* 27 (3): 11-21.

_____. 2006. *Introduzione alla politica mondiale*. Milano: Franco Angeli.

Frieden, Jeffry A., and David A. Lake, eds. 2000. *International Political Economy: Perspectives on Global Power and Wealth*. New York: St. Martin's Press.

Gilpin, Robert. 2001. *Global Political Economy: Understanding the International Economic Order*. Princeton, NJ: Princeton University Press.

Grilli di Cortona, Pietro. 2009. *Perché gli stati diventano democratici*. Rome: Laterza.

Held, David, and Anthony McGrew, eds. 2003. *The Global Transformations Reader*, 2nd ed. Cambridge: Polity Press.

Hintze, Otto. (1929) 1990. *Storia, sociologia, istituzioni*. Edited by G. Di Costanzo. Naples: Morano.

Huntington, Samuel P. 1991. *The Third Wave: Democratization in the Late Twentieth Century*. Norman, OK: University of Oklahoma Press.

Keohane, Robert O., and Helen V. Milner, eds. 1996. *Internationalization and Domestic Politics*. Cambridge: Cambridge University Press.

Keohane, Robert O., and Joseph S. Nye. 1977. *Power and Interdependence: World Politics in Transition*. Boston: Little Brown.

Kozhemiakin, Alexander V. 1998. *Expanding the Zone of Peace? Democratization and International Security*. London: MacMillan.

Levitsky, Steven, and Lucan A. Way. 2010. *Competitive Authoritarianism: Hybrid Regimes After the Cold War*. New York: Cambridge University Press.

Linz, Juan J., and Alfred Stepan. 1996. *Problems of Democratic Transition and Consolidation: Southern Europe, South America, and Post-Communist Europe*. Baltimore: Johns Hopkins University Press.

Lipset, Seymour M. 1960. *Political Man*. Garden City, NY: Doubleday.

Mansfield, Edward D., and Marc L. Busch. 1995. "The Political Economy of Non-Tariff Barriers: A Cross-National Analysis." *International Organization* 49 (4): 723-49.

McFaul, Michael, Amichai Magen, and Kathryn Stoner-Weiss. 2007. "Evaluating International Influences on Democratic Transitions: Concept Paper." Stanford, CA: Center on Democracy, Development, and Rule of Law, Freeman Spogli Institute for International Studies. http:// iis-db.stanford.edu/res/2278/Evaluating_International_Influences_-_ Transitions_-_Concept_Paper.pdf.

Miller-Adams, Michelle. 1999. *The World Bank: New Agendas in a Changing World*. London: Routledge.

Morlino, Leonardo. 1998. *Democracy Between Consolidation and Crises*. Oxford: Oxford University Press.

_____. 2011. *Changes for Democracy: Actors, Structures, and Processes*. Oxford: Oxford University Press.

Morlino, Leonardo, Bjoern Dressel, and Riccardo Pelizzo. 2011. "The Quality of Democracy in Asia-Pacific: Issues and Findings." *International Political Science Review* 32 (5): 491-511.

O'Donnell, Guillermo. 1996. "Illusions About Consolidation." *Journal of Democracy* 7 (2): 34-51.

_____. 2010. *Democracy, Agency, and the State: Theory with Comparative Intent*. Oxford: Oxford University Press.

O'Donnell, Guillermo, Philippe C. Schmitter, and Laurence Whitehead. 1986. *Transitions from Authoritarian Rule*. Baltimore: Johns Hopkins University Press.

Pisciotta, Barbara. 2002. *Istituzioni europee e consolidamento democratico: Le politiche di privatizzazione e tutela della concorrenza in Polonia, Ungheria e Repubblica Ceca*. Naples: ESI.

_____. 2010. "L'Europa post-comunista dal crollo del muro di Berlino all'integrazione europea." *Rivista di studi politici internazionali* 77 (1): 77-91.

Pridham, Geoffrey. 1997. "The International Dimension of Democratization: Theory, Practice and Inter-Regional Comparison." In *Building Democracy? The International Dimension of Democratization in Eastern Europe*, edited by Geoffrey Pridham, Eric Herring, and George Sanford, 7-29. Leicester: Leicester University Press.

Reuveny, Rafael, and Aseem Prakash. 1999. "The Afghanistan War and the Breakdown of the Soviet Union." *Review of International Studies* 25: 693-708.

Rogowski, Ronald. 1987. "Trade and the Variety of Democratic Institutions." *International Organization* 41 (2): 203-23.

Rokkan, Stein. 1974. "Entries, Voices, Exits: Toward a Possible Generalization of the Hirschman Model." *Social Sciences Information* 13 (1): 39-53.

Rosenau, James. 1969. "Toward the Study of National-International Linkages." In *Linkage Politics*, edited by James Rosenau, 44-63. New York: The Free Press.

Russett, Bruce. 1993. *Grasping the Democratic Peace*. Princeton, NJ: Princeton University Press.

Sanford, George. 1997. "Communism's Weakest Link—Democratic Capitalism's Greatest Challenge: Poland." In *Building Democracy? The International Dimension of Democratization in Eastern Europe*, edited by Geoffrey Pridham, Eric Herring, and George Sanford, 170-96. Leicester: Leicester University Press.

Schmitter, Philippe C. 1996. "The Influence of International Context upon the Choice of National Institutions and Policies in Neo-Democracies." In *The International Dimensions of Democratization: Europe and the Americas*, edited by Laurence Whitehead, 27-54. Oxford: Oxford University Press.

————. 2012. "Ambidextrous Democratization and its Implications for MENA." September. Florence: European University Institute. http://www.eui.eu/Documents/DepartmentsCentres/SPS/Profiles/Schmitter/AmbidextrousDemocratization.pdf.

Schmitter Philippe C., and Imco Brouwer. 2000. "Promozione e protezione della democrazia: Il concetto, le ricerche, la valutazione." *Rivista italiana di scienza politica* 30 (2): 187-226.

Schmitter, Philippe C., and T. L. Karl. 1994. "The Conceptual Travels of Transitologists and Consolidologists: How Far to the East Should They Attempt to Go?" *Slavic Review* 53: 173-85.

Schwartz, Herman M. 2000. *States versus Markets: The Emergence of a Global Economy*, 3d ed. London: MacMillan.

Spizzo, Daniel, and Barbara Pisciotta. 2005. "L'impatto dell'Ue sul processo di democratizzazione dei paesi dell'Europa centro-orientale: performances nazionali e infranazionali." In *Quale Europa? L'Unione Europea oltre la crisi*, edited by Gianfranco Baldini, 53-83. Soveria Mannelli, IT: Rubbettino.

Stoner, Kathryn, Larry Diamond, Desha Girod, and Michael McFaul. 2013. "Transitional Successes and Failures: The International-Domestic Nexus." In *Transitions to Democracy: A Comparative Perspective*, edited by Kathryn Stoner and Michael McFaul, 3-24. Baltimore: Johns Hopkins University Press.

Stoner, Kathryn, and Michael McFaul, eds. 2013. *Transitions to Democracy: A Comparative Perspective*. Baltimore: Johns Hopkins University Press.

Strange, Susan. 1996. *The Retreat of the State*. Cambridge: Cambridge University Press.

Thompson, William R. 1993. "The Consequences of War." *International Interactions: Empirical and Theoretical Research in International Relations* 19 (1-2): 125-47.

Tolstrup, Jakob. 2010. "When Can External Actors Influence Democratization? Leverage, Linkages, and Gatekeeper Elites." Working Paper No. 118, July. Stanford, CA: Center on Democracy, Development, and Rule of Law, Freeman Spogli Institute for International Studies. http://iis-db.stanford.edu/pubs/22947/NO_118_Tolstrup_When_can_External_Actors_Influence_Democratization.pdf.

Whitehead, Laurence. 1996. "Three International Dimensions of Democratization." In *The International Dimensions of Democratization: Europe and the Americas*, edited by Laurence Whitehead, 5-25. Oxford: Oxford University Press.

———. 1999. "Eastern Europe a Decade Later: Geography and Democratic Destiny." *Journal of Democracy* 10 (1): 74-79.

Williamson, Jeffrey G. 2006. "Globalization, Income Distribution and History." In *Inequality and Economic Integration*, edited by Francesco Farina and Ernesto Savaglio, 9-32. New York: Routledge.

Woods, Ngaire. 2006. *The Globalizers: The IMF, the World Bank, and Their Borrowers*. Ithaca, NY: Cornell University Press.

Zakaria, Fareed. 1997. "The Rise of Illiberal Democracy." *Foreign Affairs* 76 (November/December): 22-41.

The Proactive International Dimension and the Breakdown of Non-Democratic Regimes

Antonino Castaldo

There is international consensus among scholars that democratic transitions are multicausal processes in which both internal and international variables are involved (Pridham 1991, 1995; Whitehead 1996; Schmitter 1996; Linz and Stepan 1996; Carothers 1999; Morlino and Magen 2008; Grilli di Cortona 2009). This chapter is limited, on the one hand, to the dependent variable consisting solely of the crisis/breakdown/transformation of non-democratic regimes in the Third Wave of democratization, and, on the other hand, to an independent variable identified solely with the international dimension of democratic transition. This factor, which can be termed the Proactive International Dimension (PID), specifically concerns that combination of actions or processes, produced by one or more international actors, that, intentionally or not, cause or contribute to the crisis/breakdown/transformation of a non-democratic regime.

This is not exclusively tied to the concept of intentionality. Actions that do not aim at destabilizing a regime, but in any case contribute directly to that result, are included in the analysis. The definition, however, excludes democratic "emulation" (Huntington 1995), as well as anything belonging to the international dimension that is not linked to an actor's explicit action, e.g. the effects of globalization or international economic crises.

Which international actors work to promote/cause the fall of non-democratic regimes? What are the motivations that drive them to act? What instruments or kinds of actions are employed? How effective have these instruments been in the cases under consideration? The answer to these questions will help us to understand the role of the PID in the breakdown of non-democratic regimes in the Third Wave of democratization (Huntington 1995).

The Proactive International Dimension:
Actors, Types of Actions, Capacity for Influence

It would be misleading to interpret the PID as a unitary actor or a collection of actors who work in unison. The only common characteristic is that they originate and are located outside the borders of the target state (Pridham 2000, 195). The range of possible actors includes: individual states (e.g. US), coalitions of states (e.g. the Allies during World War II), international and supranational organizations (e.g. UN, EU, IMF), political parties, unions, churches, and NGOs, among others. The underlying motivations for actions that promote/cause the fall of an autocracy include: interests linked to the security of the international actors; the need to preserve peace and the stability of the international system; the actual intention to encourage the spread of democracy (Castaldo 2014, 33-34). It is important to underline that the first two are fundamental, while the third often appears more like a public justification of actions that are, in fact, motivated by international security and stability objectives, rather than being a real motivation in itself.

It is important to make distinctions among the various actions of the PID, separating those that can temporarily undermine/suspend the formal sovereignty of the target state from those that do not threaten formal sovereignty, even though they have actual influence on it. Although there is no deterministic connection, it is likely that the kinds of actions that undermine the formal sovereignty of a state have a greater chance of playing a prominent role in an autocracy's breakdown. Actions that can limit/suspend the formal sovereignty of a target state can include: a) military intervention and b) inter-state conflict and its internal effects.

Intervention is a coercive action that officially makes recourse to military force. According to Tillema, interventions can be considered "military operations undertaken openly by a state's regular military forces within a specific foreign land in such a manner as to risk immediate combat" (1994, 251). In this optic, intervention constitutes a distinct category of "militarized international behavior" that: a) requires the use of force; b) often foresees a limited number of soldiers falling in battle; c) is described by the target state as a hostile act (Kegley and Hermann 1996, 311). A broad interpretation of this concept envisions the intervention resulting in a full-fledged military conflict, either brief or of medium-long duration, between the target state and the international actor, including consideration of a military occupation. What distinguishes it from a generic inter-state conflict is the intention, even if not overriding, to influence the internal order of the target state, promoting/causing the autocracy's fall. Interesting examples are Grenada (1983), Panama (1989), Afghanistan (2001), and Iraq (2003).

Table 1. Third Wave cases where military intervention or peace-keeping were employed[1]

Case	Year	Principal external actors
Central African Repub.	1979	France
Grenada	1983	US
Panama	1989	US
Cambodia	1991-93	UN
Mozambique	1992-94	UN
Haiti	1994	US/UN
Lesotho	1998	SADC[2]
Serbia	1999-2000	NATO/UN
Afghanistan	2001	US, Allies
Iraq	2003	US, Allies
Liberia	2003	UN, ECOWAS

Inter-state conflict and its internal effects represent a coercive action with official recourse to military force that does not include the breakdown of the non-democratic regime among its stated goals. The target state is involved in an inter-state war from which it will emerge defeated or extremely weakened. This is a classic reference to the scapegoat theory: an autocracy, delegitimized internally, attempts to stimulate a rally-around-the-flag effect by embarking on an external military adventure (Panebianco 1997, 76ff.). The failure of this strategy, whether by military defeat or the conflict's profound political and socio-economic consequences, exhausts the regime's residual legitimacy and causes its fall (Schmitter 1996, 35). In these cases, there is not a clear intention to influence the type of regime in the target state. Although the war's consequences are partly responsible for the regime's breakdown, these are unintended consequences of intentional actions (Grilli di Cortona 2014, 32). The classic examples are Portugal (1960s and '70s), Greece (1974), Argentina (1982), Uganda (1979) and the USSR (1979-89).

The second group of actions, which do not formally undermine the target state's sovereignty, include: a) covert operations; b) negative conditionality (sanctions); c) positive conditionality; d) diplomatic pressure; e) democratic assistance. Covert operations are a type of coercive action, including possible use of military force, intentional in nature, but unofficial. These are often clandestine military actions, conducted by the special forces of the international actor or via the recruitment/training/support of guerillas affiliated with opposition groups. It is important to make a distinction between this type of action, characterized by military goals, and peaceful assistance given to internal opposition groups. The classic case is Nicaragua (1980s).

Sanctions are political, economic and diplomatic measures of a coercive nature that do not envisage the use of military force, and aim to provoke a change in one or more policies of a given country (Smith 1995). These can consist of financial restrictions, arms embargoes, cuts in assistance, commercial sanctions, non-issuance of visas, etc. Sanctions can run from "comprehensive" to "targeted" or "smart" (Drezner 2011). The first type is based on the "punishment theory" (Lektzian and Souva 2007, 850), which assumes that socioeconomic problems inflicted on the population will translate into a loss of legitimacy for the regime and political pressure to conform to international demands (Kerr and Gaisford 1994). Smart sanctions are more recent, and aim to resolve some potential problems with comprehensive sanctions, such as the emergence of a rally-around-the-flag effect[3] (Allen 2005; Galtung 1967). Smart sanctions directly strike the regime's leaders, oligarchs, and socioeconomic elites (Giumelli 2011; Lektzian and Souva 2007; Major and McGann 2005). According to Brooks (2002) comprehensive sanctions should be more effective against democracies while smart sanctions should work better against non-democratic regimes. In any case, if the objective is regime change, then Dashti-Gibson, Davis, and Radcliff (1997) and Elliott (2002, 171) maintain that comprehensive sanctions have a major chance for success. Some cases include: South Africa (1970s and 1980s), Cambodia (1997), Haiti (1991, 1994), and Peru (1992).

If sanctions represent the stick in the process of promoting democracy, positive conditionality (Schmitter 1986; Pridham 1991), devoid of coercive elements and deriving its ability to influence from the concession of advantages in exchange for internal political decisions, plays the role of the carrot. A regime can secure advantages, including diplomatic recognition, the promise to be included in a supranational community, economic aid, development programs, or commercial contracts (Horng 2003; Piccone 2004). On the other hand, they are obliged to make progress in the development of democratic institutions (Murphy 1999), e.g. respect for political and civil rights, protection of internal minorities, and respect for the principles of liberal democracy. There are numerous examples of positive conditionality from Africa and Latin America.

Diplomatic pressure is often the first kind of action employed to promote the crisis/breakdown/transformation of an autocracy. This can take many different forms and often can overlap with the types of actions already discussed (Diamond 2011) but certain aspects merit highlighting. First of all is so-called "quiet diplomacy": confidential diplomatic contacts, conducted by ambassadors or emissaries of international organizations, with the objective of convincing regimes to liberalize and democratize. Various examples of the positive application of quiet diplomacy can be found in Africa,[4] as well as in Latin America in the 1970s and 1980s, especially on the part of the US, thanks to the ambassadors ("freedom pushers") appointed with a mandate to push regimes to democratize (Huntington 1995, 116). Particularly important is an international actor's withdrawal of political approval or support for an autocracy, even if not necessarily reflecting the desire to promote its fall. The more crucial the support of an external actor for a regime's economic/ military survival, and from the ideological point of view, the more the withdrawal of that support can play an essential role in the regime's fall. Good examples are the change in Soviet foreign policy towards Eastern Europe, as well as Africa, in the 1980s, and the US withdrawal of support for South American regimes in the 1970s (Dix 1982, 567; Sikkink 1996).

A final mention should be made of "democratic assistance" activities: advice and consultation on drafting constitutions and establishing democratic judicial systems, training for state employees, monitoring elections, financial assistance, support for political parties and training for party officials, professional training for members of NGOs and interest groups and their socialization toward democratic norms, etc. Particularly in the crisis/breakdown/ transformation phase, it is important to highlight the role of peaceful external support for internal opposition groups. Classic examples are the democratic development programs carried out by the National Endowment for Democracy (NED) in Latin America, but also in Poland in the 1980s (Carothers 1996).

Which factors influence the efficacy of such external actions in promoting/causing the fall of an autocratic regime? Answering this question is complicated due to the wide variation in the cases and the number of variables that have to be considered. The following is an attempt to catalog these factors.

The first group of factors concerns the strength of the institutions and economy of the target state. One must consider the

- size of the economy;
- state's coercive capability;
- strength of the regime's dominant political party;
- state's discretionary control of the economy;
- dependence on foreign assistance and raw materials;
- strategic importance, including geographic location and wealth in raw materials, especially petroleum.

The PID's influence potentially will be most important in weak states with small economies that are heavily dependent on foreign assistance and raw materials, e.g. Sub-Saharan Africa (Levitsky and Way 2010, 41; Schmitter 1996, 48).

The second factor to consider are "black knights" (Hufbauer, Schott, and Elliott 1990, 12) which, by providing economic, military and diplomatic support to target states, can condition and/ or impair the PID's ability to exert influence. Since the end of the Cold War, Russia, China, Japan, and France have played this role at times (Levitsky and Way 2010, 41).

A third element concerns linkage to the West (Levitsky and Way 2010, 43-4). This concept identifies the density of economic, political, diplomatic, social, and organizational ties, as well as the flow of capital, goods and services, people, and information between the target state and the major pro-democratic international actors (US, EU, IMF, World Bank, etc.). A high level of linkage will amplify the influence of external pressure.

The fourth and final factor refers to the congruity between the type of actions employed and the kind of legitimacy that the autocracy enjoys (e.g. theocratic or hereditary factors; political ideology; electoral autocracy; performance legitimacy; external legitimization) (Burnell 2006, 548-49). Understanding the predominant sources of legitimacy is important for determining which kind of action to employ: the congruity between these and the target state's type of legitimacy will amplify the PID's efficacy. For example, economic sanctions will be more effective than diplomatic pressure if applied to a regime based on performance legitimacy, while diplomatic pressure will be more effective in cases of external legitimization.

In relation to other variables, the PID can assume a principal, concurrent or marginal role. The PID constitutes the principal variable when it comes close to being the sufficient condition for the fall of an autocracy. Even if other variables are present, the international variable is crucial to producing the result; without the PID, the regime's fall would not occur in a given limited time period. The concurrent role is something very close to being a necessary condition. In this case, the PID is not, by itself, sufficient to provoke the regime's fall, even if in certain cases it represents the detonator. It still has considerable weigh, however. The explanation for the breakdown can be found in the interactions between the PID and the other variables involved. Lastly, a marginal role indicates that the international variable represents a condition that is neither necessary nor sufficient. The PID is present, but the effect it produces on the regime's fall is residual, and subordinated to the role played by the other variables. The PID effect is often indirect, at most amplifying the role of the crucial variables. The objective in the following pages is to identify the principal actors, the kinds of actions, and in particular the role (principal, concurrent, marginal) of the PID in some of the most important national cases in each world region during the Third Wave of democratization, focusing our attention on the interaction between this variable and the others involved.

Southern Europe

The "Carnation Revolution" in Portugal on April 25, 1974 launched the Third Wave of democratization. In Portugal and Greece, unlike in Spain, the PID had a significant concurrent role, along with inter-state conflict and its internal effects. At the time of its fall, the Portuguese regime was in a state of obsolescence, Caetano having succeeded Salazar only a few years before. Although the state was fairly strong, thanks to its pervasive penetration of society,[5] Portugal had a weak economy, was dependent on foreign energy sources, and was severely damaged by the weight of colonial wars. Beginning in the 1960s, the military was engaged in the repression of independence movements in Portugal's African colonies. The economic unsustainability of these conflicts, which consumed large portions of the state budget, and the inability to secure a military victory had seriously undermined the regime's legitimacy in sectors crucial for its stability. The middle ranks of the army, directly involved in the colonial wars, were especially receptive to the influence of anticolonial ideology (Morlino 1986). The oil crisis of 1973 exacerbated the economic crisis (Germano, Grilli di Cortona and Lanza 2014, 48). Interaction among all these factors led to the coup that ended the Portuguese regime. While the role of the colonial wars appeared to be central, it did not by itself produce the end result (Germano, Grilli di Cortona and Lanza 2014, 47-48; Huntington 1995, 75, 77; Pridham 2000, 289-90; Schmitter 1996, 35).

The Greek military regime had been in power only a few years (beginning in 1967) when the transition began. Its legitimacy based on anti-Communism, the Greek regime was born as a temporary solution and never succeeded in consolidating itself (Contogeorgis 2003, 17). With a weak economy dependent on foreign energy sources, the regime was poorly institutionalized and had a fragmented elite. The oil crisis of 1973 further damaged the country's already exhausted economy and weakened the regime (Germano, Grilli di Cortona and Lanza 2014, 43). To try to stimulate a rally-around-the-flag effect by procuring an external enemy, the 1974 attempt to overthrow President Makarios III of Cyprus created the conditions for a military conflict. Turkey responded by invading Cyprus. The Greek army's refusal to embark on a war they would have lost put an end to the regime's residual legitimacy, and ended with its replacement by a transition government (Huntington 1995, 78; Germano, Grilli di Cortona and Lanza 2014, 43-44). The Cyprus crisis was the detonator for the regime's fall (Germano, Grilli di Cortona and Lanza 2014, 44; Schmitter 1996, 35), but it might not have produced this result without the regime's already serious loss of legitimacy, and the disastrous state of the country's economy (Pridham 2000, 289).

Latin America

In evaluating the PID's importance in Latin America, we must principally highlight the role of the United States of America. US policy toward this continent changed radically from the 1960s to the 1980s (Grilli di Cortona 2014, 31). The "geopolitical dependency hypothesis" (Muller 1985, 451, 466) maintains that the bipolar confrontation and the need to contain Communist expansion in the 1960s led the US to undermine certain Latin American democratic experiences, facilitating the emergence of, or at least supporting, solidly anti-Communist military regimes (Sanchez 2003, 238). US economic, military (including covert operations), ideological (development of the "national security doctrine") and diplomatic support was often fundamental for the stability of these regimes (Sanchez 2003, 238). The American attitude changed with the emergence of a new human rights policy developed by Congress beginning in 1973 (Smith 1994, 241; Huntington 1995, 114). This was further accelerated with the election of Carter, who made human rights one of the cornerstones of his foreign policy (Smith 1994, 245). Carter pulled support from a good number of South American military regimes, removing one of their principal sources of legitimacy (Sikkink 1996, 107). In addition, Carter promoted policies of pressure and conditionality to combat systematic violations of human rights. Even if not its explicit goal, this policy contributed to weakening these regimes (Smith 1994, 241). For a brief period in the 1980s, Reagan pushed back the hands of the clock, giving priority to fighting Communism. However, thanks in part to the diminished perception of the Soviet threat, in his second term Reagan also placed human rights and democracy promotion at the center of his foreign policy (Carothers 1991, 150, 255; Smith 1994, 286-87; Huntington 1995, 114).

Grenada was the most straightforward case of democratic transition in Latin America and the Caribbean. In power for only a few years, the New Jewel Movement (NJM) was facing a crisis due to the failure of its economic policy and a conflict within its authoritarian elite that led to the assassination of Maurice Bishop, charismatic leader of the NJM, by the most orthodox Marxist-Leninist faction of the movement, led by Bernard Coard (Connaughton 2008; Williams 1997). Still, absent the 1983 US military intervention (Operation Urgent Fury), the regime's structure (Henfrey 1984) and the absence of a strong internal opposition probably would have permitted the NJM to survive. Therefore, the PID was the sufficient cause for the fall of the non-democratic regime.

In Panama, even conflict within the authoritarian elite did not prevent Noriega from firmly holding on to power for most of the 1980s, surviving attempts to remove or politically weaken him (Levitsky and Way 2010, 173). Proof of the regime's strength was its ability to resist the internal and international pressure applied prior to the military intervention. Demonstrations by the internal opposition never succeeded in making a dent in Noriega's hold on power, or the popular support he enjoyed (Levitsky and Way 2010, 171, 178). Diplomatic pressure, withdrawal of economic and military assistance, and economic and commercial sanctions did not have the desired effect, in part thanks to the assistance Noriega received from other states such as Libya, which acted as a sort of black knight (Levitsky and Way 2010, 173-75, 178; Carothers 1991, 255). The military operation Just Cause (1989) represented, by itself, the cause of the Panamanian regime's fall.

Haiti's case is more complex, since at least four regimes fell during the period under consideration. The PID had an important role in all of these, but had its greatest influence in the fall of the Cedras regime (1994). Only seven months after the Aristide government came to power in the first-ever democratic elections in Haiti's history (1990), the army seized power, placing Cédras at the head of a military junta. Condemnation by the international community (UN, OAS, and the US in particular) was immediate (Diamond 2011, 139; Mobekk 2001, 174). In the following three years, many PID actions were employed (diplomatic pressure, economic and commercial sanctions, a naval blockade), not only to restore the legitimate, democratically elected government, but also because of the brutal methods the regime used to suppress the opposition. Despite the state's extreme weakness, its socioeconomic structure, and its dependence on international aid (Levitsky and Way 2010, 173), the inability of these PID instruments to bring about the regime's fall (Giumelli 2011, 58; Von Hippel 2000, 98-99) almost led to a military intervention (Operation Uphold Democracy, 1994). The US military was already deployed and waiting for the order to move into action when, because of this pressure, Cédras relinquished power (Diamond 2011, 122, 140; Von Einsiedel and Malone 2006; Mobekk 2001, 174-75; Schmitter 1996, 45; Gros 1997). The military intervention was transformed into a peacekeeping mission conducted under UN aegis. This action was the sufficient cause for the Haitian regime's fall (Levitsky and Way 2010, 171-74).

In the case of Guyana, the PID (with the US in the lead) adopted a package of actions aimed at destabilizing the regime of the People's National Congress (PNC), a party of the country's Black minority that came into power in the 1960s. Supported initially by the US and Britain, it was led by Forbes Burnham until his death in 1985, and then by Desmond Hoyte. With the Cold War winding down, the US under Carter withdrew support from the Guyanese regime. Reagan increased the pressure, USAID offices in Guyana were closed and international loans blocked. These measures produced a rapid decline in the Guyanese economy, already extremely fragile and dependent on foreign assistance, indicating that international conditionality had decisive influence. At the end of the 1980s, free elections became the prerequisite for aid. Thanks to this pressure, elections were called in 1992. The Carter Center largely ran the elections, which removed the regime's ability to manipulate them (Levitsky and Way 2010, 148). Regime repression had undermined the opposition's ability to exercise influence (Premdas 1993, 48), but the PID actions created the economic crisis that weakened the regime to the point of forcing it to give in to international conditionality, which constituted the principal variable in its fall.

The US ability to influence the Dominican Republic was so great that it was able to bring down the Balaguer regime in 1978 using only diplomatic pressure (Diamond 2011, 121; Levitsky and Way 2010, 134-35). This derived from: a tradition of direct US interference (i.e. the 1916-1924 occupation and the 1965-1966 military intervention); the state's weakness in the face of migratory waves from Haiti; severe poverty; a weak economy totally dependent on foreign energy sources and on commercial relations with the United States; enormous quantities of economic and military aid from the US (Levitsky and Way 2010, 133). The non-democratic Dominican regime established after the American military intervention that ended the 1965-1966 civil war enjoyed full US support (Prince 1996; Conaghan and Espinal 1990). This situation changed, however, during the 1970s, with Carter's human rights policy (Sikkink 1996). After the effective repression of opposition groups, in particular the *Partido Revolucionario Dominicano* (PRD), which boycotted elections in 1970 and 1974, it was American pressure (Hartlyn 1991) that forced the regime to cease its repressive policies and allow opposition parties to participate in more open and fair elections in 1978 (Arthur 2011; Conaghan and Espinal 1990). The regime's loss of popular consensus led to the PRD candidate's landslide victory (Conaghan and Espinal 1990). After it became apparent that the PRD would win, the US role emerged even more clearly when it withheld support for a coup organized by soldiers loyal to Balaguer (Arthur 2011). In this context, the PID was sufficient to explain why the regime fell.

Nicaragua's case is particularly interesting, as the interaction of various international actors brought about regime change. The fall of the Somoza regime in 1979 was principally due to ever more effective military actions by the *Frente Sandinista de Liberación Nacional* (FSLN). This is not to underestimate the consequences for the regime's legitimacy and military capacity of the US withdrawal of support, sanctions, and cutoff of assistance (Smith 1994, 245, 247, 250-51). Because the Sandinista regime, established in 1979, effectively repressed internal opposition (Levitsky and Way 2010, 145), the process that led to the Sandinistas' fall originated in the international dimension (Levitsky and Way 2010, 141, 145), with prominent roles for the US, USSR and President Arias of Costa Rica. There were several different PID actions: covert operations, sanctions, positive conditionality, diplomatic pressure, and democratic assistance. The principal US instrument of pressure was a covert operation, long an open secret, that included economic,

military, logistic, and diplomatic support for the Contras guerillas ($19 million in 1981; $24 million in 1983; $1 million a month
via Saudi Arabia beginning in mid-1984; $27 million in 1985; $100
million in 1986) (Carothers 1991, 83, 89). Added to this during the
1980s were: economic sanctions and the 1985 commercial embargo
(Carothers 1991, 84-85, 90-91); diplomatic pressure, including frequent bilateral contacts aimed at promoting the peace process; joint
US-Honduras military exercises on the Nicaraguan border (Carothers 1991, 84-87); non-lethal assistance to opposition groups in the
1990 elections ($12.7 million), as well as international monitoring
of those elections (Levitsky and Way 2010, 142-44; Whitehead 1996,
80; Carothers 1991, 95; Lean 2007).

In this period, the USSR played the role of the black knight, furnishing the Sandinistas with 4.5 billion dollars between 1981 and
1989 (Orozco 2002, 54). The diplomatic efforts of Costa Rican president Arias generated two agreements (Esquipulas II, 1987; Tesoro
Beach, 1989)[6] that led to the 1990 elections, won by the opposition.
The interaction of these factors was responsible for the Sandinista
regime's fall (Diamond 2011, 122). The enormous amount of money supplied by the USSR had countered the effects of the embargo
and the Contras' military operations, but the cutoff of these funds
beginning in 1986 made the economic consequences of American
pressure and guerilla operations unsustainable[7] (Levitsky and Way
2010, 141; Roberts 1990). It forced the Sandinistas to participate in
the peace process promoted by Arias, which they saw as a way to
block increased assistance to the Contras by the American Congress (Carothers 1991, 105-107). To make this succeed, the Sandinistas had to ensure an impeccable electoral process, by definition
out of their control, which led to their defeat in the 1990 elections
(Levitsky and Way 2010, 141, 145; Whitehead 1996, 84-85). The PID,
therefore, was the sufficient cause for the regime's fall (Levitsky
and Way 2010, 141).

In Argentina the PID played a concurrent role. The Argentine
military regime was subject to sanctions and diplomatic pressure,
as well as being involved in an inter-state conflict. Following the establishment of Carter's human rights policy, in 1978 the US blocked
military assistance to Argentina (Sikkink 1996, 97; Smith 1994, 245),
voted down or abstained on 23 out of 25 Argentine requests for in-

ternational loans, and clearly expressed its concerns about respect for human rights to all three Argentine military juntas (Sikkink 1996, 97, 115). If in 1980 sanctions were loosened, with the aim of obtaining Argentine cooperation for the grain embargo against the USSR, sanctions on arms sales remained in force until 1983 (Sikkink 1996, 97). Although they did not have a decisive impact, these actions exacerbated the legitimacy crisis (Diamond 2011, 121) stemming from the following factors: the regime's failed attempt to revive an economy seriously scarred by the 1973 oil crisis; the "dirty war" to suppress internal opposition; divisions within the military elite; loss of support from the Catholic Church and entrepreneurs; and the growing activism of internal opposition groups, despite repression. This, along with a lack of options, led Galtieri to bet on a rally-around-the-flag effect in 1982 by invading the Malvinas/ Falkland Islands, which Great Britain controls but Argentina claims (Grilli di Cortona 2009, 47). The British intervention and Argentina's consequent military defeat cancelled out any residual legitimacy the regime still possessed, bringing it to an end (Huntington 1995, 78; Whitehead 1996, 63; Schmitter 1996, 35). As this was the result of interaction between internal and international factors, the role of the PID was concurrent.

In most of the other cases in Latin America, the PID's role appears marginal. This is not to suggest that it had no role or no effect, but only that it was not a necessary and/or sufficient condition. In most cases, the PID reinforced key variables explaining regime change, even without an important direct impact. For example, in Chile, withdrawal of support from the Pinochet regime, pressure not to annul the 1988 referendum on renewing its mandate, and economic and diplomatic support for internal opposition groups did not represent necessary and/or sufficient conditions for the regime's fall. However, they contributed to reinforcing those internal variables that were directly responsible for the transition, especially the opposition (Carothers 1991, 162, 163; Diamond 2011, 122). In the same manner, in Uruguay the PID (American pressure during the Carter Administration) had a considerable indirect effect in strengthening the pro-democratic faction of the military and internal opposition (Sikkink 1996, 106, 107, 115), but did not contribute directly to the regime's fall.

Asia

In the Asian Third Wave the PID's role was rather limited. There is only one identifiable case where it had a principal role, i.e. Afghanistan. In other cases, the role was marginal. The fall of non-democratic regimes on this continent is principally the result of internal factors and international factors not linked to explicit actions by an external actor. For example, the transformation of the Mongolian regime stemmed in good part from the authoritarian elite's perception of the breakdown of Soviet Communism and the necessity of a rapprochement with the West in order to obtain enough assistance to replace the economic relationship with the USSR (Fish 1998).

In Afghanistan, PID actions were primarily sanctions applied when the Taliban seized power in 1996, and then military intervention after Afghanistan-based Al Qaeda carried out the September 11, 2001 attacks. In resolution 1076 of 1996, the UN had asked all member states to cease arms shipments to both the Taliban government and internal opposition groups, followed on December 17, 1996 by EU common position 746 (Giumelli 2011, 70). These and other measures adopted in subsequent years had little effect either in moderating the Taliban's policies on human rights or bringing about the regime's fall. The most important armed opposition, the Northern Alliance, made up of Tajiks, Uzbeks, Hazara and ethnic Pashtun minorities, financed by Iran, Russia and India, only represented a limited threat to the regime and succeeded in gaining control of only a small and poor part of territory (Dobbins et al. 2003, 129). In response to the September 11, 2001 terrorist attack, the US launched Operation Enduring Freedom (OEF), with the goal of eradicating Al Qaeda and the Taliban from Afghanistan. The operation included strong military and economic support for the Northern Alliance, enabling them to obtain early and unexpected military successes, conquering Kabul in mid-November 2001 (Dobbins et al. 2003, 129-30). The successes of the Northern Alliance, so ineffectual in previous years despite funding from Iran, Russia and India, were attributable to the support from OEF. Consequently, the PID (OEF) was the variable sufficient to explain the fall of the Taliban regime (Suhrke 2008).

In most of the other Asian cases, the PID played a marginal role.

South Korea is one example. The PID actions, mostly by the US, were diplomatic pressure and democratic assistance. Because of intense protests by opposition forces, American support for President Chun Doo Hwan was replaced by cautious but ever more constant pressure by Reagan and the Department of State for an opening to the opposition, increased moderation in dealing with public protests, and for Chun to keep his promise to leave office peacefully at the end of his term in 1988, along with a stern warning to the military not to attempt a coup (Saxer 2002, 63; Smith 1994, 280-81; Huntington 1995, 118; Diamond 2011, 122). In addition, via the National Endowment for Democracy, the Americans provided economic and political support for the opposition. By and large, at the origin of the South Korean transition were the internal opposition's intense pressure and the authoritarian leadership's awareness that it could not prolong its permanence in power (Smith 1994, 280-81). The PID actions reinforced a trend already in motion that, predictably, would have arrived at the same result. In the Philippines, American diplomatic pressure contributed to convincing Marcos to leave power after the electoral defeat of 1986 (Diamond 2011, 121-22; Haynes 2001). In any case, this pressure was applied when the crisis was already underway, thanks to the opposition's mobilization and the regime's inability to combat the Communist guerillas, resulting in divisions in the army and a weakening of the regime, along with a serious economic crisis and the opposition of the Catholic Church (Pei 1998; Huntington 1995, 77).

Post-Communist Europe

Although marked by nationally specific courses of action and geographical differences, the PID's role in this region has been important. The following analysis focuses not on the countries created with the break-up of the USSR, as the dissolution of a state is not considered a PID factor, but rather on East Central Europe and the Balkans.

Although there were cases of military intervention and sanctions (Serbia) and of inter-state war (USSR in Afghanistan), diplomatic pressure, in the form of withdrawal of support and stimuli to adopt a particular set of reforms, was the action that most influenced the breakdown of non-democratic regimes in East Central Europe. The principal actor was the Soviet Union. In the context of bipolar confrontation, relations between Eastern European countries and the USSR were based on the Brezhnev Doctrine, making the countries of the Soviet Bloc penetrated political systems. Such control[8] prevented any political evolution not approved by Moscow. The cases of Hungary (1956), Czechoslovakia (1968) and Poland (1956, 1970, 1980-81) demonstrate how prepared the USSR was to intervene to block unwanted reform (Batt 1997, 155; Niklasson 1994, 202).

A series of actions by the reformist leadership that came into power in the USSR in the second half of the 1980s made a substantial contribution to regime change in Eastern Europe. It is unlikely that the objective was to promote the fall of these regimes (Light 1997, 134). The "Gorbachëv Effect" can be summarized as the withdrawal of Soviet willingness to intervene, including militarily, in the internal affairs of satellite states to preserve the status quo[9] and the application of pressure to implement reforms that Gorbachëv himself was carrying out in the USSR (Light 1997, 133; Niklasson 1994, 203). These were not, however, obligatory, as in the past, since in 1985 Gorbachëv had renounced the so-called principle of "Socialist Internationalism," under which the USSR had supervised internal policies and approved changes in leadership in East European countries (Light 1997, 140, 142).

The Polish case featured a long tradition of strong internal opposition. There were important protests in 1956, 1968, 1970-71, and 1976, ending with the imposition of martial law after protests led by Solidarity in 1980-81.[10] These demonstrations were repressed, sometimes violently, thanks to USSR support. The emergence of Gorbachëv's leadership had several consequences. It reactivated internal pressure for reform both by the opposition and regime moderates. Also, it convinced the Communist leadership that change was inevitable (Niklasson 1994, 210-211, 212). The Polish regime received Gorbachëv's pressure positively (Light 1997, 140), relaxing its repressive policies, allowing Solidarity to reconstitute, and conceding limited reforms in the system. The telephone call of August 22, 1989, in which Gorbachëv pressured Jaruzelski to enter a non-Communist government, is only one example of the role the

PID had in the Polish transition (Light 1997, 141; Niklasson 1994, 211). Gorbachëv's withdrawal of support, including military support, took away the regime's principal source of legitimacy, and the instruments it needed to deter or repress internal opposition, indicating the concurrent nature of the PID's role.

In Hungary as well, Gorbachëv's reforms met a positive reception (Light 1997, 140). The principal difference with Poland resided in the long-standing moderation of the Hungarian leadership, thanks to which it was able to take the initiative and control the transition. Since the 1960s, the Communist leadership had undertaken a gradual reform process aimed at reacquiring popular consensus lost after the 1956 Soviet intervention. The New Economic Mechanism (NEM) of the 1970s was intended to enlarge the private sector. In 1983, an electoral reform was adopted that, within a single-party system, allowed non-Communists to be elected to parliament. The economic and political crises of the 1980s, however, increased internal pressure for change, even within the Communist Party (Batt 1997, 161). It was also thanks to Gorbachëv's reforms that in May 1988, János Kádar was replaced as party leader by a moderate directorate. In addition, Moscow's non-intervention when the Hungarian leadership dismantled the Iron Curtain on the Austrian-Hungarian border (May 1989) and thus made it possible for East Germans to reach West Germany (September 1989), convinced the Hungarians that there would be no external opposition to a regime change (Light 1997, 140). In essence, as in Poland, Gorbachëv's reforms had convinced the Communist leadership that change was inevitable (Niklasson 1994, 212). In this transition as well the PID played a concurrent role.

The leadership of the German Democratic Republic, on the other hand, stubbornly refused to accept the reforms promoted by the USSR (Light 1997, 140). Since 1986, Honecker had made it clear the German regime had no need for change (Niklasson 1994, 212). Mass protests, suppressed by the regime, began in summer 1987 at the same time the Soviets were pressuring East European regimes to reform. These were repeated in January 1988 on the anniversary of the death of Rosa Luxemburg and Karl Liebknecht. Added to Gorbachëv's pressure was the decision by the Hungarian government in May 1989 to open the frontier with Austria and allow free passage of East Germans to West Germany, further weakening the Honecker regime (Light 1997, 142; Niklasson 1994, 211; Pridham 2000, 285). Beginning in October 1989, there were enormous popular demonstrations in Leipzig and Berlin. In the same month, during a visit marking the anniversary of the birth of the German Democratic Republic, Gorbachëv pressured Honecker to make concessions and refused to supply troops to suppress the demonstrations (Light 1997, 142; Whitehead 1996, 371). Faced with public pressure, and absent Soviet support, the Communist leader had no choice but to resign, triggering the regime change that occurred only a few weeks after the fall of the Berlin Wall. Without the support and legitimacy provided by the USSR, a regime like that of East Germany, with no internal legitimacy, could not last. This withdrawal of support, along with the popular protest, was the principal factor in the regime's fall. The PID's role therefore was concurrent.

The Czechoslovak leadership also refused to accept the reforms promoted by Gorbachëv (Light 1997, 140). Miloš Jakeš, who replaced Gustáv Husák in 1987, was also profoundly conservative, and responded to the failure of his reform initiative with increased repression. The purges following the 1968 Soviet intervention had excluded reformers from the Czechoslovak leadership (Niklasson 1994, 213). In addition, repression had limited the emergence of a strong internal opposition (Batt 1997, 161). The Czechoslovak ruling class, therefore, was dominated by orthodox factions, completely dependent on Moscow for their legitimacy (Niklasson 1994, 213). In this country the Gorbachëv effect was clearly the origin of the regime's fall (Batt 1997, 161), removing any legitimacy that remained to the regime[11] and indirectly encouraging the emergence of an opposition that, beginning in March 1988, was capable of organizing protests much larger than those in Poland and Hungary. Therefore, the 1989 "Velvet Revolution" was an excellent example of the PID's concurrent role.

A heavy dependency on Moscow, both for legitimacy and economically because of its chronic budget deficits, made Bulgaria one of the regimes most loyal to the USSR (Niklasson 1994, 213). Živkov, therefore, officially embraced *perestroika*, announcing reforms in 1987 that were, however, barely implemented (Light 1997, 140; Niklasson 1994, 213). The centralization of power in Živkov's hands, and the control guaranteed by the secret police, limited the socio-political importance of opposition to the regime. This situation changed in 1987 with the proliferation of protests both within and without the party. The serious economic crisis and pressure from Moscow were the reasons for this change. In 1987 Gorbachëv openly admonished the Bulgarian leader to speed up reforms (Light 1997, 142). Because of the opposition's weakness, change originated within the single party. In November 1989, Mladenov, leader of the reformist faction, obtained Živkov's resignation, thereby initiating the regime's transformation under the control of the reformist Communist leadership (Kolarova and Dimitrov 1996). It is certain that Mladenov consulted with Gorbachëv: returning from a visit to China shortly before Živkov's resignation, the reformist leader stopped in Moscow (Light 1997, 142). It is likely that he got Gorbachëv's green light for his succession (Niklasson 1994, 213). In this case the PID played a particularly important concurrent role in the transition.

In conclusion, abandonment of the Brezhnev Doctrine and diplomatic pressure for reform, especially in 1987-1989 (Light 1997, 138), left East European leaders helpless before their populations, orphaned of the principal source of their legitimacy. It gave Communist party reformist factions and opposition groups a greater awareness of the possibilities for reforming or overthrowing their respective regimes (Bratton and van de Walle 1997, 29; Sanford 1997, 176-77; Whitehead 1996, 371). Although the Gorbachëv effect cannot be considered a sufficient condition for the fall of the Eastern European regimes, it did represent a necessary condition (Light 1997, 133; Batt 1997, 155; Schmitter 1996, 27; Niklasson 1994, 206; Pridham 2000, 285). Maintaining the Brezhnev Doctrine would have altered both the time and character (certainly more violent) of regime change in Eastern Europe (Light 1997, 149; Whitehead 1996, 372).

Serbia, on the other hand, is a case of a principal role for the PID. The PID worked against the Milošević regime by employing democratic assistance, diplomatic pressure, sanctions, and a military intervention. Beginning in 1992, the international community imposed sanctions with the goal of persuading Milošević to end support for Serbian aggression in Bosnia and Croatia. The most important of these were exclusion from the World Bank and denial of access to IMF financing (Levitsky and Way 2010, 107). The necessity of having Milošević's support for the peace process in Bosnia obliged international actors to moderate the sanctions' actual effects (Levitsky and Way 2010, 104). In combination with the regime's coercive capability, it permitted Milošević to survive this phase, but not without difficulty.

The Dayton Accords (1995), which ended the Yugoslav conflict, enabled the West to intensify diplomatic pressure and make the sanctions more effective. The US and EU froze the overseas assets of the regime's elite, prohibited new foreign investment, blocked the Serbian airline from flying to western countries, and banned issuance of visas to the regime's most important figures (Levitsky and Way 2010, 105, 109, 110). Ethnic cleansing in Kosovo, visible to the world's media, obliged the PID to intervene militarily in 1999 (Levitsky and Way 2010, 109). Sanctions and 78 days of NATO bombing[12] devastated the Serbian economy, forcing Milošević[13] to withdraw from Kosovo and call early elections for October 2000 (Diamond 2011, 122-23; Levitsky and Way 2010, 109). The international community intervened heavily on the side of the opposition, furnishing financing of between $40 and $70 million, creating a united anti-Milošević front (Levitsky and Way 2010, 111). His electoral defeat led to the fall of the regime.

A fragmented opposition, although active during all of the 1990s, would never have been able to bring down a regime like that of Milošević, which had popular consensus and a considerable capacity for repression. In addition to international financing, the victory of the opposition in the 2000 election resulted, above all, from the devastating effects on the economy of the sanctions and the military intervention, and the consequent weakening of the regime's coercive ability and consensus (Diamond 2011, 122; Levitsky and Way 2010, 104, 109-10). The loss of Kosovo was a severe blow to Milošević's image (Levitsky and Way 2010, 109-110). All of these factors demonstrate that the PID was the sufficient condition for the regime's fall.

It is worth noting the PID's role also in the breakdown of the Communist regime in the USSR. The PID actions in this case were inter-state warfare and its internal effects, plus diplomatic pressure.

The arms race triggered by Reagan, which should be considered a form of diplomatic pressure, worsened the Soviet economy's crisis (Pridham 2000, 290). The consequences of the war in Afghanistan were especially important (1979-89), in particular the Red Army's inability to win the war (Huntington 1995, 77). There were various internal effects, linked, for example, to the Communist leadership's perception of the Red Army and of its potential effectiveness for use internally to control the non-Russian republics and abroad to preserve the Soviet empire (Reuveny and Prakash 1999). It is difficult, however, to judge the weight of these factors against the others involved in the fall of the USSR, such as the failure of the planned economy and the consequent economic crisis (Kort 1992), the emergence of a reformist leadership, (Adomeit 1994), the breakdown of Communist regimes in Eastern Europe, and the increasingly loud demands by many Soviet republics for more autonomy or total independence (Carrère d'Encausse 1993).

Africa

About a third of the countries involved in the Third Wave were located in Africa. With this large number of cases, all possible types of PID action were present, playing all possible roles (principal, concurrent, marginal), with the full range of international actors involved. For this area as well, the analysis here is limited to cases where the PID's role was principal or concurrent.

Mozambique is among the cases where the PID played the principal role. Different international actors employed assistance, diplomatic pressure, conditionality, covert operations and military interventions (a peace-keeping operation). With independence, Mozambique became the theater of a civil war that to a large extent reflected the bipolar confrontation (Levitsky and Way 2010, 246; Gomes Cravinho 1998). Set against the *Resistência Nacional Moçambicana* (RENAMO), which had covert support from South Africa and Rhodesia (Moran and Pitcher 2004), was the *Frente de Libertação de Moçambique* (FRELIMO), a single party heading a Marxist-Leninist-inspired regime (Pitcher 2002), supported by the USSR with ideological cover, arms, and petroleum, $150 million a year in the 1980s (Alden 2001, 94). Withdrawal of external support by both sides in the 1980s compromised the ability of the two parties to continue the conflict and, unintentionally, amplified the effectiveness of international conditionality, especially important because, at the beginning of the 1990s, international assistance constituted 75% of the country's GDP (Levitsky and Way 2010, 247; Peiffer and Englebert 2012, 362-64). The indispensable nature of this aid drove FRELIMO to abandon its Marxist-Leninist orientation, concede some forms of political liberalization (Alden 2001), and enter into peace negotiations, sponsored by the international community, which led to the deployment of a multinational force of 7,500 men, the UN Operation in Mozambique (ONUMOZ) (Levitsky and Way 2010, 248; Manning and Malbrough 2010; Alden 2001; Gomes Gravinho 1998). Finally, different types of assistance were provided for the 1994 elections. RENAMO received several million dollars to provide some balance to the electoral competition, as FRELIMO had control of the state's resources. In addition, 2,500 international observers monitored the elections (Levitsky and Way 2010, 249). The timing was particularly important. During the 1970s and 1980s, internal factors such as the economic crisis[14] and the presence of an armed opposition did not produce regime change. International conditionality, supported by ONUMOZ and amplified by Soviet and South African withdrawal of support (Peiffer and Englebert 2012, 362-64), therefore constituted, albeit in a weak form, the sufficient cause of the regime's transformation (Bratton and van de Walle 1997, 182).

There are numerous other cases where the PID played a concurrent role. South Africa is an interesting, if complicated, example. The principal actions of the US, UN, and European Economic Community were sanctions and diplomatic pressure, although it is necessary to carefully consider the withdrawal of Soviet support from the African National Congress and actions set in motion by foreign private financial institutions. In 1973 the UN declared apartheid a "crime against humanity" and in 1977 encouraged the adoption of an embargo on arms sales to South Africa. Beginning in 1985, after the declaration of a state of emergency by the Botha government, the European Economic Community, the Commonwealth, US, and other states and international institutions adopted increasingly stringent financial and commercial sanctions (Omer-Cooper 1998;

Huntington 1995, 120; Smith 1994, 278). Although the estimates fix the direct impact of the sanctions on South Africa's GDP at 0.5% (Levy 1999, 7) the psychological effect on the White political and socio-economic elite should not be underestimated (Diamond 2011, 123; Von Hippel 2000, 98). In addition, the sanctions also should be evaluated on the basis of their importance for the protagonists in the transition. At the beginning of negotiations, for example, Mandela and the ANC asked that the sanctions be maintained until the regime had been effectively dismantled (Levy 1999, 10). The psychological effect was amplified by diplomatic pressure and the unanimous international condemnation of apartheid. In 1989, informal meetings were held in Great Britain among representatives of the ANC, the National Party, various African states, the US and the USSR. In September the US stressed that, if Mandela was not released within six months, President Bush would approve an extension of the sanctions.

The economic dimension was crucial in launching the transition. In the mid-1980s the South African public debt was $24 billion, two-thirds of which was short-term. This situation made the South African economy vulnerable, dependent on the readiness of foreign investors to refinance the public debt (Levy 1999, 5). Before financial sanctions, which exacerbated the situation, it was foreign banks that suspended investment in South African debt. After the state of emergency was declared, Chase Manhattan Bank, followed by other banks, announced that it would not extend further credit to South Africa (Levy 1999, 5). The impact was extremely important, even though not generated by a desire to bring about regime change. Socio-political instability made investment in South African sovereign debt risky (Levy 1999, 6). Another crucial element that inadvertently favored the South African regime's transformation was the withdrawal of Soviet support from the ANC (Bratton and van de Walle 1997; Smith 1994, 279). This had a dual effect. On one hand, it undercut the ANC's ability to continue its armed resistance, making it more open to negotiations. On the other, it reassured the White political and socio-economic elite that regime change would not mean the adoption of a planned economy (Levy 1999, 11). The most important factors in the internal dimension were the crisis of the South African economic model and the robust activism of the internal opposition and civil society, e.g. churches, unions, and business associations (Wood 2001). Underpinning regime change, therefore, were interactions between internal and international factors, most especially those linked to the PID, highlighting its concurrent role in the transition.

In Malawi the PID worked via conditionality and diplomatic pressure. In the context of the bipolar confrontation, the West had long supported the Hastings Banda regime. This support ended with the end of the Cold War, and when Western democratic conditionality took hold (Levitsky and Way 2010, 283). With the Vatican's encouragement, on March 8, 1992 eight Catholic prelates published an open letter criticizing the regime (Levitsky and Way 2010, 284). The arrest on April 6 of Chihana, one of the principal internal opposition leaders, and the popular demonstrations of May 6-7, brutally repressed by the regime, convinced international donors (Paris Conference, May 11-13) to suspend all non-humanitarian assistance[15] until democratic reforms had been implemented (Levitsky and Way 2010, 284; Venter 1995). The country's extreme poverty, enormous public debt ($1.5 billion) and growing difficulty in making interest payments (Venter 1995), its chronic dependence on international assistance,[16] the absence of black knights (Levitsky and Way 2010, 282), as well as Banda's advanced age, which provoked an intense succession struggle with a lack of military support for the designated heir (Levitsky and Way 2010, 283), combined to make it impossible for the regime to resist international pressure for long. Only a few months after the interruption of assistance, Banda allowed a referendum on the introduction of a multi-party system (October 18, 1992), marking the beginning of the democratic transition (Diamond 2011, 124; Levitsky and Way 2010, 283; Bratton and van de Walle 1997, 182; Venter 1995). Although elements of regime crisis were already present due to internal factors, the PID, in particular conditionality expressed via freezing international aid, was a necessary condition for the regime's fall.

Uganda's path toward a multi-party democracy has been a tortured one, characterized by civil wars and coups. The major non-democratic regimes have been those of Milton Obote (1966-71), Idi Amin (1971-79), again Obote (1980-85), Okello (1985-86) and, beginning in 1986, Museveni. PID actions have influenced the fate of these regimes to varying degrees. The democratic transition, inter-rupted many times, began with multi-party elections after the fall of the Amin regime in 1979. The principal PID actions in this case were diplomatic pressure, inter-state conflict, and its internal ef-fects, which then evolved into a military intervention. The immedi-ate recognition of Amin's regime in 1971, and the Western support he briefly enjoyed, already had been withdrawn by 1972 because of the regime's brutality and Amin's rapprochement with the USSR and Libya (Rake 1998). The atrocities and the ethnic strife the re-gime incited, especially to the detriment of the Langi and Acholi ethnic groups, leaving 300,000 dead in 1971-79, compromised the regime's internal legitimacy (Jennings 2010; Carbone 2003). In Oc-tober 1978, Amin tried to divert the attention of the armed forces from their internal divisions, which had generated several coup at-tempts, by acquiring an external enemy, specifically by invading Tanzania. This backfired, leading the Tanzanian regime to encour-age formation of a united political front among Ugandan dissidents and exiles to depose Amin. In January 1979, the Tanzanian army and the Uganda National Liberation Front (UNLF) invaded Ugan-da and met with little resistance, taking the capital by April 1979 (Rake 1998; Hansen and Twaddle 1995, 139). Although the detona-tor was military defeat, the speed with which this happened, along with repeated attempted coups (Rake 1998), demonstrate how little legitimacy the regime had because of internal factors. However, the lack of international support and military defeat represented the necessary conditions for the fall of the Amin regime. On the other hand, in Museveni's slow transition to democracy, still in progress today, diplomatic pressure and conditionality are more subtle, the PID having a marginal role (Keating 2011; Hansen and Twaddle 1995, 150).

Liberia's case is particularly complex. Since 1980 there have been a succession of coups, non-democratic regimes, and civil wars. Focusing strictly on the process that led to the fall of Liberian president Charles Taylor (2003), the principal international actors were the Economic Community of West African States (ECOWAS), in which Nigeria played the key role, the US, UN, and neighbor-ing countries like Guinea and the Ivory Coast. Practically all PID instruments were present, although only some of these effectively influenced the regime's fall. In 1999, a new armed opposition formed, Liberians United for Reconciliation and Democracy (LURD), which, thanks to support from Guinea (Outram 2004, 625), opened the door to another civil war. At the beginning of 2003, another armed opposition emerged, the Movement for Democracy in Liberia (MODEL), supported by the Ivory Coast (Moran and Pitcher 2004, 506). As the civil war deepened, it attracted the attention of the international community. In September 2002, the International Contact Group on Liberia (ICGL) was created, consisting of the UN, African Union, ECOWAS, Morocco, Nigeria, Senegal, EU, France, Great Britain and the US (Outram 2004, 626). The objective was to bring the belligerent parties to the table to negotiate a cease-fire agreement. Only in April 2003 did the LURD agree to negotiate with the regime, and on June 4 peace negotiations began in Accra, Ghana (Outram 2004, 627).

It is possible that the renewal and extension of sanctions (including commercial) and the arms embargo (May 2003) contributed to this increased inclination toward negotiation. During the negotiations, the UN Special Court for Sierra Leone issued an arrest warrant for Taylor, charging him with war crimes, crimes against humanity and grave violations of international law (McGovern 2008). This was taken as a clear signal, and was followed by a coup attempt by Vice-President Blah, allegedly with US backing, foiled, however, by Taylor on June 5 (Outram 2004, 627). The LURD in the north and MODEL in the south had at this point taken control of most of the country (MacQueen 2006, 223; Moran and Pitcher 2004, 506). Also on June 5, the opposition launched an attack on the capital, Monrovia, the only area still under Taylor's control. Despite the cease-fire agreement signed a few days before, they attacked the capital again at the end of the month. The humanitarian crisis increased international pressure on Taylor. US president Bush formally asked for his ouster at the end of June; the Nigerian president offered him asylum on the condition that he remain out of Liberian politics; the UN peacekeeping mission was preceded by 1,300 Nigerian soldiers sent as ECOWAS peacekeepers (Moran and Pitcher 2004, 506; Outram 2004, 627). In exchange for some concessions, on June 6 Taylor accepted the Nigerian offer and, after the deployment of the UN mission at the beginning of August, left power in the hands of Vice President Blah (MacQueen 2006, 223; Outram 2004, 627; McGovern 2008). International pressure was without a doubt very strong, including the threat of a direct military intervention by units of the US Navy that were positioned off the coast, and deployment of the UN peacekeeping mission. However, these factors cannot be considered sufficient for Taylor's fall. We must remember that the armed opposition at that point controlled most of the country and was laying siege to Taylor's last stronghold, the capital Monrovia. In conclusion, the regime's breakdown was due to the coordinated contributions of LURD and MODEL's military victories and pressure by the international community (Moran and Pitcher 2004, 516), making the PID's role concurrent.

The Central African Republic also has experienced a succession of non-democratic regimes, coups and a transition process never fully completed. As the principal former colonial power, France has on many occasions played a fundamental role in the country's political life. Most PID instruments were employed at varying times, with varying levels of effectiveness. The regime established by Bokassa in 1966 broke down in 1979, thanks to a coup supported by the French army (MacQueen 2006, 207). The change in the French presidency in 1981 led to withdrawal of support for the Dacko regime, which was persuaded to cede power to the military, giving birth to the Kolingba regime (Englebert 1998, 288). The actions by France were very close to being the sufficient condition for the fall of these regimes, making the PID role almost the principal one. The fall of the Kolingba regime formally occurred with multi-party elections in 1993. The PID played a crucial role on more than one occasion (MacQueen 2006, 207). The legalization of political parties, for example, granted in 1991 was, even by Kolingba's own admission, the result of pressure by international donors, together with the activism of the domestic opposition, which had a role in influencing the international community's policy (Englebert 1998, 289). Elections, originally set for the end of 1992, were postponed several times. Thanks to French pressure, these finally took place in August 1993. In the same vein, it was the French threat to suspend bilateral cooperation that convinced Kolingba to withdraw the decrees by which he intended to subvert the elections that were not going his way (Englebert 1998, 290). The extreme weakness of institutions and of the socio-economic dimension, combined with strong pressure from the internal opposition, prevented the regime from holding out against international conditionality, and were necessary for the fall of the regime, which indicates a concurrent role for the PID.

In Mali the PID involved diplomatic pressure, conditionality and democratic assistance. For historical reasons, France, the ex colonial power, played an important role in the political life of the country, and specifically in the fall of the Moussa Traoré regime in 1991, which launched the transition (Diamond 2011, 124). After months of opposition demonstrations and popular protests, violently repressed, the regime's fall occurred via a coup carried out by Amadou Touré. The precarious economic conditions and negative social effects of World Bank and IMF restructuring in the 1980s had undermined the Traoré regime's popular consensus. In particular, the necessity for drastic cuts in public administration had serious repercussions for employment and swelled the opposition's ranks (Vengroff and Kone 1995, 46). International assistance took on a crucial role for the regime. At the beginning of the 1990s, it constituted 30% of GDP (Levitsky and Way 2010, 297; Vengroff and Kone 1995, 46). France provided significant funding for both the army and the salaries of civil servants (Peiffer and Englebert 2012, 363; Turrittin 1991, 99). Mitterrand's change in policy towards Africa at the 1990 Franco-African Summit in La Baule made France's aid distribution dependent on the implementation of democratic reforms, leaving the Traoré regime only the option of repression (Peiffer and Englebert 2012, 363). In addition, it seems that, in the weeks before the Traoré regime's fall, Amadou Touré made a trip to France, leading to the belief that there may have been French involvement in the coup (Turrittin 1991, 102). Finally, various international actors had provided important financing to opposition groups, which quickly transformed into political parties between the 1980s and 1990s (Vengroff and Kone 1995, 47). Without a doubt, popular mobilization, the economic crisis and the winds of change generated by the fall of the Communist regimes also had a crucial role in the Traoré regime's fall. Conditionality and pressure from donor nations, especially France, were equally vital in arriving at this result. The withdrawal of international aid at that particular historical moment denied the Traoré regime the resources it needed to remain in power. The PID's role nonetheless should be considered concurrent.

There are also many cases in which the PID played a marginal role in the fall of African regimes. Nigeria's case is particularly interesting. After having annulled the results of the 1993 elections, judged by international observers to have been free and fair, and to the general condemnation of the international community, Abacha took power (Giumelli 2011, 69). The US, Great Britain, and the EU imposed sanctions and strengthened them several times, but excluded the regime's fundamental resource, petroleum (Giumelli 2011, 70). In addition, many of the measures had no significant effect, because of defections by France, Germany, and Japan in the implementation phase (Diamond 2011, 125; King 1999; Osaghae 1998). The regime fell in 1998 when the dictator died. It is rumored that Abacha did not die of a heart attack but rather was poisoned by his military colleagues, tired of the country's international isolation (Diamond 2011, 126). In fact, right after Abacha's death, the military began the democratic transition. This unsubstantiated interpretation could upend negative opinions on the effectiveness of sanctions in the fall of the Abacha regime. In any case, there is no concrete proof, and the failure of some states to implement sanctions, sparing at least some key economic sectors, leads us to believe that the PID's impact was marginal.

Conclusions

The general objective of this chapter is to evaluate the PID's role in the crisis/breakdown/transformation of non-democratic regimes in the Third Wave. In analyzing some of the most important cases (about 30 out of more than 80) in all the geographic areas involved, considerable challenges derived from the extraordinary variation in terms of time period, geographical location, socio-economics, culture, etc. and the number of variables involved. Nonetheless, taking into account both the overall analytical framework and the idiosyncrasies of variables and cases, it is possible to suggest conclusions specific to each geographic area. These conclusions take into account the interactions between the PID and the other variables involved.

In both Southern European cases considered here, the PID played a concurrent role through the same type of action, i.e. inter-state conflict and its internal effects. The similarities were determined in part by the same international context (effects of the Cold War on the European chessboard and the 1973 oil crisis) and in part by the economic and political weakness of the Portuguese and Greek regimes, both with legitimacy crises and deeply dependent on foreign energy sources. These weaknesses, in the absence of black knights, interacted with the actions taken by the PID, which was enough to undermine the already weak legitimacy of the two regimes and contributed to their fall.

In evaluating the weight of the PID in Latin America, two factors are especially important: 1) there was an international actor (the US) with the ability and will to act as the hegemonic power in the region; 2) changes in the international context had considerable influence on the international actors involved. In Latin America, one can see all PID instruments in action and the PID playing principal, concurrent, and marginal roles. Comparative analysis of the Latin American cases shows that the PID has a greater capacity for influence in countries where:

- dimensions are small;
- the economy is weak;
- dependency on international assistance is strong;
- geostrategic importance is accentuated, e.g. in terms of bi-polar confrontation, but black knights are absent;
- there is a tradition of external interference.

Due also to these factors, the capacity of the principal external international actor, the United States, to exercise influence varies significantly. It is more pronounced, in fact, in Central America and the Caribbean, with a concentration of cases of the PID having the principal role and of more invasive actions.[17] In South America, on the other hand, there is a preponderance of cases in which the PID plays a marginal role in the fall of non-democratic regimes (Carothers 1991, 249-53; Whitehead 1996, 63).

The PID's role in Asia, on the other hand, has been extremely limited. The fall of non-democratic regimes in Asia is principally the result of internal factors and international factors not linked to explicit actions by an external actor. The only case of a principal

196 Crisis and Breakdown of Non-Democratic Regimes

role was Afghanistan, in which a military intervention was effective, given the country's severely compromised socio-economic and institutional situation, with an absence of black knights able to counterbalance PID pressures. Although in certain cases (South Korea, the Philippines) there was a certain linkage to the West, in particular to the US, the PID involved little more than diplomatic pressure, playing a marginal role in the fall of those regimes. Importantly, however, in both cases strong internal oppositions were present.

In evaluating the PID's role in East Central Europe and the Balkans the two primary factors worth mentioning are: 1) the presence of a dominant international actor (USSR) whose actions, even unintentionally (Light 1997, 134) contributed heavily to regime change; 2) the extreme importance of change in the international context. Despite the presence of military interventions (Serbia) and interstate conflicts (USSR) the most frequent PID action was diplomatic pressure, specifically withdrawal of support and stimulus to adopt a particular set of reforms, the so-called "Gorbachëv effect" (Light 1997, 133; Niklasson 1994, 203). In most cases in this region, the PID played a concurrent role.

The factors that contributed to the ability of the PID to influence outcomes in East Central Europe were:

- economic weakness due to the failure of planned economies;
- dependence on the USSR's economy, due to inclusion in the Soviet Bloc;
- dependence on the USSR for instruments of repression of last resort to contain internal opposition;
- the end of the antidemocratic black knight role played by the USSR until the end of the 1980s;
- extreme dependence on the USSR for legitimacy;
- the change in the Soviet attitude under Gorbachëv in the second half of the 1980s, which led to the explosion of the legitimacy crises that hit practically all the East European regimes.

The concurrent nature of the PID's role originated in the interactions between the pressures it exercised, the action of internal opposition, and a potent emulation effect after the explosion of the first cases.

The non-democratic African regimes fell primarily in the decade between 1980 and 1990, which demonstrated the weight of
a new Soviet foreign policy (Light 1997, 44; Herbst 1990) and the
changed policy of Western conditionality (Bratton and van de Walle
1997, 135), as well as the role of ex-colonial powers, France in particular. Thanks to the large number of cases in this region, about a
third of the total, they run the full gamut in terms of both actions
and the role of the Proactive International Dimension. In general,
the PID's influence on the fall of African regimes was amplified by:
- the presence of problems of stateness;
- civil wars;
- weak economies, especially where valuable natural resources were absent;
- a strong dependence on international assistance;
- little geostrategic importance;
- the absence or withdrawal of black knights;
- maintenance of close ties to ex-colonial powers.

   The interaction of the PID with the economic variable was decidedly strong, not only in crises that augmented dependence on
international aid, but also in states possessing rare natural resources where international actors were less willing to intervene to bring
about a regime's fall (Nigeria). We should note the important role
in many cases, e.g. South Africa, of internal oppositions (Bratton
and van de Walle 1997) that were able to connect with and benefit
from assistance from international actors .

   Both the analysis of individual cases and the conclusions regarding each geographic region demonstrate the utility and the
effectiveness of the framework adopted. Albeit in specific, case-
by-case fashion, the strength of the state and the economy, the presence or absence of black knights, linkage to the West, and the types
of sources of legitimacy in a given state can be used to explain the
role (principal, concurrent, marginal) of the PID in the transition
processes of the Third Wave.

   Another generalization emerging from this analysis is that PID
actions that do not undermine the formal sovereignty of the target
state are more likely to be ineffective if, despite even extreme weakness, e.g. economic, the target state retains one or more of the following attributes:

- a strong coercive ability;
- a very weak opposition;
- the presence of black knights;
- geostrategic importance.

Under these conditions, it is probable that necessity and emergencies (genocide, threats to the international actor's security, etc.) will lead to direct interventions. Actions that undermine the sovereignty of a target state are more likely to succeed in causing a regime to fall, implying a more important role for the PID. But does this effectiveness of the PID necessarily persist in the subsequent democratization process?

All things being equal, and regardless of the specific instruments it employs, it is likely that the PID's influence will be greater if there is a hegemonic power in the region that has the means and the political will to act, whether or not it intends to promote the fall of a regime. This observation finds confirmation, for example, in the US role in Central America and the Caribbean, the USSR's role in East Central Europe, and the generally small role of the PID in Asia.

One hesitates to identify a hegemonic international power in the case of the so-called Arab Spring, even though the countries of the region, and everyone else for that matter, has kept a constant watch for signs of Washington's intentions. Without underestimating the domestic drivers, both economic and political, of attempted change in the Middle East and North Africa, it is clear that the international dimension has been vitally important. This perhaps goes back to the 2003 invasion of Iraq, which at least may have demonstrated to the Arab publics that even the most brutally efficient dictatorships need not last forever (Husain 2013; Makiya 2013).

But what about a Proactive International Dimension, defined above as "that combination of actions or processes, produced by one or more international actors, that, intentionally or not, cause or contribute to the crisis/breakdown/transformation of a non-democratic regime"? One may quibble that the US and Europe have not always been "proactive" with respect to the Arab Spring, if we exclude the Libyan case. It may have been precisely US and/or European decisions *not* to take certain actions that established a permissive environment for, or helped stimulate, regime crisis/breakdown (Hollis 2012). Kivimäki (2013), for example, argues that the US, notably under the Obama Administration, relaxed its support for repression by Middle Eastern autocracies, opening the way to regime change. Kissinger in 2012 noted that the US administration had been "successful in avoiding placing America as an obstacle to the revolutionary transformations" in the Arab world, terming this "not a minor achievement."[18] One can argue, in fact, that decisions not to act are very much a type of action, perhaps especially for the US in the Middle East (Hamid 2015).

The Arab Spring may be a good illustration, however, of why including "intentionally or not" when defining the PID is a good idea. Unintentional consequences of international action, both positive and negative, have abounded. The success of reform in Tunisia frankly seems to owe little to international efforts, and a great deal to the Tunisians themselves. An Islamist government came to power in Egypt via elections that the Western powers precipitously demanded, only then to welcome a return to military authoritarianism. The Libyan case illustrated once again the difficulty outside powers have in foreseeing the longer-term effects of military interventions in unfamiliar territory.

Concerns about further unintended consequences, notably in Syria, have been increasingly evident. The vigorous Syria debate in the US as 2015 was ending pointed out, among other things, the difficulty of reliably connecting the Proactive International Dimension to positive, long-term transformation of autocratic regimes, and the need for better insight into such connections.

Endnotes

[1] More recent cases have been excluded (for example, Libya) as they occurred after the conventional time frame of the Third Wave of democratization (1974-2004).
[2] Southern African Development Community
[3] See Amuzergar (1997) on Iran and Schreiber (1973) on Cuba.
[4] "Notably, international donors remained important players in African transitions, though they were more effective at inducing political liberalization through quiet diplomatic persuasion than through highly publicized suspensions of aid" (Bratton and van de Walle 1997, 186).

[5] The *Polícia Internacional e de Defesa do Estado* – PIDE (International Police and State Defense), the secret political police, had an extensive network of informers and was very efficient in repressing dissent. It is no surprise then that the revolution was the work of actors inside the dominant coalition (army), and not of the opposition (Morlino 1986).

[6] See Whitehead (1996, 91-93, 104-107) and Carothers (1991, 91-94).

[7] 30,000 dead and 9 billion dollars in destruction (Orozco 2002, 68).

[8] The leaders of Communist parties were appointed and supervised by Moscow; the security forces were run by the Soviet secret services; military structures were merged in the Warsaw Pact Organization, economies were linked to and dependent on that of the USSR via the Council for Mutual Economic Assistance (Batt 1997, 155).

[9] In his speech of November 2, 1987 in commemoration of the 70th anniversary of the Bolshevik revolution, Gorbachëv emphasized the independence of all the Communist parties and their sovereignty in resolving their own internal problems. The same message was repeated in Prague (April 1987), Belgrade (March 1988) and Warsaw (July 1988) (Niklasson 1994, 202).

[10] Note the Western economic sanctions in response to implementation of martial law (Sanford 1997).

[11] Besides pressure for opening, in 1989 Gorbachëv made it understood that he did not support Jakeš (Light 1997, 141-42).

[12] The NATO bombing inflicted between $30 and $40 billion in damage to the Serbian economy (Levitsky and Way 2010, 109).

[13] With its decision not to play the black knight and to provide only meager support, Russia contributed to Milošević's choice to give in to Western pressure (Levitsky and Way 2010, 105).

[14] From 1980 to 1986 the GDP dropped 9% annually (Manning and Malbrough 2010).

[15] For example, a loan for $74 million was frozen in May 1992 (Diamond 2011, 124).

[16] The blocking of international loans denied the regime the resources needed to pay the salaries of public servants (Levitsky and Way 2010, 284).

[17] In three out of six cases (Grenada, Panama and Haiti) the US directly intervened militarily.

[18] "A New Doctrine of Intervention?" *Washington Post*, March 30, 2012, https://www.washingtonpost.com/opinions/a-new-doctrine-of-intervention/2012/03/30/gIQAcZL6lS_story.html.

Reference List

Adomeit, Hannes. 1994. "Gorbachev, German Unification, and the Collapse of Empire." *Post-Soviet Affairs* 10 (3): 197-230.

Alden, Chris. 2001. *Mozambique and the Construction of a New African State*. Basingstoke, UK: Palgrave.

Allen, Susan H. 2005. "The Determinants of Economic Sanctions Success and Failure." *International Interactions* 31 (2): 117–38.

Amuzegar, Jahangir. 1997. "Adjusting to Sanctions." *Foreign Affairs* 76 (3): 31–41.

Arthur, C. 2011. "The Dominican Republic: History." In *South America, Central America and the Caribbean 2012*, edited by Europa Publications, 401-4. London: Routledge.

Batt, Judy. 1997. "The International Dimension of Democratization in Hungary, Slovakia and the Czech Republic." In *Democracy Building? The International Dimension of Democratisation in Eastern Europe*, edited by Geoffrey Pridham, Eric Herring and George Sanford, 164-79. London: Leicester University Press.

Bratton, Michael, and Nicholas van de Walle. 1997. *Democratic Experiments in Africa*. Cambridge: Cambridge University Press.

Brooks, Risa A. 2002. "Sanctions and Regime Type: What Works and When?" *Security Studies* 11 (4): 1–50.

Burnell, Peter. 2006. "Autocratic Opening to Democracy: Why Legitimacy Matters." *Third World Quarterly* 27 (4): 545-62.

Carbone, Giovanni M. 2003. "Political Parties in a 'No-Party Democracy': Hegemony and Opposition Under 'Movement Democracy' in Uganda." *Party Politics* 9 (4): 485-501.

Carothers, Thomas. 1991. *In the Name of Democracy. U.S. Policy toward Latin America in the Reagan Years*. Berkeley, CA: University of California Press.

———. 1996. "The Resurgence of United States Political Development Assistance to Latin America in the 1980s." In *The International Dimensions of Democratization: Europe and the Americas*, edited by Laurence Whitehead, 125-45. Oxford: Oxford University Press.

———. 1999. *Aiding Democracy Abroad: The Learning Curve*. Washington, DC: Carnegie Endowment for International Peace.

Carrère d'Encausse, Hélène. 1993. *The End of the Soviet Empire: The Triumph of the Nations*. New York: Basic Books.

Castaldo, Antonino. 2014. *Dall'imposizione al successo: La democratizzazione tedesca in prospettiva comparata*. Naples: Editoriale Scientifica.

Conaghan, Catherine M., and Rosario Espinal. 1990. "Unlikely Transitions to Uncertain Regimes? Democracy Without Compromise in the Dominican Republic and Ecuador." *Journal of Latin American Studies* 22 (3): 553-74.

Connaughton, Richard. 2008. "Grenada 1983." *The RUSI Journal* 153 (1): 74-79.

Contogeorgis, Georges D. 2003. "La dictadura militar en Grecia (1967-1974) ¿Cómo enfocar el fenómeno autoritario?" *Studia Historica: Historia Contemporánea* 21: 17-43.

Dashti-Gibson, Jaleh, Patricia Davis and Benjamin Radcliff. 1997. "On the Determinants of the Success of Economic Sanctions." *American Journal of Political Science* 41 (2): 608–618.

Diamond, Larry. 2011. *Lo spirito della democrazia: La battaglia per costruire società libere nel mondo*. Milan: Edizioni Ariele. Italian translation of *The Spirit of Democracy: The Challenge of Building Free Societies Throughout the World*. New York: Henry Holt and Company, 2008.

Dix, Robert H. 1982. "The Breakdown of Authoritarian Regimes." *The Western Political Quarterly* 35 (4): 554-573.

Dobbins, James, John G. McGinn, Keith Crane, Seth G. Jones, Rollie Lal, Andrew Rathmell, Rachel Schwanger, and Anga Timilsina. 2003. *America's Role in Nation-Building: From Germany to Iraq*. Santa Monica, CA: RAND.

Drezner, Daniel W. 2011. "Sanctions Sometimes Smart: Targeted Sanctions in Theory and Practice." *International Studies Review* 13 (1): 96–108.

Elliott, Kimberly. 2002. "Analyzing the Effects of Targeted Sanctions." In *Smart Sanctions*, edited by David Cortright and George Lopez. New York: Rowman and Littlefield.

Englebert, Pierre. 1998. "The Central African Republic: Recent History." In *Africa South of the Sahara 1999*, 28th ed., 299-309. London: Europa Publications Limited.

Fish, Steven M. 1998. "Mongolia: Democracy without Prerequisites." *Journal of Democracy* 9 (3): 127-141.

Galtung, Johan. 1967. "On the Effects of International Economic Sanctions: With Examples from the Case of Rhodesia." *World Politics* 19 (3): 378–416.

Germano, Luca, Pietro Grilli di Cortona, and Orazio Lanza. 2014. *Come cadono i regimi non democratici: Primi passi verso la democrazia nei paesi della "terza ondata."* Naples: Editoriale Scientifica.

Giumelli, Francesco. 2011. *Coercing, Constraining and Signaling*. Colchester, UK: ECPR Press.

Gomes Cravinho, Joao. 1998. "Mozambique: Recent History." In *Africa South of the Sahara 1999*, 28th ed., 728-35. London: Europa Publications Limited.

Grilli di Cortona, Pietro. 2009. *Come gli stati diventano democratici*. Rome: Laterza.

_____. 2014. "Crisi e crollo dei regimi non democratici. Condizioni e tendenze nella terza ondata." In *Come cadono i regimi non democratici: Primi passi verso la democrazia nei paesi della"terza ondata,"* edited by Luca Germano, Pietro Grilli di Cortona, and Orazio Lanza, 1-36. Naples: Editoriale Scientifica.

Gros, Jean Germain. 1997. "Haiti's Flagging Transition." *Journal of Democracy* 8 (4): 94-109.

Hamid, Shadi. 2015. "Islamism, the Arab Spring, and the Failure of America's Do-Nothing Policy in the Middle East," *The Atlantic* online, October 9. http://www.theatlantic.com/international/archive/2015/10/middle-east-egypt-us-policy/409537/.

Hansen, Holger B., and Michael Twaddle. 1995. "Uganda: The Advent of No-Party Democracy." In *Democracy and Political Change in Sub-Saharan Africa*, edited by John A. Wiseman, 137-51. London: Routledge.

Hartlyn, Jonathan. 1991. "The Dominican Republic: The Legacy of Intermittent Engagement." In *Exporting Democracy: The United States and Latin America, Case Studies*, edited by Abraham F. Lowenthal, 53-92. Baltimore: Johns Hopkins University Press.

Haynes, Jeffrey. 2001. *Democracy in the Developing World: Africa, Asia, Latin America and Middle East.* Cambridge: Polity Press.

Henfrey, Colin. 1984. "Between Populism and Leninism: The Grenadian Experience." *Latin American Perspectives* 11 (3): 15-36.

Herbst, Jeffrey I. 1990. "The Fall of Afro-Marxism." *Journal of Democracy* 1 (3): 92-101.

Hollis, Rosemary. 2012. "No Friend of Democratization: Europe's Role in the Genesis of the 'Arab Spring'." *International Affairs* 88 (1): 81-94.

Horng, Der-Chin. 2003. "The Human Rights Clause in the European Union's External Trade and Development Agreements." *European Law Journal* 9 (5): 677-701.

Hufbauer, Gary C., Jeffrey J. Schott and Kimberly A. Elliott. 1990. *Economic Sanctions Reconsidered: History and Current Policy*, 2nd ed. Washington, DC: Institute for International Economics.

Huntington, Samuel P. 1995. *La terza ondata: I processi di democratizzazione del XX secolo.* Bologna: Il Mulino. Italian translation of *The Third Wave of Democratization in the Late Twentieth Century.* Norman, OK: University of Oklahoma Press, 1991.

Husain, Ed. 2013. "Did Iraq War Give Birth to the Arab Spring?" *CNN* online, March 18. http://www.cnn.com/2013/03/17/opinion/iraq-war-arab-spring-husain/

Jennings, Michael. 2010. "Uganda: Recent History." In *Africa South of the Sahara 2011*, 1287-94. London: Routledge.

Keating, Michael F. 2011. "Can Democratization Undermine Democracy?

204 Crisis and Breakdown of Non-Democratic Regimes

Economic and Political Reform in Uganda." *Democratization* 18 (2): 415-42.

Kegley Charles W., Jr., and Margaret G. Hermann. 1996. "How Democracies Use Intervention: A Neglected Dimension in Studies of the Democratic Peace." *Journal of Peace Research* 33 (3): 309-22.

Kerr, William A., and James D. Gaisford. 1994. "A Note on Increasing the Effectiveness of Sanctions." *Journal of World Trade* 28 (6): 169–76.

King, Toby. 1999. "Human Rights in European Foreign Policy: Success or Failure for Post-Modern Diplomacy?" *European Journal of International Law* 10 (2): 313–37.

Kivimäki, Timo. 2013. "The United States and the Arab Spring." *Journal of Human Security* 9 (1): 15-26.

Kolarova, Rumyana, and Dimitr Dimitrov. 1996. "The Roundtable Talks in Bulgaria." In *The Roundtable Talks and the Breakdown of Communism*, edited by John Elster, 178-212. Chicago: University of Chicago Press.

Kort, Michael. 1992. *The Rise and Fall of the Soviet Union*. New York: Franklin Watts.

Lean, Sharon F. 2007. "Democracy Assistance to Domestic Election Monitoring Organizations: Conditions for Success." *Democratization* 14 (2): 289-312.

Lektzian, David, and Mark Souva. 2007. "An Institutional Theory of Sanctions Onset and Success." *Journal of Conflict Resolution* 51 (6): 848–71.

Levitsky, Steven, and Lucan A. Way. 2010. *Competitive Authoritarianism: Hybrid Regimes After the Cold War*. New York: Cambridge University Press.

Levy, Philip I. 1999. "Sanctions on South Africa: What Did They Do?" *The American Economic Review* 89 (2): 415-20.

Light, Margot. 1997. "The USSR/CIS and Democratisation in Eastern Europe." In *Democracy Building? The International Dimension of Democratisation in Eastern Europe*, edited by Geoffrey Pridham, Eric Herring, and George Sanford, 133-153. London: Leicester University Press.

Linz, Juan J., and Alfred Stepan. 1996. *Problems of Democratic Transition and Consolidation: Southern Europe, South America and Post-Communist Europe*. Baltimore: Johns Hopkins University Press.

MacQueen, Norrie. 2006. *Peacekeeping and the International System*. London: Routledge.

Major, Solomon, and Anthony J. McGann. 2005. "Caught in the Crossfire: 'Innocent Bystanders' as Optimal Targets of Economic Sanctions." *Journal of Conflict Resolution* 49 (3): 337–59.

Makiya, Kanan. 2013. "The Arab Spring Started in Iraq." *New York Times*, April 6. http://www.nytimes.com/2013/04/07/opinion/sunday/the-arab-spring-started-in-iraq.html?_r=0.

Manning, Carrie, and Monica Malbrough. 2010. "Bilateral Donors and Aid Conditionality in Post-Conflict Peace-Building: The Case of Mozambique." *Journal of Modern African Studies* 48 (1): 143-69.

McGovern, Mike. 2008. "Liberia: The Risks of Rebuilding a Shadow State." In *Building States to Build Peace*, edited by Charles. T. Call (with Vanessa Wyeth), 335-62. Boulder, CO: Lynne Rienner.

Mobekk, Eirin. 2001. "Enforcement of Democracy in Haiti." *Democratization* 8 (3): 173-88.

Moran, Mary H., and Mary A. Pitcher. 2004. "The 'Basket Case' and the 'Poster Child': Explaining the End of Civil Conflicts in Liberia and Mozambique." *Third World Quarterly* 25 (3): 501-19.

Morlino, Leonardo. 1986. "Dall'autoritarismo alla democrazia: Spagna, Portogallo e Grecia." In *La storia: I grandi problemi dal Medioevo all'età contemporanea: Dal primo al secondo dopoguerra*, vol. 4, edited by Nicola Tranfaglia and Massimo Firpo, 761-88. Milan: Garzanti.

Morlino, Leonardo, and Amichai Magen. 2008. "Methods of Influence, Layers of Impact, Cycles of Change: A Framework for Analysis." In *International Actors, Democratization and the Rule of Law: Anchoring Democracy*, edited by Amichai Magen and Leonardo Morlino, 26-52. London: Routledge.

Muller, Edward N. 1985. "Dependent Economic Development, Aid Dependence on the United States, and Democratic Breakdown in the Third World." *International Studies Quarterly* 29 (4): 445–69.

Murphy, Sean D. 1999. "Democratic Legitimacy and the Recognition of States and Governments." *International and Comparative Law Quarterly* 48 (3): 545-81.

Niklasson, Tomas. 1994. "The Soviet Union and Eastern Europe, 1988-9: Interactions Between Domestic Change and Foreign Policy." In *Democratization in Eastern Europe: Domestic and International Perspectives*, edited by Geoffrey Pridham and Tatu Vanhanen, 191-219. London: Routledge.

Omer-Cooper, J.D. 1998. "South Africa: History." In *Africa South of the Sahara 1999*, 974-84. London: Europa Publications Limited.

Orozco, Manuel. 2002. *International Norms and Mobilization of Democracy: Nicaragua in the World*. Aldershot, Hants., England: Ashgate.

Osaghae, Eghosa E. 1998. *Crippled Giant: Nigeria Since Independence*. Bloomington, IN: Indiana University Press.

Outram, Quentin. 2004. "Liberia: Recent History." In *Africa South of the Sahara 2005*, 34th ed., 619-29. London: Europa Publications.

Panebianco, Angelo. 1997. *Guerrieri democratici: La democrazia e la politica di potenza*. Bologna: Il Mulino.

Pei, Min X. 1998. "The Fall and Rise of Democracy in East Asia." In *Democ-*

racy in East Asia, edited by Larry Diamond and Marc Plattner, 57-78. Baltimore: Johns Hopkins University Press.

Peiffer, Caryn, and Pierre Englebert. 2012. "Extraversion, Vulnerability to Donors, and Political Liberalization in Africa." *African Affairs* 111 (444): 355–78.

Piccone, Theodore J. 2004. "International Mechanisms to Protect Democracy." In *Protecting Democracy: International Responses*, edited by Morton H. Halperin and Mirna Galic, 101-126. Lanham, MD: Lexington Books.

Pitcher, Mary A. 2002. *Transforming Mozambique: The Politics of Privatization, 1975–2000*. New York: Cambridge University Press.

Premdas, Ralph, ed. 1993. *The Enigma of Ethnicity: An Analysis of Race and Ethnicity in the Caribbean and the World*. Trinidad: University of the West Indies Press.

Pridham, Geoffrey. 1991. "International Influences and Democratic Transition: Problems of Theories and Practices in Linkage Politics." In *Encouraging Democracy: The International Context of Regime Transition in Southern Europe*, edited by Geoffrey Pridham, 1-28. Leicester: Leicester University Press.

_____. 1995. "The International Context in Democratic Consolidation: Southern Europe in Comparative Perspective." In *The Politics of Democratic Consolidation: Southern Europe in Comparative Perspective*, edited by Richard Gunther, P. Nikiforos Diamandouros and Hans-Jürgen Puhle, 166-203. Baltimore: Johns Hopkins University Press.

_____. 2000. *The Dynamics of Democratization. A Comparative Approach*. London: Continuum.

Prince, R. 1996. "Dominican Republic: History." In *South America, Central America and the Caribbean 1997*, 275-76. London: Europa Publications Limited.

Rake, Alan. 1998. "Uganda: Recent History." In *Africa South of the Sahara 1999*, 1110-16. London: Europa Publications Limited.

Reuveny, Rafael and Aseem Prakash. 1999. "The Afghanistan War and the Breakdown of the Soviet Union." *Review of International Studies* 25 (4): 693-708.

Roberts, Kenneth M. 1990. "Bullying and Bargaining: The United States, Nicaragua, and Conflict Resolution in Central America." *International Security* 15 (2): 67-102.

Sanchez, Peter M. 2003. "Bringing the International Back In: US Hegemonic Maintenance and Latin America's Democratic Breakdown in the 1960s and 1970s." *International Politics* 40: 223-47.

Sanford, George. 1997. "Communism's Weakest Link – Democratic Capitalism's Greatest Challenge: Poland." In *Democracy Building? The In-*

ternational Dimension of Democratisation in Eastern Europe, edited by Geoffrey Pridham, Eric Herring and George Sanford, 170-96. London: Leicester University Press.

Saxer, Carl J. 2002. *From Transition to Power Alternation: Democracy in South Korea, 1987-1997*. New York: Routledge.

Schmitter, Philippe C. 1986. "An Introduction to Southern European Transitions from Authoritarian Rule: Italy, Greece, Portugal, Spain, and Turkey." In *Transitions from Authoritarian Rule: Southern Europe*, edited by Guillermo O'Donnell, Philippe C. Schmitter, and Laurence Whitehead, 3-10. Baltimore: Johns Hopkins University Press.

_____. 1996. "The Influence of the International Context Upon the Choice of National Institutions and Policies in Neo-Democracies." In *The International Dimensions of Democratization: Europe and the Americas*, edited by Laurence Whitehead, 26-54. Oxford: Oxford University Press.

Schreiber, Anna P. 1973. "Economic Coercion as an Instrument of Foreign Policy: US Economic Measures Against Cuba and the Dominican Republic." *World Politics* 25 (3): 387–413.

Sikkink, K. 1996. "The Effectiveness of US Human Rights Policy, 1973-1980." In *The International Dimensions of Democratization: Europe and the Americas*, edited by Laurence Whitehead, 93-124. Oxford: Oxford University Press.

Smith, Alastair. 1995. "The Success and Use of Economic Sanctions." *International Interactions* 21 (3): 229-45.

Smith, Tony. 1994. *America's Mission: The United States and the Worldwide Struggle for Democracy in the Twentieth Century*. Princeton, NJ: Princeton University Press.

Suhrke, A. 2008. "Democratizing a Dependent State: The Case of Afghanistan." *Democratization* 15 (3): 630-48.

Tillema, Herbert K. 1994. "Cold War Alliance and Overt Military Intervention, 1945-1991." *International Interactions* 20 (3): 249-78.

Turrittin, Jane. 1991. "Mali: People Topple Traoré." *Review of African Political Economy* 18 (52): 97-103.

Vengroff, Richard, and Moctar Kone. 1995. "Mali: Democracy and Political Change." In *Democracy and Political Change in Sub-Saharan Africa*, edited by John A. Wiseman, 45-70. London: Routledge.

Venter, Denis. 1995. "Malawi: the Transition to Multi-Party Politics." In *Democracy and Political Change in Sub-Saharan Africa*, edited by John A. Wiseman, 152-92. London: Routledge.

Von Einsiedel, Sebastian, and David M. Malone. 2006. "Peace and Democracy for Haiti: A UN Mission Impossible?" *International Relations* 20: 153-74.

Von Hippel K. 2000. "Democracy by Force: A Renewed Commitment to Nation Building." *The Washington Quarterly* 23 (1): 95-112.

Whitehead, Laurence, ed. 1996. *The International Dimensions of Democratization: Europe and the Americas.* Oxford: Oxford University Press.

Williams, Gary. 1997. "Prelude to an Intervention: Grenada 1983." *Journal of Latin American Studies* 29 (1): 131-69.

Wood, Elisabeth J. 2001. "An Insurgent Path to Democracy: Popular Mobilization, Economic Interests, and Regime Transition in South Africa and El Salvador." *Comparative Political Studies* 34 (8): 862-88.

An Alternative Geopolitics
of Democratization

Eric R. Terzuolo

Twenty-five years after the fall of the Berlin Wall, advocates and scholars of democratization were asking whether democratic change on a par with the remarkable "Third Wave" ever would return, and, if not, what would replace it. A roughly equal mix of new democratizations and of reversals (Plattner 2014)? To take only a few examples, events in Ukraine recalled the political challenges for countries with large minority populations, especially those linked to a powerful neighboring state. Hungary, long a democratization success story, was sliding ever further into "illiberal democracy." Aggression by the Islamic State spotlighted the weakness of an elected Iraqi government rigidly controlled by the Shiite majority. The "Arab Spring" gave way, for the most part, to renewed authoritarianism or factional warfare, although democracy in Tunisia was surprisingly sturdy, and Morocco continued a low-key yet significant internal reform process (Bernard 2013). Indonesia, the world's largest Muslim-majority country, completed another democratic hand-over of authority, voting for good governance, though not all signs were positive (Freedom House 2015). In other words, a complex picture.

The scholarly literature on democratization, rooted in the discipline of political science, has focused on the search for valid generalizations. But one also must consider the specificities of individual national cases, or even sub-national cases, e.g. Iraqi Kurdistan. "Outliers," cases that contradict the predictions of theory or simply buck trends at the global, regional, sub-regional, or "neighborhood" levels, are numerous.

Some geographical thinking may be useful. "All existing democracies are territorially based," after all (Whitehead 1999, 75). Despite the claims of numerous intellectuals that globalization has rendered the nation state irrelevant (Andrei 2009), democracy is among the attributes that so far have been largely confined to the nation state. The distribution of democratization in both space and time seems anything but accidental. Location is significant, though it needs to be understood on a number of different geographical scales. The characteristics of populations, again mapped on a range of geographical scales, also matter, as do the economic and natural resources those populations may control. Through such factors, geography shapes the specific interests and objectives of political actors, whether promoters or opponents of democracy. In this sense, there exists a "geopolitics of democratization" which goes deeper than just "great power politics," for which "geopolitics" often serves, imprecisely, as a synonym.[1] But it is best to think in terms of a geopolitical "approach" to democratization, rather than a full-fledged geopolitical "theory" thereof.

Geography, Geopolitics, and Democratization

Geographical and geopolitical dimensions occasionally figure in reflections on democratization. With the 25th anniversary of the fall of the Berlin Wall approaching, for example, the *Washington Post* picked up on a research study demonstrating that the degree and type of economic and political transformation in the post-Communist countries correlated strongly with geography, specifically with the political and economic characteristics of a given country's closest non-Soviet-Bloc neighbor as of 1990 (Treisman 2014). Attention to the geography/democracy nexus, however, has varied from one academic discipline to another.

Comparative politics specialists initially relied on internal factors to explain democratization, but then made a "spatial turn," explaining the success or failure of democratic transitions based on a country's proximity to or distance from Western Europe. While the just-mentioned study continues in this vein, other comparativists swung back to challenge the relevance of geography, arguing that it could be a proxy for deeper historical differences among countries, or for policy choices made in Western capitals (Kopstein 2009).

Some lament the "ghostly presence of democracy" as a field of study and research in academic geography and its sub-disciplines (Barnett and Low 2004, 1), noting in particular the "relative silence on democracy in human geography" (Stokke 2009, 739), a field purportedly gripped by a romantic and ideologically rooted fascination with social protest against democracy as it actually exists (Barnett and Low 2004; Staeheli 2010). *Political* geographers, in turn, are charged with abandoning state-centered approaches and consequently neglecting democracy, which primarily plays out in the state (Barnett and Low 2004).

Anyone who proposes a "geopolitics of democratization" focused on the *nexus* between geography and politics should bear in mind that, in the English-speaking world at least, geopolitics is poorly developed, and has been an "unfashionable brand of political science " (Whitehead 2002, 258). The democratization literature tends to employ "geopolitics" as a synonym for "great power politics" or *Realpolitik*. Academic critics of democratization as it actually has occurred are quite ready to treat democratization and democracy promotion as a "hegemonic geopolitical tool" of the Western powers, intent on promoting liberal economics, imposing their views of gender roles on countries undergoing political transition (Horn 2010), or exercising out and out imperialism (Slater 2008). There is, of course, nothing scandalous in suggesting that major international actors, whether themselves democratic or undemocratic, act on the basis of national interests shaped in part by geographical factors (Cavatorta 2001). But the suggestion that the established democracies are totally cynical in the promotion of democracy also seems difficult to swallow.

Perhaps the clearest statements on the geography/democracy nexus are still those of Laurence Whitehead (1999, 75), who underlines how "geopolitical constraints and crosscurrents can powerfully affect: 1) the interstate distribution of democracy; 2) the scope of democracy *within* the states affected; and 3) the viability of the resulting democratic regimes." Though he too uses "geopolitics" primarily as a synonym for great power politics, Whitehead is sensitive to the complex and multiple roles of geographical factors in politics. Strictly geographical characteristics, e.g. physical location or island status, can interact with internal political dynamics and with external political pressures in a variety of ways, and with a variety of outcomes. Democracy requires inter alia a "restatement of the territorial scope and limits of the polity to be democratized [which] may not always reaffirm inherited boundaries." Whitehead underlines in fact how national borders may not coincide with the territorial distribution of peoples. He cites Albania and Croatia, as cases in which democratization only was possible if states left significant portions of their core national group outside their boundaries.

Defining a "geopolitics of democratization" is not simple. O'Loughlin et al. (1998) employ the term, but do not offer a clear definition of what constitutes "geopolitics," other than perhaps democracy promotion efforts by some states. Manlio Graziano (2012) in a piece on the "geopolitics of democracy" for *Limes*, the Italian journal of geopolitics, discusses a series of potentially relevant factors, from regional contexts to income levels to connections between capitalism and democracy. But in the end he too does not deliver a clear definition.

In the search for a better definition, one might turn to Yves Lacoste, the innovative and controversial French geographer who is a pillar of modern geopolitical thought (Claval 2000; Hepple 2000). Geopolitical analysis, in Lacoste's view, should focus on "rivalries for power on a given territory," and he takes a broadly inclusive view of relevant actors, contextual factors, instruments of power, and territories on which those rivalries take place (Castets 2014). A genuinely geopolitical approach, for Lacoste, cannot be strictly "geographical" or "political," and cannot treat these as alternative explanations. The focus must be on how geographical factors, including economic and cultural ones, shape the political process, helping define competing interests and creating or constraining political options.

By extension, this does not allow for a neat separation between internal and external factors in democratic transitions. Thus a geopolitical approach is broadly consistent with current efforts in democratization studies to focus on "the interaction between domestic actors and international actors in bringing about transitional opportunities" (Stoner, Diamond, Girod, and McFaul 2013, 4) or in conditioning the outcomes of democratization processes (Levitsky and Way 2010). Geopolitical analysis can complement this approach by adding a focus on how *context* can condition external/ internal interactions.

In addition to spatial dimensions, *time* is also a relevant dimension in geopolitical analysis, which treats current problems as rooted in histories that must be understood. As Lacoste puts it: "One cannot do geopolitics without taking into account the history of the territory in question, the events that shaped it" (Castets 2014). A current high-profile example is Hungary, where the self-described illiberal democrat Orbán has played to notions of Hungarian exceptionalism and enduring anger over the loss of two thirds or more of "historic" Hungarian lands in the post-Word War I settlement. But territories have multiple *histories*, with multiple authors, not just *a* history. The multiplicity of narratives is evident as well for pre-existing patterns of modernization or the formative experience of nation building, which have been cited to account for variation in democratization (Kopstein 2009). A historical factor that receives considerable attention in the democratization literature is an area's history of colonization. Not all agree, however, that colonialism has a systemic effect, and some suggest that its impact "may have been exaggerated" (Teorell 2010, 7). In sum, the historical dimension is complex.

All this is not to argue for geographical or geopolitical determinism. As with the influence of external *actors* (Tolstrup 2010), the influence of external conditioning factors is filtered through the thought and action of local democratizers, or *gatekeeper elites*, as Tolstrup terms them. The same can well be said for *internal* conditioning factors. The fundamental untidiness of geopolitics makes it important to look at how specific people assess and act upon the nexus of geographical and political factors at a given time, i.e. human agency. Three broad categories of geopolitical factors are worth examining: 1) territory and location; 2) identity and territorial distribution of populations; 3) resources, man-made or natural, and their distribution. An important recent study implicitly recognized the importance of such factors when it pointed out the need to control for "geographic location, gross domestic product [GDP] per capita, [and] degree of ethnic homogeneity" (Stoner et al. 2013, 6) when comparing specific national cases of democratization.

Territory and Location

The concepts of "territory" and "location" sound simple, but in fact are not. Lacoste's core idea of "geographical reasoning" stresses the need to consider situations by looking at multiple geographical scales of analysis, which can bring to light different intersections between competing groups. What seems a relatively simple situation when viewed on a large-scale map, for example, may prove to be a great deal more complex as one moves down to smaller scale maps and the importance of entities with little weight in the "big picture" starts coming to light.

The maps relevant to geopolitical analysis not only can include different scales, but also can map different characteristics. Maps indicating national or territorial borders are the ones we know best, but physical geography, for example, also can have strong implications for politics. The first group of democracies to emerge "often possessed geostrategic positional advantages (maritime insulation in the cases of Britain and the United States, mountains in the case of Switzerland) that made them less vulnerable to external attack"* (Rasler and Thompson 2005, 222). Vulnerable states were more likely to centralize power and control of resources. Distributions of population groups and resources also are worth mapping for geopolitical analysis.

A list of relevant geographical scales could include: global; continental; sub-continental; groups of bordering states ("neighborhoods"); dyads of two bordering states; individual states within their recognized borders; sub-national administrative districts; areas distinguished by predominance of certain racial/ethnic/cultural/religious groups; degree and type of industrialization or resource extraction; degree of urbanization.

Global-level analysis can be problematic. Geopolitics is innately skeptical of claims that globalization is erasing regional, national, and territorial differences, and has a healthy respect for concrete power. Consequently, the spectacularly diverse and divided Group of 77, for all its ambitious claims, does not pass muster as a geopolitically relevant unit at the global level. The "West," on the other hand, still can demonstrate a sense of common interest and the ability to marshal resources to preserve that interest.

The highest-level geographical units that seem relevant to a geopolitics of democratization are the continents, more commonly, though not always consistently, referred to in the literature as "regions."[2] The image of democratization leapfrogging "through southern Europe and Latin America, then to Eastern Europe and Asia, and finally to Africa" (Kauffman 2010, 363) is attractive, but certainly reductive. Mainwaring and Pérez-Liñán (2007) in fact lament a shortage of attention to the regions in the field of comparative politics, and argue forcefully for regional specificities and for the role of regional dynamics in shaping democracy. Møller and Skaaning (2013) in turn underline regional differences in prospects for a "reverse wave," i.e. a retreat from democratization. Regions in fact may be difficult to compare when it comes to democratization. Some scholars try to square the circle, arguing that regions are comparable, while also stressing "the specific historical, cultural, and institutional matrix of each region" (van Beek 2005, 22).

Continents or regions are also not monoliths. Groupings of less than continental or regional scale require attention. The area once referred to as the "Indian subcontinent," which includes the world's most populous democracy and presents enormous cultural and other differences from East Asia, might best be examined primarily at the sub-continental rather than at the Asian or Asian-Pacific level. North Africa routinely is examined as distinct from Sub-Saharan Africa, but is distinct also from the Middle East, with which it often is grouped. Eurasia makes sense as a world region for the study of democratization, but contains sub-regions, such as the Caucasus and Central Asia, that are both strongly characterized and internally diverse when examined closely. Europe too can be usefully divided into sub-regions, given the different histories of democratization in Western, Southern, East Central, and Southeastern Europe. One also must be open to reflection on groupings of countries that historically have not been assigned a shared identity, but stand out together as outliers within a broader regional or continental context. On the 2015 Freedom House map of the world, for example, Bolivia (often classified as Andean) and Paraguay (part of Latin America's Southern Cone) form a large partly free area surrounded by free countries. Another striking outlier is Mongolia, a free country in largely unfree Eurasia, surrounded by China and Russia, and almost bordering on Kazakhstan.

The distinction between regional and sub-regional dimensions is relevant when thinking about the role of what are usually termed "regional organizations." The democratizing role of bodies such as the African Union, Council of Europe, European Union, and Organization of American States has received considerable scholarly attention, though evidence of such a role is not universally strong (Teorell 2010, 7). The EU, notably, may constitute a geographical scale unto itself when it comes to geopolitical analysis. Its membership does not include all states in what is normally considered geographical Europe, and its center of gravity remains distinctly in Western Europe. It might be seen as a collection of sub-regions (some central, some peripheral), heavily engaged at the regional level.

Sub-regions, even those long and widely recognized as such, may or may not stand out dramatically within their regions. The Caucasus and Central Asia, for example, with their overall poor democratic performance, are in line with the overall dismal situation in Eurasia, which Freedom House (2015, 11) rated as the second worst world region, after the Middle East. On the other hand, in Sub-Saharan Africa, with its large number of unfree countries, Southern Africa stands out as free.

The sub-regions, in turn, can present significant differences from one country to another. Unlike the other Central Asian countries, all unfree according to Freedom House (2015), Kyrgyzstan still was classified as partly free, despite a deteriorating situation, while Turkmenistan and Uzbekistan made it onto the "Worst of the Worst" list. Unlike partly free Georgia and Armenia (the latter scoring notably less well than the former), Azerbaijan was deemed unfree, with a deteriorating situation, and earned special mention in the Freedom House report as an overlooked autocracy (2015, 7). In West Africa, where partly free countries prevail, Benin, Ghana, and Senegal stand out as free. Indeed, the first two confounded the expectations of Levitsky and Way (2010) that they would lapse into "unstable authoritarianism," instead going further toward democracy (Slater 2011).[3] In North Africa, a sub-region long considered to have important common elements, the extent of democratization varies dramatically, with free Tunisia and partly free Morocco sharing the sub-region with unfree Algeria and Libya, with unfree Mauritania and Egypt as bookends.

Negative sub-regional outliers could include Venezuela. Its partially free Freedom House rating marks it off from its free neighbors (Brazil and Guyana), and it compares unfavorably with Colombia, the other large country of Caribbean South America, although Colombia too is considered only partially free. Unfree Zimbabwe is also an outlier, sandwiched between the free countries of Southern Africa and the mostly partially free countries to the northeast

Such diversity within sub-regions argues for caution in assessing diffusion effects, widely considered to be an important determinant of democratization. Li and Reuveny (2003) showed democratic diffusion to have a positive effect. Teorell, in partnership with Hadenius (2007) and individually in 2010, confirmed this, but highlighted the need for further case studies to shed light on the mechanism of democratic diffusion. Proximity in and of itself clearly does not guarantee democratic diffusion, or the preservation of democracy once established. Hungary, for example, has been losing ground in the Freedom House ratings due to the action of the Orbán government, and seems not to benefit from being surrounded by neighbors with "perfect" democracy scores.

In addition, it is important to remember that borders within a sub-region can be secure or insecure, and relationships between neighboring states can range from friendly to conflictual. Sometimes, in fact, a pair of neighboring states, a "dyad," requires particular focus. Such links can have either positive or negative effects on a process like democratization. A strategic rivalry with another state can "distort democratization processes" (Rasler and Thompson 2005, 223), as the case of Croatia and its rivalry with Serbia arguably demonstrated for some time. It may indeed be that "the most conflict-prone dyads are those that pair a democracy with an autocracy" (Rasler and Thompson 2005, 224). But nationalist rivalry does not require stark differences in political systems. The Turkish military was still keeping a watchful eye on domestic politics when Greek-Turkish rivalry contributed to the 1974 overthrow of the military dictatorship in Greece, when the Colonels proved unable to counter the Turkish incursion into northern Cyprus. At the other end of Southern Europe, the 1974 overthrow of the dictatorship in Portugal helped create the context in which Spain began moving toward democracy following Franco's death the following year. For a less encouraging example, one might look to Belarus, where Lukashenko's authoritarianism has benefited greatly from Russian support.

As already noted, the crucial container of democracy has been and remains the individual state. But we must be wary of taking national borders as givens, when in fact they often are contested. Many of the positive democracy outliers do have some type of un-resolved territorial issue with neighboring states, although Tunisia, the success story of the Arab Spring, does not have any.[4] Govern-ing regimes in negative democracy outliers seem inclined to ex-ploit territorial disputes for purposes of internal political mobiliza-tion. For the Castro regime in Cuba, the only unfree country in the Western Hemisphere according to Freedom House, the extraterri-torial status of Guantanamo Bay, dating back to the aftermath of the 1898 Spanish-American War, remains a useful tool for focusing animus against the United States. Venezuela has a large number of disputed territorial claims, and its border with US-backed Colom-bia became a politically convenient flashpoint during the Chavez years. In Azerbaijan, the perception that Armenia unjustly seized the Nagorno-Karabakh region has been an important tool "for the ruling elite to use in maintaining its power" (Bunce and Wolchik 2013, 405). In fact, when and how political regimes decide to ex-ploit territorial disputes for internal political purposes, and to what extent territorial disputes become excuses for not addressing inter-nal democratic shortfalls, merits attention.

The importance of the national scale of analysis is so self-ev-ident that it is not easy to find studies of democracy and democ-ratization on smaller geographical scales. Still, "in recent years, there has been a growing interest in the spatially uneven nature of democracy at the subnational level" (Behrend, 2011, 150). In its 2015 report, for example, Freedom House assessed the state of de-mocracy in 13 "Disputed Territories." Only Northern Cyprus, con-tested by Turkey and Cyprus, was classified as free, and most of the rest were unfree. Other territories contested between dyads of states included Abkhazia and South Ossetia (Georgia/Russia), the Crimea (Ukraine/Russia), Indian and Pakistani Kashmir, Nagorno-Karabakh (Azerbaijan/Armenia), and Transnistria (Moldova/Rus-sia). Other cases involved disputes between states and movements or entities not universally recognized as states: the Gaza Strip and the West Bank, Somaliland, Tibet, and the Western Sahara. In truth, this is only a very partial listing of territories that are to some degree contested,[5] and the political fallout of such disputes for the contending parties and their degree of democratic development merits attention.

Even in less dramatic situations, degrees and rates of democratization can vary from one sub-national region to another. Russia provided an example of this (Lankina and Getachew 2006), with responses to efforts by the central government to reassert authority in the regions also varying (Lankina 2009). And long ago Yves Lacoste, engendering no small wave of outrage, asserted that regions, even in highly centralized France, could have their own individual geopolitics.[6] Of more current concern, a recent study points out that Kurdistan Regional Government elections "have very little in common with elections in the rest of Iraq" (Aziz 2014, 67). A better understanding of how democracy has developed in Iraqi Kurdistan might help explain its relatively sturdy response to Islamic State aggression, as compared to the conflicted and initially totally inefficient response of the central Iraqi state.

Identity and Territorial Distribution of Populations

Whatever geographical scale we have in mind, borders as such matter less than the fact that they create bounded *populations*. The differing characteristics and distributions of population groups are politically important, and often contribute to tensions and conflicts. The more sanguine among us see a dynamic process of inventing new identity narratives, facilitating a "democratic culture of inclusion" (van Beek 2005, 33). But redefinition of identity in fact is often about exclusion, e.g. wiping away vestiges of multiethnic identity in the successor states of Yugoslavia.

Ethnolinguistic Fractionalization

Our collective memory is full of dramatic images of interethnic violence. From a democratization perspective, ethnic homogeneity may look like a good thing, which "can no doubt alter the probability of regime type change, or at least the probability that changes persist" (Rasler and Thompson 2005, 59). The impact of ethnolinguistic fractionalization on democratization, however, is open to debate, as reflected in the chapter by Grilli di Cortona and Di Sotto in this collection. In a 1999 study, Barro found "only a marginally significant effect" (cited in Teorell and Hadenius 2007, 75). And Teorell (2010, 9) later would state quite forcefully: "Heterogeneous populations did not hurt democracy during the Third Wave [of democratization]."

But the literature offers other perspectives as well. There is evidence that population diversity can strain political systems. Horowitz (2014, 5) argues that: "In societies severely divided by ethnicity, race, religion, language or any other form of ascriptive affiliation, ethnic divisions make democracy difficult, because they tend to produce ethnic parties and ethnic voting." Ethnic majorities generally dominate minority groups, although in an undemocratic society like Syria's a minority can dominate the majority, with "explosive consequences" (18n). Peaceful agreement on mechanisms to ameliorate such situations is rare, and the problem is widespread. Examining 123 countries in Asia, Africa, the Middle East, Eastern Europe, the former Soviet Union and the Caribbean between 1980 and 2010, Horowitz found that 78 of them had experienced one or more cases of serious ethnic conflict, and that only 20 of those countries had reached agreements on interethnic power sharing at the central government level. Other studies as well confirm that the presence of ethnic minorities is a hindrance to democratic transitions. In new democracies, for example, economic cleavages compete with ethnicity as the conditioning political factor, but ethnicity prevails where income inequality is low (Epstein, Levantoğlu, and O'Halloran 2012).

Might degrees of ethnolinguistic fractionalization help account for positive and/or negative democracy outliers in regions or subregions? Desmet, Ortuño-Ortín, and Wacziarg (2009) provide a useful scale of ethnolinguistic fractionalization by country, and their analysis suggests that deep, historic cleavages between linguistic families[7] are better predictors of civil conflict and the extent of redistribution than are more recent and more superficial ethnolinguistic divisions.

Comparing language family (level one) fractionalization among democracy outliers does not lead, however, to an entirely clear picture. Bolivia, already mentioned as a negative democracy outlier in South America, has a high degree of level one fractionalization (0.647 out of 1.00). In the Caucasus, things are more complicated. Unfree Azerbaijan has a far from negligible score (0.346), but partially free Georgia actually has a somewhat higher index of fractionalization (0.435). In North Africa, free Tunisia's index is very low (0.005), as is partially free Morocco's (0.008), but this does not mark them off dramatically from unfree Algeria (0.009) or Libya (0.015).

Interestingly, however, Tunisia's fractionalization score remains very low even when looking at more recent and arguably superficial linguistic divisions, plateauing at 0.012 at level 6 in the hierarchy Desmet, Ortuño-Ortín, and Wacziarg employ. The other North African countries all have higher scores. Algeria plateaus at level 6 at 0.313, roughly similar to Libya (0.362), with Morocco at 0.466. In West Africa, the positive outliers all have level one fractionalization scores below 0.02: Benin 0.014, Ghana 0.000, and Senegal 0.017. Compared to some other West African countries, notably Nigeria (0.434), and perhaps Cameroon (0.211) and Gabon (0.115), these scores look low, but low level one scores are fairly common in West Africa. In sum, ethnolinguistic fractionalization seems to offer no clear and automatic explanation for varying levels of democracy from one country to another. But it does seem worth considering in a geopolitical analysis of democracy's trajectory in any given country.

It is important to bear in mind also that ethnolinguistic groups can themselves be fractionalized in various ways. Among many ethnolinguistic groups, tribal or clan affiliations can easily prevail over loyalties to the broader group. This can have strongly anti-democratic implications, e.g. in Azerbaijan, where the Aliyev regime has used clan ties, among other instruments, to "co-opt potential opposition" (Bunce and Wolchik 2013, 421).

Religious Fractionalization

Religion is, of course, a highly significant identity component, which can either closely overlay ethnicity or cut across ethnic lines. Shiite Arabs in Iraq, for example, may feel more drawn to their co-religionaries in Iran than to Sunni Arabs in Iraq, despite an ample history of Arab-Persian antagonism. And 2014 events in Iraq also brought to light the remarkable religious diversity among the Kurds. Teorell and Hadenius (2007, 81) found that a country's degree of "religious fractionalization has a clearly significant and negative impact" on democratization. They found that the proportion of Muslims in a country's population was among the most important determinants of democratization, and that the relationship was negative. However, while religious fractionalization broadly speaking had a negative impact on democratization, adherence to differing forms of Christianity had no significant impacts. (Admittedly, those who recall the role of the Serbian Orthodox Church in supporting the nationalist program of Slobodan Milošević may have some doubts about this.)

Teorell (2010, 8) later offered a more nuanced view, arguing that the Muslim gap in democracy was in fact largely an Arab gap. Democratic sentiments of Muslims are no weaker than those expressed by other religious groups, hence "the cultural interpretation of the Muslim gap rests on shaky micro-foundations." Nasr (2005) had underlined an impressive emergence, beginning in 1990, of what he termed "Muslim Democracy," though admitting that the rise of Islamic-oriented democratic parties had taken place in large Muslim-majority countries—Bangladesh, Indonesia, Malaysia, Pakistan, and Turkey—that were *not* part of the Arab world.[8] Elshtain (2009) later eloquently laid out three credible and coexisting views on the relationship between Islam and democracy: the optimists, the hopeful, and the dubious or outright despairing.

Looking at individual national cases of particular interest, it is hard to see a clear and simple pattern in the relationship between democracy and religion, or, perhaps more precisely, the religious composition of national populations. The conduct of the Muslim Brotherhood as the undisputed, for a time, governing party in Egypt, suggests that some of the literature may have been much too sanguine (Wittes 2008; Kurzman and Naqvi 2010). But one can draw encouraging lessons from the conduct of Ennahda in Tunisia. And while Freedom House (2015) continued to rate Indonesia as only partly free, it also recognized the 2014 elections in the world's largest Muslim-majority country as largely open and fair, providing the elected leader with a strong mandate. Indonesia is widely considered a case of successful democratic transition (Aspinall and Mietzner 2013). And while, in the Caucasus, majority Muslim Azerbaijan is a negative democracy outlier, numerous other factors, notably an economy dependent on energy exports, may be more significant.

The notable religious homogeneity of Latin America obviously has not prevented significant divergences in the history and practice of democracy at the national level, although the Americas now include only one country that Freedom House rates as not free (Cuba), which is perhaps especially striking for a region that is still largely part of the developing world. The three positive democratic outliers in West Africa, in turn, do not present a consistent pattern when it comes to religious composition and degree of diversity. Benin is highly diverse, scoring a 7.2 out of 10 on the Pew Research Center's Religious Diversity Index.[9] Ghana (4.7) is moderately diverse, while Senegal (0.8) is on the low end. In addition, while both Benin and Ghana have Christian majorities, Senegal's population is overwhelmingly Muslim.

This varied range of associations between democracy and religious composition once again argues for caution in making generalizations. There is certainly ample reason to believe that religion, and especially the presence of Islam, can be an important factor in political development, but one should evaluate it on a case-by-case basis.

Culture (?)

Ethnicity and religion are part of what we loosely term "culture," a concept that sometime finds its way into discussions of democracy, and whether democracy has different forms and meanings to people in different world regions. Some views are quite sanguine. Introducing a four-continent comparative study of democratizations, for example, van Beek (2005, 24) refers to "geocultural regions" and "geocultural boundaries." The basic premise of the authors is that "people with different historical and cultural backgrounds are likely to create different types of democracy for themselves and the better the fit between structure and culture, the better the prospects for consolidation and ultimately for the persistence of democracy in a given society." Indeed, the aforementioned tendency to examine democratization continent-by-continent risks validating the idea that there are culture zones with specific democratization styles and propensities.

Regimes such as that of the PRC, for example, which are frankly hostile to meaningful democratization, present themselves self-servingly as defenders of "Asian-style democracy" against Western democratic imperialism. But the notion that Asians have desires and expectations of democracy different from those of Western counterparts is in fact highly questionable. Dalton and Ong (2005) tested this hypothesis using data from the 2000-2002 World Values Survey, comparing views of authority in China, Japan, Singapore, South Korea, Taiwan, and Vietnam with those in Australia, Canada, New Zealand, and the US, finding no sharp differences. This suggests that one should be careful of using "culture," a poorly defined concept, to explain democratization. It does not seem fruitful to discuss democratization from the perspective of a "clash of civilizations" (Huntington 1993), and generalizations about the intrinsically democratic or undemocratic nature of certain groups or regions get us nowhere.

Distribution of Population Groups

However one defines the crucial identity components of a given population, geopolitical analysis requires putting it on maps. Our default approach is to focus on populations of states within their internationally recognized borders. National population size does have important implications, including perhaps for democratization. Teorell and Hadenius (2007, 82), for example, rank population size among the most important determinants of democratization, concluding that a small population has a "significant and positive...impact on democratization."

But national borders, even if widely recognized and not actively contested, only help us understand part of the story. Many geopolitically relevant characteristics do not necessarily follow the borders of political geography. Industrial and resource-extraction regions, for example, can run across borders, with significant political implications. Perhaps even more important, though, is how the territories in which given ethnic, cultural, or racial groups are predominant do not necessarily coincide with official borders.

Examples of this abound, and the ability of political regimes to deal with the issue of divided populations varies markedly. Some of the most dramatic instances of large population groups divided by borders can be found in Africa, where imperial powers drew borders for their own political convenience, dividing large population groups, and left these divisions as legacies of colonialism. The Ewe, for example, provided a national leader in Ghana and have not been heavily engaged in ethnic politics there, while in Togo they have been the less favored of the two main ethnic groups and have encountered repression and restrictions.[10] Looking elsewhere, the Pashtuns, who are the source of the Taliban, are divided only formally by the porous Afghanistan/Pakistan border. The result is enormous strain on the politics of both countries.

The end of the Cold War opened up a remarkable phase of democratization, but also of conflicts that illustrated how the "legacy of irredentism or the myth of a divided nation that needs to be reunited within one territorial unit...can 'override' democratization processes" (Rasler and Thompson 2005, 223). The collapse of the Soviet Union left large ethnic Russian populations, or Russophile ethnic minority populations, in many of non-Russian former Soviet republics, as the government of Ukraine has been painfully aware of late. Georgia, however, is a positive democracy outlier in the Caucasus sub-region *despite* the loss of significant territories inhabited by non-Georgian ethnic groups in the 2008 conflict with Russia. By 2013, with the election of a new leadership replacing wartime president Saakashvili, Georgia appeared to have swallowed its losses and to be seeking improved relations with its much larger and more powerful neighbor.[11]

The distribution of populations is also a dynamic phenomenon. Migration, both external and internal, is creating economic, social, security, and political challenges. Many developing countries, for example, are being left with increasingly severe shortages of medical personal, as indigenously trained doctors or nurses depart for greener pastures. And one wonders about the long-term demographic, economic, social, and political implications of the dramatic departure of women of childbearing age from a country like Moldova.[12]

Both the arrival of migrant groups at their destinations and their departure from their places of origin can have political implications. Addressing migratory flows can become a major political challenge even for long-consolidated democracies, as the harsh immigration debate in the US and Europe demonstrates. Gebremedhin and Mavisakalyan (2013) demonstrate a positive correlation between share of immigrant population and political instability, especially in countries with assimilative immigration laws (i.e. that facilitate acquisition of host country citizenship) and which one thus might be tempted to consider "more" democratic. On the other hand, in an unusual study that examines the impact of migration on democracy in the *sending* country, Pfutze (2012) finds a positive effect of outward migration on Mexican democracy. In any case, migration is a sensitive point of intersection between human geography and politics.

Resources and Their Distribution

Beyond the distribution of population groups on given territories, geopolitical analysis requires attention to the resources these populations possess, and how they are managed. Debate over the relationship between national wealth and democracy goes back over fifty years, at least to Lipset's seminal article "Some Social Requisites of Democracy; Economic Development and Political Legitimacy" of 1959.[13] Lipset's thesis routinely is simplified into a negation that democracy is possible in poor countries, although his actual view was considerably more nuanced (Diamond, Fukuyama, Horowitz, and Planner 2014, 91). Some explicitly reject the linkage between economic prosperity and democratization (Stoner et al. 2013, 14-16). Economic factors, including levels of socioeconomic development and short-term economic performance, do rank among major determinants of democratization for Teorell and Hadenius (2007, 70, 82), although said link emerges from a large-sample study primarily because of the "tendency among less-modernized countries to revert towards authoritarianism."

In other words, one should be wary of economic determinism. Teorell's later research (2010, 12) does not bear out the prediction of economists that "decreasing income inequality triggers democratization." And Diamond argues that, while national poverty does make democratization difficult, "we shouldn't discount the possibility of democratic transitions in unlikely places, even if the odds are against it" (Diamond et al. 2014, 91). Estimates of a threshold economic level for democratization vary dramatically, from Zakaria's $5000-10,000 per annum to a mere $730 annual threshold for middle class status according 2010 analyses from the African Development Bank and the Asian Development Bank. Per capita GDP was lower in Tunisia, Egypt, and Syria prior to the "Arab Spring" than it was in China, where no comparable democracy movements surfaced (Graziano 2012). Turkey and Azerbaijan had almost identical per capita GDPs in constant terms when they attempted democratic transitions (in 1983 and 2005 respectively), but only Turkey was successful.[14] Chile, Iran, Poland, and Ukraine also had similar economic levels at the time of their attempted transitions, and Iran did not make it (Stoner et al. 2013, 14).

A focus on economics at the national level is in any case reductive, and the concept of geographical scales of analysis can offer additional insights. Relative wealth and distribution of resources at the global, continental, and sub-continental levels all can shape the thought and action of democratizers at the national level. Uneven distribution of wealth and resources among areas within a given country, and between urban and rural areas, are in fact the *norm*, even in the most consolidated democracies, and certainly feed into the political process. In an established democracy like Italy's, for example, there is still marked variation in economic output by sub-national unit, associated with varying levels of social capital and of effective governance (Helliwell and Putnam 1995). And in the run-up to the violent dissolution of Yugoslavia, resource transfers from the wealthier component republics to the poorer ones were an important, yet often neglected, flashpoint. Secessionism, which certainly can have an impact on democratization, seems to thrive in relatively wealthy sub-national units (Sorens 2005).

Frankly, there does not appear to be a democratization literature that focuses on the impact of sub-national economic differences and offers a systematic analysis. But this can and should be addressed in case-by-case analyses of democratization, since subnational differentiation can put democracy under stress or shove democratization onto the back burner for national elites. It also can exacerbate intrastate violence, as in the case of Nepal, where conflict during the Maoist insurgency was most intense in areas with low human development indicators and land ownership (Murshed and Gates 2004).

The literature on the relationship between natural resource wealth and democracy, on the other hand, is very rich. Ross's widely referenced article from 2001, "Does Oil Hinder Democracy?"[15] remains a major point of reference, with its straightforward affirmation that "oil and mineral wealth tends to make states less democratic" (328). But Ross himself, in an unpublished paper from 2009,[16] offers the more nuanced conclusion that "oil wealth strongly inhibits democratic transitions in authoritarian states" and that, while the negative effect is increasing, "oil's undemocratic effects are uneven" (2). He notes, for example, that oil has not inhibited democratic transition in Latin America. Teorell and Hadenius (2007, 83) had found some confirmation of Ross's 2001 findings, but attributed this to "a much larger share of upturns in democracy among countries not dependent on oil relative to the oil-rich countries." They also had seen the oil effect as more restricted to the Middle East, and found no effect for non-fuel metals and ores.

A recent meta-analysis (Ahmadov 2014) examines 29 studies reporting almost 250 distinct estimates of the impact of oil on democracy. The statistically significant results overwhelmingly indicate negative relationships between oil and democracy (86% to only 14% positive). But this relationship varies across world regions and institutional contexts. In the Middle East and North Africa, and also in Sub-Saharan Africa, oil has a significant negative impact on democracy. In Latin America, on the other hand, the association is positive. Also, the "broader set of political and economic institutions associated with OECD membership" (1261) has a positive effect on the oil/democracy relationship. Institutions associated with past status as a British imperial possession, on the other hand, are not significant.

Another recent study confirms the importance of looking at the oil/democracy relationship in nuanced fashion, with attention not just to broadly regional but national specificities. Liou and Musgrave (2014) focus on seven countries that became economically reliant on oil exports following the shock of 1973: Algeria, Ecuador, Gabon, Indonesia, Mexico, Nigeria, and Trinidad and Tobago. They find dramatically different impacts on democracy (measured by Polity scores). Trinidad and Tobago was substantially unaffected by oil-reliance. Ecuador, under military rule as of 1972, actually democratized after becoming oil-reliant. In Nigeria, outcomes were mixed, with higher democracy scores, at some points, than would have been expected. Algeria and Gabon, on the other hand, confirmed the pessimists' view of the oil/democracy connection, and Mexico as well experienced a deterioration of democracy after becoming oil-reliant.

Recent events in Iraq have reminded us that the internal politics of oil remain vexing. In 2014, for example, under pressure for funds to arm itself against the advance of the Islamic State, the Kurdistan Regional Government was seeking to sell five tankers full of crude oil, loaded at the Turkish port of Ceyhan. This despite the fact that the Iraqi constitution, laboriously hammered out under US supervision, had made oil revenues the property of the Iraqi people, not of those population groups dominant in the areas where it was extracted.[17]

Water is another scarce and inequitably distributed resource that is a potential object of interstate and intrastate conflict (Yoffe and Ward 1999). Gizelis and Wooden (2010, 451) point out that the role of political institutions and governance in addressing the risks of water-related conflict has received little scholarly attention. Their research finds that "democratic state institutions reduce the likelihood of intrastate conflict; democratic institutions are also more likely present in countries with greater availability of freshwater resources per capita." The American geographer John Agnew (2011, 1) used his presidential address to the Association of American Geographers to argue, in fact, for attention to practical politics, which is "at work around the world in managing water problems." He criticized human and physical geographers for being "dismissive of the possibilities of democratic politics" to address crises in water provision. With respect to water as well, in other words, the nexus of geography and politics merits more sustained reflection.

Conclusions

A comprehensive geopolitical theory of democracy and democratization does not exist. Nor should we expect it to. The big ideas of geopolitical thinkers born in the Victorian age, such as Halford Mackinder (Heartland) or Friedrich Ratzel (*Lebensraum*), have gone out of style, perhaps rightly so. Lacoste's currently more influential approach is focused on specific situations, examined in depth, though also on a number of different geographical planes. This idiographic approach could be seen as clashing with the nomothetic inclinations of political science, devoted to developing and testing theory. But geopolitical analysis also may be complementary. Even a theoretically very sophisticated approach such as that of Levitsky and Way (2010) seemingly cannot eliminate the problem of outliers, whether more successful at democratizing than theory would suggest, or less successful. The need for case-by-case analysis is unlikely to disappear.

Without any pretense of being exhaustive, it is possible to propose a list of factors in human, political, and economic geography that should be considered when analyzing the specific trajectories of regime change and democratization:

1. Location, considered on a series of different geographical scales;
    a. Global
    b. Continental
    c. Sub-continental
    d. Smaller groups of bordering states ("neighborhoods"), including dyads of two bordering states
    e. Individual states within their recognized borders
    f. Sub-national administrative districts
    g. Areas distinguished by predominance of racial/ethnic/cultural/religious groups, degree and type of industrialization or resource extraction, or degree of urbanization.

2. Identity, size, and territorial distribution of populations, as defined by:
    a. Ethnicity, with particular attention to trans-border ethnic groups

    b. Religion
    c. Culture (potentially)

3. Resources, by type, extent, and how distributed, including:
    a. GDP at the national and subnational unit levels
    b. Natural resources
      i. Petroleum
      ii. Natural gas
      iii. Other mineral resources
      iv. Water

This is just a list, not a theory in disguise. No factors on this list, taken either singly or in groups, can provide a satisfactory, parsimonious explanation of democratization. They do not offer, nor should they be understood as, a way of circumventing the crucial and complex role of human agency. On the other hand, they form an important part of the context for said agency, and help shape the options and choices that both democratizers and their opponents must confront.

Endnotes

[1] In fairness, great power politics *is* highly relevant to prospects for successful democratization. See the chapters on international political factors in this volume, as well as Ghia Nodia, "The Revenge of Geopolitics," *Journal of Democracy* 25 (4): 139-50.

[2] Rather than comparing a wide range of modestly differing ways of dividing the world, it makes sense to provide one example, from the influential *Freedom in the World* reports by Freedom House: Americas, Asia-Pacific, Eurasia, Europe, Middle East and North Africa, and Sub-Saharan Africa.

[3] Stoner and McFaul (2013) in fact treat Ghana as a case of successful incremental transition to democracy.

[4] Based on the *CIA World Factbook* listing of international disputes, accessed Nov. 27, 2015, https://www.cia.gov/library/publications/the-world-factbook/fields/2070.html.

[5] See preceding note.

[6] See for example the highly critical review by Isabel Boussard of Lacoste's three-volume *Géopolitiques des régions françaises* (Paris: Fayard, 1986) in

Vingtième Siècle: Revue d'histoire 16 (October-December 1987): 121-25.

[7] As illustrative examples, they cite the divisions between the Indo-European and Dravidian language families in Pakistan, and among the Niger-Congo, Nilo-Saharan, and Afro-Asiatic families in Chad.

[8] From a current perspective, however, one might have doubts about Nasr's analogy between parties like Turkey's AKP and the Christian Democratic parties that emerged in Western Europe after the Second World War.

[9] Accessed Nov. 27, 2015, http://www.pewforum.org/2014/04/04/religious-diversity-index-scores-by-country/.

[10] See the data from the University of Maryland's Minorities at Risk project, accessed Nov. 27, 2015, http://www.cidcm.umd.edu/mar/assessments.asp?regionId=6.

[11] See BBC News Europe, "Five Years On, Georgia Makes Up with Russia," June 24, 2013, http://www.bbc.com/news/world-europe-23010526.

[12] On the complex Moldovan migration situation, see European University Institute Migration Policy Centre, *MPC Migration Profile: Moldova*, June 2013, http://www.migrationpolicycentre.eu/docs/migration_profiles/Moldova.pdf.

[13] *American Political Science Review* 53 (March): 69-105. See the more detailed discussion in Luca Germano's chapter in this volume.

[14] Recent events in Turkey, admittedly, remind us that a successful transition may not automatically imply the long-term persistence of democracy.

[15] *World Politics* 53: 325-61.

[16] http://www.sscnet.ucla.edu/polisci/faculty/ross/Oil%20and%20Democracy%20Revisited.pdf.

[17] Steve Mufson, "How the US Got Mixed Up in a Fight Over Kurdish Oil—With a Unified Iraq at Stake," *The Washington Post*, August 4, 2014, http://www.washingtonpost.com/business/economy/how-the-us-got-mixed-up-in-a-fight-over-kurdish-oil--with-a-unified-iraq-at-stake/2014/08/04/4a00a6e2-1900-11e4-9e3b-7f2f110c6265_story.html. Some would argue that Kurdistan is the portion of post-Saddam Iraq in which governance has been the most democratic.

Reference List

Agnew, John. 2011. "Waterpower: Politics and Geography of Water Provision." *Annals of the Association of American Geographers* 101 (3): 463-76.

Ahmadov, Anar K. 2014. "Oil, Democracy, and Context: A Meta-Analysis." *Comparative Political Studies* 47 (9): 1238-67.

Andrei, Mădălina. 2009. "Geopolitics, power, and governmentality." *Geopolitics, History, and International Relations* 1 (1): 192-96.

Aspinall, Edward, and Marcus Mietzner. 2013. "Indonesia: Economic Crisis, Foreign Pressure, and Regime Change." In *Transitions to Democracy: A Comparative Perspective*, edited by Kathryn Stoner and Michael McFaul, 144-67. Baltimore: Johns Hopkins University Press.

Aziz, Sardar. 2014. "The Kurdistan Regional Government Elections: A Critical Evaluation." *Insight Turkey* 16 (3): 67-76.

Barnett, Clive, and Murray Low. 2004. "Introduction: Geography and Democracy." In *Spaces of Democracy: Geographical Perspectives on Citizenship, Participation, and Representation*, edited by Clive Barnett and Murray Low, 1-22. London: SAGE.

Behrend, Jacqueline. 2011. "The Unevenness of Democracy at the Subnational Level: Provincial Closed Games in Argentina." *Latin American Research Review* 46 (1): 150-76.

Beissinger, Mark R. 2008. "A New Look at Ethnicity and Democratization." *Journal of Democracy* 19 (3): 85-97.

Bernard, Dalila. 2013. "Maroc: la révolution des petits pas?" In *Moyen-Orient 2012: bilan géopolitique*, edited by Institut MEDEA, 90-93. Paris: Editions du Cygne.

Bunce, Valerie J., and Sharon L. Wolchik. 2013. "Azerbaijan: Losing the Transitional Moment." In *Transitions to Democracy: A Comparative Perspective*, edited by Kathryn Stoner and Michael McFaul, 400-28. Baltimore: Johns Hopkins University Press.

Castets, Caroline. 2014. "Yves Lacoste: La géopolitique, ça sert encore 'à faire la guerre.' " *Le nouvel économiste*, January 7. http://www.lenouveleconomiste.fr/yves-lacoste-la-geopolitique-ca-sert-encore-a-faire-la-guerre-21105/.

Cavatorta, Francesco. 2001. "Geopolitical Challenges to the Success of Democracy in North Africa: Algeria, Tunisia, and Morocco." *Democratization* 8 (4): 175-94.

Claval, Paul. 2000. "*Hérodote* and the French Left." In *Geopolitical Traditions: A Century of Geopolitical Thought,* edited by Klaus Dodds and David Atkinson, 239-67. London and New York: Routledge.

Dalton, Russell J., and Nhu-Ngoc T. Ong. 2005. "Authority Orientations and Democratic Attitudes: A Test of the 'Asian Values' Hypothesis." *Japanese Journal of Political Science* 6 (August): 211-31.

Desmet, Klaus, Ignacio Ortuño-Ortín, and Romain Wacziarg. 2009. *The Political Economy of Ethnolinguistic Cleavages.* Working Paper 15360. Cambridge, MA: National Bureau of Economic Research.

Diamond, Larry, Francis Fukuyama, Donald L. Horowitz, and Marc F. Plattner. 2014. "Reconsidering the Transition Paradigm." *Journal of Democracy* 25 (1): 86-100.

Elshtain, Jean Bethke. 2009. "Religion and Democracy." *Journal of Democracy* 20 (2): 5-17.

Epstein, David, Bahar Leventoğlu, and Sharyn O'Halloran. 2012. "Minorities and Democratization." *Economics and Politics* 24 (November): 259-78.

Freedom House. 2015. *Freedom in the World 2015.* https://freedomhouse.org/sites/default/files/01152015_FIW_2015_final.pdf.

Gebremedhin, Tesfaye A., and Astghik Mavisakalyan. 2013. "Immigration and Political Instability." *Kyklos* 66 (August): 317-41.

Gizelis, Theodora-Ismene, and Amanda E. Wooden. 2010. "Water Resources, Institutions, and Intrastate Conflict." *Political Geography* 29: 444-53.

Graziano, Manlio. 2012. "Geopolitica della democrazia." *Limes* (March), http://www.limesonline.com/cartaceo/geopolitica-della-democrazia?prv=true.

Helliwell, John F., and Robert, D. Putnam. 1995. "Economic Growth and Social Capital in Italy." *Eastern Economic Journal* 21 (Summer): 295-307.

Hepple, Leslie W. 2000. "Lacoste, *Hérodote* and French Radical Politics." In *Geopolitical Traditions: A Century of Geopolitical Thought*, edited by Klaus Dodds and David Atkinson, 268-301. London and New York: Routledge.

Horn, Denise M. 2010. *Women, Civil Society, and the Geopolitics of Democratization.* New York: Routledge.

Horowitz, Donald L. 2014. "Ethnic Power Sharing: Three Big Problems." *Journal of Democracy* 25 (2): 5-20.

Huntington, Samuel P. 1993. "The Clash of Civilizations." *Foreign Affairs* 72 (Summer): 22-49.

Kauffman, Craig M. 2010. "Democratization." In *Encyclopedia of Political Theory*, edited by Mark Bevir, 362-70. Thousand Oaks, CA: SAGE.

Kopstein, Jeffrey. 2009. "Geography, Post-Communism, and Comparative Politics." In *The Spatial Turn*, edited by Barney Warf and Santa Arias, 77-87. Routledge Studies in Human Geography. Abingdon, UK: Routledge.

Kurzman, Charles, and Ijlala Naqvi. 2010. "Do Muslims Vote Islamic?" *Journal of Democracy* 21 (2): 50-64.

Lankina, Tomila. 2009. "Regional Developments in Russia: Territorial Fragmentation in a Consolidating Authoritarian State." *Social Research* 76 (Spring): 225-56.

Lankina, Tomila V., and Lullit Getachew. 2006. "A Geographic Incremental Theory of Democratization: Territory, Aid, and Democracy in Postcommunist Regions." *World Politics* 58 (4): 536-82.

Levitsky, Steven, and Lucan A. Way. 2010. *Competitive Authoritarianism: Hybrid Regimes After the Cold War.* New York: Cambridge University Press.

Li, Quan, and Rafael Reuveny. 2003. "Economic Globalization and Democracy: An Empirical Analysis." *British Journal of Political Science* 33 (January): 29-54.

Liou, Yu-Ming, and Paul Musgrave. 2014. "Refining the Oil Curse: Country-Level Evidence from Exogenous Variations in Resource Income." *Comparative Political Studies* 47 (11): 1584-610.

Mainwaring, Scott, and Aníbal Pérez-Liñán. 2007. "Why Regions of the World Are Important: Regional Specificities and Region-Wide Diffusion of Democracy." In *Regimes and Democracy in Latin America: Theories and Methods*, edited by Gerardo L. Munck, 199-229. New York: Oxford University Press.

Møller, Jørgen, and Svend-Erik Skaaning. 2013. "The Third Wave: Inside the Numbers." *Journal of Democracy* 24 (4): 97-109.

Murshed, S. Mansoob, and Scott Gates. 2004. *Spatial Horizontal Inequality and the Maoist Insurgency in Nepal.* Research Paper No. 2004/43, July. World Institute for Development Economics Research. United Nations University.

Nasr, Vali. 2005. "The Rise of 'Muslim Democracy'." *Journal of Democracy* 16 (2): 13-27.

O'Loughlin, John, Michael D. Ward, Corey L. Lofdahl, Jordin S Cohen, David S. Brown, David Reilly, Kristian S. Gleditsch, and Michael Shin. 1998. "The Diffusion of Democracy, 1946-1994." *Annals of the Association of American Geographers* 88 94): 545-74.

Pfutze, Tobias. 2012. "Does Migration Promote Democratization? Evidence from the Mexican Transition." *Journal of Comparative Economics* 40: 159-75.

Plattner, Marc F. 2014. "The End of the Transitions Era?" *Journal of Democracy* 25 (3): 5-16.

Rasler, Karen, and William R. Thompson. 2005. *Puzzles of the Democratic Peace: Theory, Geopolitics, and the Transformation of World Politics.* New York: Palgrave Macmillan.

Slater, Dan. 2011. Review of *Competitive Authoritarianism: Hybrid Regimes After the Cold War*, by Steven Levitsky and Lucan A. Way. *Perspectives on Politics* 9 (June): 385-8.

Slater, David. 2008. "Imperial Powers and Democratic Imaginations in a Global Era." In *Globalization: Theory and Practice*, 3rd ed., edited by Eleonore Kofman and Gilian Youngs, 40-56. New York: Continuum.

Sorens, Jason. 2005. "The Cross-Sectional Determinants of Secessionism in Advanced Democracies." *Comparative Political Studies* 38 (April): 304-326

Staeheli, Lynn A. 2010. "Political Geography: Democracy and the Disorderly Public." *Progress in Human Geography* 34 (1): 67-78.

Stokke, Kristian. 2009. "Human Geography and the Contextual Politics of Substantive Democratization." *Progress in Human Geography* 33 (6): 739-42.

Stoner, Kathryn, Larry Diamond, Desha Girod, and Michael McFaul. 2013. "Transitional Successes and Failures: The International-Domestic Nexus." In *Transitions to Democracy: A Comparative Perspective*, edited by Kathryn Stoner and Michael McFaul, 3-24. Baltimore: Johns Hopkins University Press.

Stoner, Kathryn, and Michael McFaul, eds. 2013. *Transitions to Democracy: A Comparative Perspective*. Baltimore: Johns Hopkins University Press.

Teorell, Jan. 2010. *Determinants of Democratization: Explaining Regime Change in the World, 1972-2006*. Cambridge: Cambridge University Press.

Teorell, Jan, and Axel Hadenius,. 2007. "Determinants of Democratization: Taking Stock of the Large-N Evidence." In *Democratization: The State of the Art*, 2nd ed., edited by Dirk Berg-Schlosser, 69-95. Opladen, Germany: Barbara Budrich Publishers.

Tolstrup, Jakob. 2010. "When Can External Actors Influence Democratization? Leverage, Linkages, and Gatekeeper Elites." Working Paper No. 118, July. Stanford, CA: Center on Democracy, Development, and Rule of Law, Freeman Spogli Institute for International Studies. http://iis-db.stanford.edu/pubs/22947/NO_118_Tolstrup_When_can_External_Actors_Influence_Democratization.pdf.

Treisman, Daniel. 2014. "Lessons from 25 Years of Post-Communism: The Importance of Reform, Democracy, and Geography." *The Washington Post*, June 10. http://www.washingtonpost.com/blogs/monkey-cage/wp/2014/06/10/lessons-from-25-years-of-post-communism-the-importance-of-reform-democracy-and-geography/.

van Beek, Ursula. 2005. "Editor's Introduction." In *Democracy Under Construction: Patterns from Four Continents*, edited by Ursula J. van Beek, 21-38. Bloomfield Hills, MI: Barbara Budrich Publishers.

Whitehead, Laurence. 1999. "Geography and Democratic Destiny." *Journal of Democracy* 10 (1): 74-9.

_____. 2002. *Democratization: Theory and Experience*. Oxford: Oxford University Press.

Wittes, Tamara Coffman. 2008. "Islamist Parties and Democracy: Three Kinds of Movements. " *Journal of Democracy* 19 (3): 7-12.

Yoffe, Shira B., and Brian S. Ward. 1999. "Water Resources and Indicators of Conflict: A Proposed Spatial Analysis." *Water International* 24 (4): 377-84.

Contributors

Antonino Castaldo is Post-Doctoral Research Fellow (FCT grant SFRH/BPD/101442/2014) at the Instituto de Ciências Sociais, Universidade de Lisboa, Av. Professor Aníbal de Bettencourt, 9, 1600-189, Lisbon, Portugal, with a research project on external democratization after war in comparative perspective. He has a PhD in Political Science from the University of Florence (2008). Over the past years, he mainly has focused on political parties and party systems, the analysis of democratization processes, and the breakdown of non-democratic regimes, publishing numerous journal articles, book chapters, and a book.

Nicoletta Di Sotto is adjunct professor at the American University of Rome and at the University of Rome 3. She holds a PhD in comparative and European politics from the University of Siena (2006). Her main research interests are ethnonationalism and ethnoregionalist parties, local politics, stateness problems, and democratization processes. She has published several journal articles, book chapters, and two books, including a 2009 study of ethnoregionalist party attitudes toward the European Union.

*Luca German*o is adjunct professor of public policy at the Department of Political Sciences, University of Rome 3. He is author of numerous studies on interest groups, democratization processes, and public policy, including books on federalism in Italy (2002) and on Italian auto giant Fiat's transformation into a global player (2009).

Pietro Grilli di Cortona was professor of political science at the University of Rome 3 and, until shortly before his untimely death in July 2015, president of the Italian Political Science Association. His numerous books included a prescient study (in 1989) of the crisis of Communist regimes in Europe, and he maintained a scholarly focus on democratic political change throughout the rest of his life. He was also the author of important works on political party and electoral systems, and on Italian politics, and a respected leader in his university's academic community.

Barbara Pisciotta is associate professor of political science at the University of Rome 3, where she teaches international relations, international politics, and democratization processes. She is author of three books and several articles, focusing in particular on consolidation of the party system in Eastern Europe, including *Alle origini dei partiti post-comunisti: La frattura di classe nell'Europa centro-orientale* (At the origins of the post-Communist parties: the class fracture in East Central Europe) of 2007.

Eric R. Terzuolo taught political and economy geography at the University of Rome 3 from 2006 to 2010, and since then has been responsible for West European area studies at the Foreign Service Institute, the professional development and training branch of the US Department of State. As a US Foreign Service Officer from 1982 to 2003, he focused on international security issues, and is the author of two books and numerous articles and book chapters on proliferation of weapons of mass destruction. He holds a doctorate in history from Stanford University.

Index

www.ingramcontent.com/pod-product-compliance
Lightning Source LLC
Chambersburg PA
CBHW020659270326
41928CB00005B/193